Disinformation and Data Lockdown on Social Platforms

This book addresses the question of how researchers can conduct independent, ethical research on mal-, mis-, and disinformation in a rapidly changing and hostile data environment.

The escalating issue of data access is thrown into sharp relief by the large-scale use of bots, trolls, fake news, and strategies of false amplification, the effects of which are difficult to quantify due to a corporate environment favouring platform lockdowns and the restriction of access to Application Programming Interfaces (APIs). As social media platforms increase obstacles to independent scholarship by dramatically curbing access to APIs, researchers are faced with the stark choice of either limiting their use of trace data or developing new methods of data collection. Without a breakthrough, social media research may go the way of search engine research, in which only a small group of researchers who have direct relationships with search companies such as Google and Microsoft can access data and conduct research.

The chapters in this book were originally published as a special issue of the journal, *Information, Communication & Society*.

Shawn Walker is Assistant Professor of Data & Society in the School of Social and Behavioral Sciences at Arizona State University.

Dan Mercea is Reader in the Department of Sociology at City, University of London.

Marco Bastos is the University College Dublin Ad Astra Fellow at the School of Information and Communication Studies.

Disinformation and Data Lockdown on Social Platforms

Edited by
Shawn Walker, Dan Mercea and Marco Bastos

Routledge
Taylor & Francis Group
NEW YORK AND LONDON

First published 2022
by Routledge
605 Third Avenue, New York, NY 10158

and by Routledge
2 Park Square, Milton Park, Abingdon, Oxon OX14 4RN

Routledge is an imprint of the Taylor & Francis Group, an informa business

Library of Congress Cataloging-in-Publication Data
A catalog record for this title has been requested

ISBN: 978-1-032-07447-4 (hbk)
ISBN: 978-1-032-07448-1 (pbk)
ISBN: 978-1-003-20697-2 (ebk)

DOI: 10.4324/9781003206972

Typeset in Minion Pro
by Newgen Publishing UK

Publisher's Note
The publisher accepts responsibility for any inconsistencies that may have arisen during the conversion of this book from journal articles to book chapters, namely the inclusion of journal terminology.

Contents

Citation Information

The chapters in this book were originally published in the journal, *Information, Communication & Society*, volume 22, issue 11 (2019). When citing this material, please use the original page numbering for each article, as follows:

Chapter 1

The disinformation landscape and the lockdown of social platforms
Shawn Walker, Dan Mercea and Marco Bastos
Information, Communication & Society, volume 22, issue 11 (2019), pp. 1531–1543

Chapter 2

After the 'APIcalypse': social media platforms and their fight against critical scholarly research
Axel Bruns
Information, Communication & Society, volume 22, issue 11 (2019), pp. 1544–1566

Chapter 3

An end to the wild west of social media research: a response to Axel Bruns
Cornelius Puschmann
Information, Communication & Society, volume 22, issue 11 (2019), pp. 1582–1589

Chapter 4

Overcoming terms of service: a proposal for ethical distributed research
Alexander Halavais
Information, Communication & Society, volume 22, issue 11 (2019), pp. 1567–1581

Chapter 5

Data craft: a theory/methods package for critical internet studies
Amelia Acker and Joan Donovan
Information, Communication & Society, volume 22, issue 11 (2019), pp. 1590–1609

Chapter 6

Diverging patterns of interaction around news on social media: insularity and partisanship during the 2018 Italian election campaign
Fabio Giglietto, Augusto Valeriani, Nicola Righetti and Giada Marino
Information, Communication & Society, volume 22, issue 11 (2019), pp. 1610–1629

Chapter 7

Algorithms and agenda-setting in Wikileaks' #Podestaemails release
Nicholas Proferes and Ed Summers
Information, Communication & Society, volume 22, issue 11 (2019), pp. 1630–1645

Chapter 8

Disinformation, performed: self-presentation of a Russian IRA account on Twitter
Yiping Xia, Josephine Lukito, Yini Zhang, Chris Wells, Sang Jung Kim and Chau Tong
Information, Communication & Society, volume 22, issue 11 (2019), pp. 1646–1664

Notes on Contributors

Amelia Acker is Assistant Professor in the School of Information at the University of Texas at Austin. She is an information scientist who researches data literacy, metadata, and information infrastructures that support long-term cultural memory.

Marco Bastos is the University College Dublin Ad Astra Fellow at the School of Information and Communication Studies and Senior Lecturer at City, University of London. He is the author of *Spatializing Social Media: Social Networks Online and Offline* (Routledge, 2021) and principal investigator in the Twitter-funded project "The Brexit Value Space and the Geography of Online Echo Chambers."

Axel Bruns is Professor in the Digital Media Research Centre at Queensland University of Technology in Brisbane, Australia. His work focuses on the study of user participation in social media spaces, and its implications for our understanding of the contemporary public sphere, drawing especially on innovative new methods for analyzing 'big social data'.

Joan Donovan is Director of the Technology and Social Change Research Project at the Shorenstein Center on Media, Politics and Public Policy at Harvard Kennedy School, where she researches media manipulation, disinformation, and adversarial media movements.

Fabio Giglietto is Associate Professor at the Department of Communication Sciences, Humanities and International Studies at the University of Urbino Carlo Bo, where he also teaches social media analysis. His main research interests are theory of information, communication, and society with a specific focus on the relationship between social systems and new technologies.

Alexander Halavais is Associate Professor of critical data studies in the School of Social and Behavioral Sciences at Arizona State University, where he researches ways in which social media change the nature of scholarship and learning and allow for new forms of collaboration and self-government. He directs the MA in Social Technologies program.

Sang Jung Kim is a doctoral student at the School of Journalism & Mass Communication, University of Wisconsin-Madison. Her interest focuses on the interaction between technology and the politics of social identities.

Josephine Lukito is a Ph.D. student at the School of Journalism & Mass Communication, University of Wisconsin-Madison, studying language and power in media texts. She is a mixed-methods researcher, specialising in critical discourse analysis, human-coded content analysis, and syntactic natural language processing tools.

Giada Marino is a PhD candidate at the University of Urbino Carlo Bo in Communication and Social Sciences. Her dissertation is focused on ephemeral user-generated content and online self-presentation.

Dan Mercea is Reader in the Department of Sociology at City, University of London. He is the author of *Civic Participation in Contentious Politics: The Digital Foreshadowing of Protest*.

Nicholas Proferes is Assistant Professor at the University of Kentucky's School of Information Science. He researches socio-technical systems, technological discourse, and users' understandings of information flow online.

Cornelius Puschmann is Senior Researcher at the Leibniz Institute for Media Research in Hamburg where he coordinates the international research network Algorithmed Public Spheres. His research interests include online hate speech, the role of algorithms for the selection of media content, and methodological aspects of computational social science.

Nicola Righetti is Research Fellow at the University of Urbino 'Carlo Bo', member of the Mapping Italian News team, and temporary professor of Sociology at the University of Verona (Italy). His research interests lie in the field of sociology of culture and communication, with a focus on digital and computational methods, data mining and text mining techniques, and R software.

Ed Summers is a PhD Candidate in the College of Information Studies at the University of Maryland. He studies how archival processes and digital preservation practices function on the web.

Chau Tong is Doctoral Candidate at the School of Journalism and Mass Communication at University of Wisconsin-Madison. Her research interests are broadly in areas of public opinion, political communication, and political behavior.

Augusto Valeriani is Associate Professor in Sociology of Communication at the Political and Social Sciences Department of the University of Bologna. His research focuses on political communication, digital media, and journalism.

Shawn Walker is Assistant Professor of Data & Society in the School of Social and Behavioral Sciences at Arizona State University. His research focuses on mis/disinformation and online resistance circulating in social media during social movements, protests, and elections, as well as the related challenges of collecting, analyzing, and preserving data from social media platforms.

Chris Wells is Assistant Professor in the Division of Emerging Media Studies and Department of Journalism at Boston University. His current research explores the dynamics and dysfunctions of the digital political information system.

Yiping Xia is a PhD student at the School of Journalism & Mass Communication, University of Wisconsin-Madison. His research is mainly concerned with political communication and social media.

Yini Zhang is a PhD candidate at the School of Journalism & Mass Communication, University of Wisconsin-Madison.

INTRODUCTION

The disinformation landscape and the lockdown of social platforms

Shawn Walker, Dan Mercea and Marco Bastos

ABSTRACT
This introduction to the special issue considers how independent research on mis/disinformation campaigns can be conducted in a corporate environment hostile to academic research. We provide an overview of the disinformation landscape in the wake of the Facebook-Cambridge Analytica data scandal and social platforms' decision to enforce access lockdowns and the throttling of Application Programming Interfaces (APIs) for data collection. We argue that the governance shift from user communities to social media algorithms, along with social platforms' intensive emphasis on generating revenue from user data, has eroded the mutual trust of networked publics and opened the way for dis/misinformation campaigns. We discuss the importance of open, public APIs for academic research as well as the unique challenges of collecting social media data to study highly ephemeral mis/disinformation campaigns. The introduction concludes with an assessment of the growing data access gap that not only hinders research of public interest, but that may also preclude researchers from identifying meaningful research questions as activity on social platforms becomes increasingly more inscrutable and unobservable.

Introduction

This Special Issue addresses the question of how researchers can conduct independent, ethical research on dis/misinformation operations in a rapidly changing and hostile data environment. The escalating issue of data access we discuss is thrown into sharp relief by the strategic use of bots, trolls, fake news, strategies of false amplification, and a corporate environment favoring platform lockdowns and the restriction of access to Application Programming Interfaces (APIs). As social media platforms increase obstacles to independent scholarship by dramatically curbing access to APIs, researchers are faced with the stark choice of either limiting their use of trace data or developing new methods of data collection. Without a breakthrough, social media research may go the way of search engine research, in which only a small group of researchers who have direct relationships with search companies such as Google and Microsoft can access data and conduct research.

The reflections that follow highlight the current scholarly predicament of grappling with the time-sensitive nature of strategic and disruptive communication in highly ephemeral dis/misinformation campaigns. These campaigns unfold in increasingly polarized, hybrid media environments where news stories are written, disseminated, and interpreted within and across intricate digital networks. While researchers are developing more sophisticated multi-method research designs and rich multi-source data sets (Chadwick, Vaccari, & O'Loughlin, 2018; Möller, Trilling, Helberger, & van Es, 2018), this methodological progress is threatened by the active resistance of social media platforms to providing support for research on topics that require greater transparency and may negatively impact their bottom line (Dance, LaForgia, & Confessore, 2018).

The disinformation landscape

The set of articles presented in this issue take stock of the epochal changes triggered by the deployment of data-driven micro-targeting in political campaigns epitomized by the Cambridge Analytica data scandal and the ensuing data lockdown enforced by social media platforms. Digital trace data has been increasingly linked to disinformation, misinformation, and state propaganda across Western industrialized democracies and countries in the Global South, where state and non-state actors seek to strategically diffuse content that heightens partisanship and erodes the general trust in democratic institutions.

Influence operations weaponizing social media have been identified in elections worldwide, with prominent examples including the 2016 US elections and the 2017 general elections in France (Bessi & Ferrara, 2016; Ferrara, 2017; Weedon, Nuland, & Stamos, 2017). This evolving disinformation landscape required the increasing adoption of specialized vocabulary associated with influence and disruptive operations to describe a set of media practices designed to exploit deep-seated tensions in liberal democracies (Bennett & Steven, 2018). The tactics documented are part of a concerted strategy to polarize voters and alienate them from the electoral process (Benkler, Faris, & Roberts, 2018). This scheme – infamously associated with Russian troll factories – took the form of misinformation, or information identified as inaccurate (Karlova & Fisher, 2013), and disinformation, or the intentional distribution of fabricated stories to advance political goals (Bennett & Steven, 2018).

Misinformation and disinformation pose a serious threat to objective decision-making by the voting public (Lewandowsky, Ecker, & Cook, 2017, p. 354). The effectiveness of dis/misinformation campaigns has in part (Benkler et al., 2018) been attributed to the manner in which they have been able to take advantage of the biases (Comor, 2001; Innis, 1982) intrinsic to social media platforms, particularly the attention economy and the social media supply chain that relies on viral content (Jenkins, Ford, Green, & New, 2013) for revenue generation. In their response, social media platforms attempted to rekindle trust by appearing to reinforce individual privacy within a newly secured user community, a set of measures that also locked academic and non-profit researchers out from studying social platforms while preserving corporate and business access to social media users' data.

Infrastructural transformation of the networked publics

This backdrop of influence operations and information warfare presents a considerable departure from years of euphoric rhetoric praising the democratization of public discourse brought by networking technology and social media platforms (Howard & Hussain, 2013). Early scholarship extolling the potential of social media for democratization and deliberation inadvertently reinforced a narrative championing communication and collaboration as expected affordances of social platforms (Loader & Mercea, 2011). By the end of the decade, however, the narrative surrounding social platforms increasingly turned to metaphors foregrounding polarization and division in a landscape marked by tribalism and information warfare (Benkler et al., 2018), enabled by a business model driven above all by the commodification of digital circulation and its capitalization on financial markets (Langley & Leyshon, 2017).

Scholarship on this hybrid media ecosystem (Chadwick, 2017) explored the technological affordances and ideological leanings that shape social media interaction, with a topical interest in the potential for civic engagement and democratic revitalization (Zuckerman, 2014). Bennett and Segerberg (2013) expanded on Olson's seminal work on the logic of collective action to explain the rise of digital networked politics where individuals would come together to address common problems. Similarly, Castells (2009) described a global media ecology of self-publication and scalable mobilization that advanced internet use and political participation (Castells, 2012).

Open platforms and unrestricted access offered the cornerstone of networked publics that reconfigured sociality and public life (boyd, 2008). The relatively open infrastructure of networked publics was also explored in scholarship detailing how online social networks support gatewatching (Bruns, 2005) and practices in citizen journalism that are central to a diverse media ecosystem (Hermida, 2010), with citizens auditing the gatekeeping power of mainstream media and holding elite interests to account (Tufekci & Wilson, 2012). By most assessments, social network sites were welcoming challengers to the monopoly enjoyed by the mass media (Castells, 2012), with only limited attention devoted to the opportunities offered to propagandists that could similarly coordinate and organize disinformation campaigns through decentralized and distributed networks (Benkler et al., 2018).

These developments challenged the very idea of networked publics and Castells' (2012) depiction of the internet as universal commons. However, the transition from narratives emphasizing open communication to concerns about information warfare was neither immediate nor trivial. With mobile platforms slowly replacing desktop-based applications, open standards gave way to centralized communication systems epitomized by social media platforms and social technologies pivoted from a business model centered on software and services to the selling and reselling of user data. These changes endangered the openness of networked publics, with the debate underpinning networks in the late 90s being replaced by a focus on the affordances of mobile apps and social platforms, whose user base largely differs from living communities of users that would come together around common interests.

Also noticeable in the transition from networked publics to social platforms was the increased commercialization of previously public, open, and often collaborative spaces that were increasingly reduced to private property. This infrastructural transformation of the networked publics continues to drive anxieties about social media platforms in the aftermath of the Cambridge Analytica data scandal, including topical issues of digital privacy, data access, surveillance, microtargeting, and the growing influence of algorithms in society. Counterbalancing reactions to these developments, distributed networks services have started in the Fediverse such as Mastodon or Pleroma. However, on the most prevalent social media platforms, the existing networked publics are defined by the technological and market exigencies of the corporations who own them.

Algorithmization of online communities

Social platforms built much of their social infrastructure on the back of networked publics and the community organization that shaped internet services in the early 90s. The drive towards community formation remains an important component of social media platforms, notwithstanding the growing trend towards data access restrictions and end-to-end encryption of their services. Indeed, on 27 February 2017, at a time when investigations into disruptive communication in the previous year's US elections were still in their infancy, the CEO of Facebook, Mark Zuckerberg, wrote in a note published on his Facebook page titled 'Building Global Community:'

> History is the story of how we've learned to come together in ever greater numbers –from tribes to cities to nations. At each step, we built social infrastructure like *communities*, media, and governments to empower us to achieve things we couldn't on our own ... Today we are close to taking our next step. Our greatest opportunities are now global ... Progress now requires humanity coming together not just as cities or nations, but also as a *global community*. (Zuckerberg, 2017, emphasis added)

Zuckerberg's vision simultaneously highlighted and projected the end of open networked publics. With increasing government pressure before the end of that same year, Zuckerberg would yield and testify before the US Congress in an investigation on Russian interference in the 2016 elections; the company would see its share price plunge amid revelations that commercial third-parties and foreign arms-length agencies were able to harness Facebook to micro-target voters (Neate, 2018). In the attempt to reverse its fortunes, Facebook launched multiple measures, including restricting third-party access to its Pages Application Programming Interface (API) that provided access to posts, comments, and metadata associated with communication on public Facebook pages (Schroepfer, 2018).

The immediate implications of this step for the – already remarkably limited – ability of independent academic researchers to form a systematic understanding of social interaction on private social media platforms (Driscoll & Walker, 2014; Skeggs & Yuill, 2015) were soon highlighted in an open letter by scholars (Bruns et al., 2018). However, at a deeper and more abstract level, one can unpick the discourse of Zuckerberg's manifesto to discern why his appropriation of the trope and exhortation of the value of community exposed, inadvertently, both the ills that plagued his platform and the steps to redress them, which were lamented as foreclosing democratic accountability (Bruns et al., 2018).

Social media platforms cannot be separated from the user communities that populate them. The business model of social platforms extracts data from community interactions (i.e., transactions among members) that can be monetized (Van Dijck, 2013; Fernback,

2007, p. 64) by a lucrative advertising business. The latter governs group interaction and individual experience alike through a set of intricate learning algorithms (Bucher, 2017). These algorithms rely on users as 'affective processors' who interpret and help govern the communities through shares, likes, retweets, and pins (Gehl, 2011; Lomborg & Kapsch, 2019). However opaque to users, algorithms generate knowledge about users beyond their immediate interactions, thereby triggering further interactions and 'imaginaries of interaction,' i.e., user theories about what the algorithm is and ought to be (Bucher, 2017).

The algorithmization of communities championed by social platforms was a milestone that instantaneously rendered networked publics into a profitable source of users' interactions. Transferring community governance from users to algorithms removed a key basis for mutual trust, opening the way for large-scale disinformation campaigns that conspicuously plagued election cycles, ethnic relations, and civic mobilization from 2016 onwards (Apuzzo & Santariano, 2019). By Facebook's own account (Weedon et al., 2017), its advertising algorithms were harnessed to segment users into belief communities that could be micro-targeted with materials that amplified their intimate political preferences. This repurposing of intimate knowledge and networked interaction for revenue-making remained the corollary of commercial social media enterprises, including the individuals and academics involved in the notorious and now defunct political consultancy firm Cambridge Analytica (Rosenberg, 2018).

The operations executed by Cambridge Analytica may have violated Facebook's terms of service (Rosenberg, 2018), but they were broadly similar to Facebook's business model that extracts commercial value from users' data. As such, they did not go against the grain of the platform's business model. On the contrary, the consultancy cynically maximized Facebook's political utility by monetizing social-psychological user traits and using granular trace data to micro-target political advertisements on the platform (House of Commons Digital, 2019). In an attempt to reassert the integrity of the user community, Facebook rolled out in 2018 a tighter data management regime that, in some assessments, equally protects users' privacy and safeguards the company's advertising business by closely guarding user data for its own corporate use only (Tufekci, 2019).

Facebook's community governance will likely continue to be contested, not least because of what it represents: a corporate hegemony that is far removed from networked publics which used to provide a counterweight to state and corporate power over individuals. Policymakers, in democratic countries, have demanded with some success more accountability from social platforms in respect to their efforts to arrest disruptive communication and preserve the intimacy of users, with the German legislation being portrayed as an exemplar (Bundeskartellamt, 2019; Volpicelli, 2019). Academics, on the other hand, have mostly been unsuccessful in their appeal to social platforms to open themselves up to a level of public scrutiny that permits investigations of its user communities by scholars. In response to Facebook's public API throttling, several prominent academic researchers stressed the following:

> Platform providers – and the research advisors they collaborate with – cannot be allowed to position themselves as the gatekeepers for the research that investigates how their platforms are used. Instead, we need far more transparent data access models that clearly articulate to platform users who may be accessing their data, and for what purposes. (Bruns et al., 2018)

Why public APIs matter

Studies in this Special Issue add to a growing body of purposeful attempts to generate meaningful, valid, and reliable results with proprietary data to which access is limited, selective, and often opaque (Driscoll & Walker, 2014). This introduction and Bruns' article, specifically, spotlight the corporate response of social media platforms – the most stringent of which has been that of Facebook, which drastically restricted access to its public APIs – to justified alarm regarding the use of personal trace data in disruptive communication (House of Commons Digital, 2019).

Public and open APIs allow researchers to retrieve large-scale data and curate databases associated with sociologically meaningful events. Without them, web interfaces have to be scraped to access the data (Freelon, 2018), which is labor-intensive and drastically limits the amount of information that can be collected and processed. Locking researchers out of the APIs constrains them to human-intensive means of data collection that cannot produce large or representative samples of real-world events, such as social movements, elections, let alone state and non-state sponsored disinformation campaigns.

Illustratively, Twitter operates three well-documented, public APIs (Twitter, 2019) in addition to its premium and enterprise offerings. Twitter's relative accessibility leads it to being vastly over-represented in social media research (Blank, 2016). Public and open APIs such as that of Twitter are an exception in the social media ecosystem. By contrast, Facebook's Public Feed API (Facebook, 2019) is restricted to a limited set of media publishers. It is against this backdrop that researchers have suggested that restrictions on data access may lead to the consideration of alternative methods (Venturini & Rogers, 2019); and, in the 'post API Age', the increased use of data collection methods that may run counter to platform terms of service such as web scraping (Freelon, 2018).

These suggestions offer a roadmap to resources researchers may leverage to implement their studies, but they underestimate the central role of APIs in providing scalable and reproducible access to data. This line of thought is epitomized in references to a 'post API Age' (Freelon, 2018) asserting that APIs are in the process of being retired. It would be more accurate to refer to a 'post-public-API age,' as Application Programming Interfaces (APIs) remain a central component of mobile and cloud-based technologies that are central to the infrastructure of social media platforms. Indeed, it is difficult to see how cloud-based business development, and web applications in general, could perform operations requiring personalization and scalability without resorting to APIs.

Perhaps more importantly, these APIs and alternative methods of data collection are not drop-in replacements. The volume, type (text, image, videos, interface, etc.), fidelity, timeliness, platform filtering, and amount of metadata vary considerably across these methods. High-volume data retrieved from APIs cannot directly replace low-volume web scraping data. Even if the volume of data collected using web scraping or APIs were identical, the metadata available via API requests is considerably different from metadata that is visible on the user-facing portions of a social media platform's website used for web scraping.

Social platform restrictions to public API access are only one aspect of the multi-faceted challenge involved in collecting digital trace data. Data access is the first in a number of steps researchers have to take as they collect, process, validate, interpret, share, and archive the data. These steps often require robust technical skills, as API endpoints for data collection were designed for programmers building application software that adds to the services offered by social platforms. As such, APIs were envisioned for purposes that differ from reproducible scientific research, a problem compounded by the significant differences between data retrieved from APIs and data visible to users on the websites and mobile apps of social platforms (Venturini & Rogers, 2019).

Locked, instable, and ephemeral

Asymmetries between information retrieved from APIs and that to which users have accessed on the web are due to social media sites being simultaneously a platform and an infrastructure (Plantin, Lagoze, Edwards, & Sandvig, 2016). Their underlying features and structures offer a rigid set of affordances, or entry points, constraining the ability to access, query, format, and collect data. These entry points take two forms: (1) interfaces for human-consumption (e.g., Facebook.com, Twitter.com, and mobile applications) and (2) software interfaces designed for consumption by computer programs called Application Programming Interfaces, with prominent examples including the Facebook Graph API, Twitter Streaming API, and Instagram API (Helmond, 2015). Social media sites have offered these website interfaces on the open web to extend their reach, decentralize data production, and centralize data collection and processing (Gerlitz & Helmond, 2013).

The underlying features of social platforms impinge on research designs and data collection, as one cannot ask questions of data that is not possible to collect. While data access is a perennial problem in social science research, a topic extensively examined in relation to survey response and privileged access to interviews (Babbie, 2010; Biernacki & Waldorf, 1981; Weller & Kinder-Kurlanda, 2016), the implications of observing dynamic content at a particular or arbitrary point in time and issues of preservation of social media data are the object of limited attention and rarely discussed in research publications. Social media posts and their accompanying metadata are fundamentally ephemeral, a term largely used as a shorthand for instability: data is constantly changing, being updated, or deleted.

The everchanging nature of social media data make it difficult for any given two researchers to collect the same exact dataset in real-time. It also makes it virtually impossible for disparate research teams to collect the same dataset retrospectively via the purchase of data from a reseller or by scraping social media websites (Burgess & Bruns, 2015). In addition to that, and perhaps more worryingly, researchers are often forbidden from sharing full datasets by the terms of service of many platforms. While some platforms, such as Twitter, allow for the sharing of each post's unique identification number, this still requires researchers to programmatically 'rehydrate' social media posts, if still accessible. While this solves the issue of informing other researchers which posts were included in the study, and also provides a method for comparing posts in different datasets, it creates at least three major issues across many social media platforms.

First, deleted posts and posts from deleted accounts cannot be retrieved from the API thereby generating orphaned data. Researchers studying misinformation are particularly interested in posts that have been deleted by users or platforms (Bastos & Mercea, 2019). Second, modified posts and modified post metadata are not flagged by APIs or web interfaces, so researchers cannot determine if a post or its metadata was changed, updated, or corrected since it was posted. Third, large datasets are difficult and time-consuming to rehydrate due to API request limits. The Twitter REST API is currently rate-limited to 150 requests per hour, returning a maximum of 100 tweets per request. While it is possible to get around these limitations by using multiple accounts simultaneously, doing so increases the technical complexity of the rehydration process.

The post IDs themselves fall under the definition advanced by Gray, Szalay, Thakar, and Stoughton (2002) of ephemeral data, since in most instances once collected these datasets cannot be reconstructed. When a post changes or disappears, it may end up being a research opportunity lost forever (Lynch, 2008) or present a false account of the phenomena under study. In the end, such obstacles to collecting and sharing datasets make it difficult and often impossible for researchers to validate or replicate studies using social media data (Felt, 2016). It additionally prevents researchers from repurposing previously collected data or expanding on research using the same dataset.

Overcoming the data access gap

Perennial issues of research replication have been compounded by social platforms' API throttling, simultaneously reducing their public accountability and increasing their opaqueness (Bastos & Mercea, 2018). Shortly after the decision to drastically limit API access, Facebook sought to counter researchers' concerns by vowing (Schrage & Ginsberg, 2018) to help the academic community gain access to social media data of public interest, starting with elections. In partnership with leading academics, public bodies, and established funding organizations, Facebook sought to collaborate with a centralized data management scheme overseen by Social Science One, an initiative that would invite and filter applications for access to datasets (for details, see commentaries of Bruns and Puschmann in this issue).

The predicament in which academics now seeking data access find themselves is evocative of the longer-standing transformation of the mission of public universities (Gumport, 1997; Walton, 2011). The erstwhile conception of universities as self-governed entities committed to the formulation, testing, and dissemination of scientific knowledge is undermined by their dependence on private enterprise and corporate activity that control data access and, to a growing extent, use. As the foundation for not only productive innovation but also new regulation, scientific knowledge could act as a restraint on corporate control (Gauchat, 2012, p. 183). However, its ability to perform this role is restricted, inter alia, by the enforcement of intellectual property rights on various aspects of research including, as described above, inputs such as data and outputs such as publications. More immediately, the creation of Social Science One as a gatekeeping body governing the relationship between Facebook and academics exemplifies a governance model that may widen the gap between data-rich industry researchers with connections to social platforms and independent researchers working outside corporations.

This divide has been characterized as the gap between 'big data rich researchers,' who have access to proprietary data and might be working in the interests of the company employing them, and the 'big data poor', or the broad universe of academic researchers whose findings may be of public interest but may ultimately be critical of social media platforms (boyd & Crawford, 2012). The data access gap not only hinders research that is peripheral to commercial interests, but it may also preclude researchers from identifying sociologically meaningful research questions because activity on social media is becoming increasingly more inscrutable and unobservable.

Alongside this apparent erosion of academic self-governance (Walton, 2011), researchers have to contend with the likelihood that social media users may not be readily open to the idea that their public communication become the object of scientific research (Fiesler & Proferes, 2018). Research entailing the automatic collection of large datasets covering long periods of time must meet expectations of non-exploitation and minimum risk/maximum benefit to informed and consenting users. To reduce the chances of causing harm to users, researchers need to find ways to obscure the presence or remove traces of any identifiable user from the data such that users are not unwillingly identified as members of an unintended community (e.g., of political dissidents).

Halavais' article (this issue) addresses some of these issues by proposing a framework of ethical distributed research involving the pragmatic partnership between users and researchers, thereby bypassing platform owners. The article suggests ways this could be accomplished and argues that the balance of power between the social media industry on one side and the users and researchers on the other has become dangerously skewed. Another innovative method to study mis/disinformation is presented by Acker and Donavan (this issue), who show how data craft through metadata manipulation and keyword squatting play a prominent role in attracting audiences. The proposed method explores data archives of disinformation offered by social media platforms and shows that such sanctioned archives prevent researchers from examining organic contexts of manipulation.

The remainder of the articles in this Special Issue tackle issues surrounding data access and ethical dilemmas in studying mis/disinformation or offer a roadmap to studying the disinformation landscape with limited or fragmented data. Bruns (this issue) outlines the societal implications of the 'APIcalypse' and reviews potential options available for researchers studying hate speech, trolling, and disinformation campaigns. The piece likewise offers a critical evaluation of Facebook's partnership with the Social Science One initiative. A response to Bruns' article is presented by Puschmann (this issue), who argues that current models of data access for social media research are also fraught with problems and pose significant risks to user privacy. The articles of Bruns and Puschmann offer opposing views of the partnerships between academics and industry seeking to address structural issues of data access.

Lastly, the Issue includes three case studies of mis/disinformation that successfully overcame the data access gap. Xia et al. (this issue) present an in-depth analysis of how the team behind an IRA Twitter account crafted the persona 'Jenna Abrams' across multiple platforms over time and describe the techniques employed to perform personal authenticity and cultural competence. Proferes and Summers (this issue) rely on a novel web archiving and scraping approach for data collection to analyze the Wikileaks' release of John Podesta's e-mails. The article details how the serialized release of batches of e-mails together with the strategic use of sequential hashtags allowed Wikileaks to game Twitter trending topics locally, nationally, and eventually worldwide. Giglietto et al. (this issue) explore partizan engagement with political news through the analysis of Twitter and Facebook interactions in the period leading up to the 2018 Italian general election. They show that polarization is not hard-wired even into highly partizan networked publics, which may engage strategically with news sources covering their favorites.

To conclude, a drive to formulate standards for public-interest research through extensive involvement of multiple stakeholders – from corporations to governments, political representatives, academic institutions, non-governmental and citizen organizations from the Global South (Milan & Treré, 2019) and North – would represent a more durable and equitable basis on which to build an alternative data governance regime to the current one. It would have to strike a balance between the accountability of all parties, their interests and rights while providing effective mechanisms to exercise a check on the power asymmetries that led to the sudden closure of the Facebook Pages API.

In that way, the data regime would have to reconcile the universalizing commercial impetus that has propelled the expansion of social platforms with the plurality of cultural, political and social communities that populate them, through a more democratic power settlement (see Laclau, 2001). It is hard to imagine, however, how the current direction of regulation that places the onus of privacy protection enforcement in the hands of social platforms (e.g., the European General Data Protection Directive, see Puschmann in this issue) may lead to such an outcome. Instead, skeptics argue that it will further consolidate their hegemony due to the high cost of privacy enforcement (Doctorow, 2019).

Disclosure statement

No potential conflict of interest was reported by the authors.

Funding

S.W. acknowledges financial support from the Arizona State University to host 'Locked out of Social Platforms: An iCS Symposium on Challenges to Studying Disinformation'. D.M. and M.B acknowledge financial support from City, University of London.

ORCID

Shawn Walker http://orcid.org/0000-0002-7052-5705
Dan Mercea http://orcid.org/0000-0003-3762-2404
Marco Bastos http://orcid.org/0000-0003-0480-1078

References

Apuzzo, M., & Santariano, A. (2019, 12 May 2019). Russia is Targetting Europe's Elections. So Are Far-Right Copycats. *New York Times*. Retrieved from https://www.nytimes.com/2019/05/12/world/europe/russian-propaganda-influence-campaign-european-elections-far-right.html

Babbie, E. R. (2010). *The practice of social research* (12th ed.). Belmont, CA: Cengage.

Bastos, M. T., & Mercea, D. (2018). The public accountability of social platforms: Lessons from a study on bots and trolls in the Brexit campaign. *Philosophical Transactions of the Royal Society A: Mathematical, Physical and Engineering Sciences*. doi:10.1098/rsta.2018.0003.

Bastos, M. T., & Mercea, D. (2019). The Brexit Botnet and user-Generated Hyperpartisan news. *Social Science Computer Review*, *37*(1), 38–54. doi:10.1177/0894439317734157.

Benkler, Y., Faris, R., & Roberts, H. (2018). *Network propaganda: Manipulation, disinformation, and Radicalization in American politics*. New York, US: Oxford University Press.

Bennett, W. L., & Segerberg, A. (2013). *The logic of Connective action: Digital media and the personalization of Contentious politics*. Cambridge: Cambridge University Press.

Bennett, W. L., & Steven, L. (2018). The disinformation order: Disruptive communication and the decline of democratic institutions. *European Journal of Communication*, *33*(2), 122–139. doi:10.1177/0267323118760317.

Bessi, A., & Ferrara, E. (2016). Social bots distort the 2016 US Presidential election online discussion. *First Monday*, *21*(11). https://firstmonday.org/article/view/7090/5653.

Biernacki, P., & Waldorf, D. (1981). Snowball sampling: Problems and techniques of chain referral sampling. *Sociological Methods & Research*, *10*(2), 141–163.

Blank, G. (2016). The digital divide Among Twitter users and Its implications for social research. *Social Science Computer Review*, *35*(6), 679–697. doi:10.1177/0894439316671698.

boyd, d. (2008). *Taken out of context: American teen sociality in networked publics*. Berkeley: University of California.

boyd, d., & Crawford, K. (2012). Critical questions for Big data. *Information, Communication & Society*, *15*(5), 662–679. doi:10.1080/1369118x.2012.678878.

Bruns, A. (2005). *Gatewatching: Collaborative online news production* (Vol. 26). New York: Peter Lang Pub Inc.

Bruns, A., Bechmann, A., Burgess, J., Chadwick, A., Clark, L. S., Dutton, W. H., … Hofmann, J. (2018). Facebook shuts the gate after the horse has bolted, and hurts real research in the process. *Internet Policy Review*. https://policyreview.info/articles/news/facebook-shuts-gate-after-horse-has-bolted-and-hurts-real-research-process/786.

Bucher, T. (2017). The algorithmic imaginary: Exploring the ordinary affects of Facebook algorithms. *Information, Communication & Society*, *20*(1), 30–44. doi:10.1080/1369118X.2016.1154086.

Bundeskartellamt. (2019). Bundeskartellamt prohibits Facebook from combining user data from different sources [Press release]. Retrieved from https://www.bundeskartellamt.de/SharedDocs/Meldung/EN/Pressemitteilungen/2019/07_02_2019_Facebook.html

Burgess, J., & Bruns, A. (2015). Easy data, hard data: The politics and pragmatics of Twitter research after the computational turn. In G. Elmer, J. Langlois, & J. Redden (Eds.), *Compromised data from social media to Big data* (pp. 93–111). London: Bloomsbury Academic.

Castells, M. (2009). *Communication power*. Oxford: Oxford University Press.

Castells, M. (2012). *Networks of outrage and hope: Social movements in the internet age*. Cambridge: Polity Press.

Chadwick, A. (2017). *The hybrid media system: Politics and power*. Oxford: Oxford University Press.

Chadwick, A., Vaccari, C., & O'Loughlin, B. (2018). Do tabloids poison the well of social media? Explaining democratically dysfunctional news sharing. *New Media & Society*, 1461444818769689. doi:10.1177/1461444818769689.

Comor, E. (2001). Harold Innis and 'The bias of communication'. *Information, Communication & Society*, *4*(2), 274–294. doi:10.1080/713768518.

Dance, G. J. X., LaForgia, M., & Confessore, N. (2018). As Facebook Raised a Privacy Wall, It Carved an Opening for Tech Giants.

Doctorow, C. (2019, 6 June 2019). Regulating Big Tech makes them stronger, so they need competition instead. *The Economist*.

Driscoll, K., & Walker, S. (2014). Working within a black box: Transparency in the collection and production of big Twitter data. *International Journal of Communication*, *8*, 1745–1764.

Facebook. (2019). Public Feed API. Retrieved from https://developers.facebook.com/docs/public_feed/

Felt, M. (2016). Social media and the social sciences: How researchers employ big data analytics. *Big Data & Society*, *3*(1), 1–15. 2053951716645828.

Fernback, J. (2007). Beyond the diluted community concept: A symbolic interactionist perspective on online social relations. *New Media & Society*, *9*(1), 49–69. doi:10.1177/1461444807072417.

Ferrara, E. (2017). Disinformation and social bot operations in the run up to the 2017 French presidential election. 2017. doi:10.5210/fm.v22i8.8005.

Fiesler, C., & Proferes, N. (2018). "Participant" perceptions of Twitter research ethics. *Social Media + Society*, *4*(1), 2056305118763366. doi:10.1177/2056305118763366.

Freelon, D. (2018). Computational research in the post-API age. *Political Communication*, 1–4. doi:10.1080/10584609.2018.1477506.

Gauchat, G. (2012). Politicization of science in the public sphere: A study of public trust in the United States, 1974 to 2010. *American Sociological Review*, *77*(2), 167–187. doi:10.1177/0003122412438225.

Gehl, R. W. (2011). The archive and the processor: The internal logic of Web 2.0. *New Media & Society*, *13*(8), 1228–1244. doi:10.1177/1461444811401735.

Gerlitz, C., & Helmond, A. (2013). The like economy: Social buttons and the data-intensive web. *New Media & Society*, *15*(8), 1348–1365.

Gray, J., Szalay, A. S., Thakar, A. R., & Stoughton, C. (2002). *Online scientific data curation, publication, and archiving*. Paper presented at the Astronomical Telescopes and Instrumentation.

Gumport, P. J. (1997). Public universities as academic workplaces. *Daedalus*, *126*(4), 113–136.

Helmond, A. (2015). The platformization of the web: Making web data platform ready. *Social Media+ Society*, *1*(2), 1–11. 2056305115603080.

Hermida, A. (2010). Twittering the news: The emergence of ambient journalism. *Journalism Practice*, *4*(3), 297–308. doi:10.1080/17512781003640703.

House of Commons Digital, C., Media and Sport Committee. (2019). *Disinformation and fake news: Final report*. Retrieved from https://publications.parliament.uk/pa/cm201719/cmselect/cmcumeds/1791/1791.pdf

Howard, P. N., & Hussain, M. M. (2013). *Democracy's fourth wave?: Digital media and the Arab spring*. Oxford: Oxford University Press.

Innis, H. A. (1982). *The Bias of communication*. Toronto: University of Toronto Press.

Jenkins, H., Ford, S., Green, J., & New, C. (2013). *Spreadable media: Creating value and meaning in a networked and London*. New York: New York University Press.

Karlova, N. A., & Fisher, K. E. (2013). A social diffusion model of misinformation and disinformation for understanding human information behaviour. *Information Research*, *18*(1). http://informationr.net/ir/18-1/paper573.html.

Laclau, E. (2001). Democracy and the question of power. *Constellations (Oxford, England)*, *8*(1), 3–14.

Langley, P., & Leyshon, A. (2017). Platform capitalism: The intermediation and capitalization of digital economic circulation. *Finance and Society*, *3*(1), 11–31. doi:10.2218/finsoc.v3i1.1936.

Lewandowsky, S., Ecker, U. K. H., & Cook, J. (2017). Beyond misinformation: Understanding and coping with the "post-truth" era. *Journal of Applied Research in Memory and Cognition*, *6*(4), 353–369. doi:10.1016/j.jarmac.2017.07.008.

Loader, B. D., & Mercea, D. (2011). Networking democracy? *Information, Communication & Society*, *14*(6), 757–769. doi:10.1080/1369118x.2011.592648.

Lomborg, S., & Kapsch, P. H. (2019). Decoding algorithms. *Media, Culture & Society*, *0*(0), 0163443719855301. doi:10.1177/0163443719855301.

Lynch, C. (2008). Big data: How do your data grow? *Nature*, *455*(7209), 28–29.

Milan, S., & Treré, E. (2019). Big data from the south(s): Beyond data Universalism. *Television & New Media*, *20*(4), 319–335. doi:10.1177/1527476419837739.

Möller, J., Trilling, D., Helberger, N., & van Es, B. (2018). Do not blame it on the algorithm: An empirical assessment of multiple recommender systems and their impact on content diversity. *Information, Communication & Society*, 1–19. doi:10.1080/1369118X.2018.1444076.

Neate, R. (2018). Over $119bn wiped off of Facebook's market cap after growth shock. *The Guardian*. Retrieved from https://www.theguardian.com/technology/2018/jul/26/facebook-market-cap-falls-109bn-dollars-after-growth-shock

Plantin, J.-C., Lagoze, C., Edwards, P. N., & Sandvig, C. (2016). Infrastructure studies meet platform studies in the age of Google and Facebook. *New Media & Society*. doi:10.1177/1461444816661553.

Rosenberg, M. (2018). Professor apologizes for helping Cambridge analytica harvest Facebook data. *New York Times*. Retrieved from https://www.nytimes.com/2018/04/22/business/media/cambridge-analytica-aleksandr-kogan.html

Schrage, E., & Ginsberg, D. (2018). Facebook launches new initiative to help scholars assess social media's impact on elections [Press release]. Retrieved from https://newsroom.fb.com/news/2018/04/new-elections-initiative/

Schroepfer, M. (2018). An update on our plans to restrict data access on Facebook | Facebook newsroom. Retrieved from https://newsroom.fb.com/news/2018/04/restricting-data-access/

Skeggs, B., & Yuill, S. (2015). The methodology of a multi-model project examining how values and value are made through Facebook relations. *Information Communication and Society*, *19*(10), 1356–1372.

Tufekci, Z. (2019, 7 March 2019). Zuckerberg's so-called shift toward privacy. *New York Times*. Retrieved from https://www.nytimes.com/2019/03/07/opinion/zuckerberg-privacy-facebook.html

Tufekci, Z., & Wilson, C. (2012). Social media and the decision to participate in political protest: Observations from Tahrir Square. *Journal of Communication*, *62*(2), 363–379.

Twitter. (2019). Documents. Retrieved from https://developer.twitter.com/en/docs

Van Dijck, J. A. (2013). *The culture of connectivity: A critical history of social media*. Oxford: Oxford University Press.

Venturini, T., & Rogers, R. (2019). "API-based research" or how can digital sociology and journalism studies learn from the Facebook and Cambridge analytica data breach. *Digital Journalism*, 1–9. doi:10.1080/21670811.2019.1591927.

Volpicelli, G. (2019). Passing laws to force Facebook to fix fake news is asking for trouble. *Wired*. Retrieved from https://www.wired.co.uk/article/dcms-report-fake-news-report

Walton, J. K. (2011). The idea of the University. In M. Bailey & D. Freedman (Eds.), *The Assault on universities* (pp. 15–26). London: Pluto Press.

Weedon, J., Nuland, W., & Stamos, A. (2017). *Information operations and Facebook*. Retrieved from.

Weller, K., & Kinder-Kurlanda, K. E. (2016). *A manifesto for data sharing in social media research*. Paper presented at the Proceedings of the 8th ACM Conference on Web Science.

Zuckerberg, M. (Producer). (2017, 03.06.2019). Building global community. Retrieved from https://www.facebook.com/notes/mark-zuckerberg/building-global-community/10154544292806634/

Zuckerman, E. (2014). New media, new civics? *Policy & Internet*, *6*(2), 151–168. doi:10.1002/1944-2866.poi360.

After the 'APIcalypse': social media platforms and their fight against critical scholarly research

Axel Bruns

ABSTRACT

In the aftermath of the Cambridge Analytica controversy, social media platform providers such as *Facebook* and *Twitter* have severely restricted access to platform data via their Application Programming Interfaces (APIs). This has had a particularly critical effect on the ability of social media researchers to investigate phenomena such as abuse, hate speech, trolling, and disinformation campaigns, and to hold the platforms to account for the role that their affordances and policies might play in facilitating such dysfunction. Alternative data access frameworks, such as *Facebook*'s partnership with the controversial Social Science One initiative, represent an insufficient replacement for fully functional APIs, and the platform providers' actions in responding to the Cambridge Analytica scandal raise suspicions that they have instrumentalised it to actively frustrate critical, independent, public interest scrutiny by scholars. Building on a critical review of *Facebook*'s public statements through its own platforms and the mainstream media, and of the scholarly responses these have drawn, this article outlines the societal implications of the 'APIcalypse', and reviews potential options for scholars in responding to it.

Introduction: end of an era

The face of scholarly social media research is changing, rapidly. For the past ten years or so – since *Facebook*'s userbase began to grow rapidly in 2008, and *Twitter*'s followed suit in 2009 – there had been a steady growth in the field, in methodological, theoretical, empirical, and organisational terms (see e.g., Baran & Ghaffari, 2017; Snelson, 2016; van Osch & Coursaris, 2014; Zimmer & Proferes, 2014). Building on increasingly large datasets, gathered through the Application Programming Interfaces (APIs) of the leading platforms, social media research had proven a particularly fertile field: driven especially by a number of leading centres for digital media research, the scholarly community developed and shared increasingly sophisticated methods and tools for gathering, analysing, and visualising social media data (Zimmer & Proferes, 2014, p. 257). These included, for *Twitter*, the public data gathering service *TwapperKeeper.com*, its open-source self-install version *yourTwapperKeeper* (2013), and subsequently especially the *Twitter Capture and Analysis*

Toolkit (*TCAT*), developed at the Digital Methods Initiative (DMI) at the University of Amsterdam (Borra & Rieder, 2014). For *Facebook*, DMI researchers developed the *Netvizz* tool (Rieder, 2013), with several other popular solutions also available. Further, commercial services such as Texifter (2018) partnered with social media platform providers to offer current and historical data and associated analytics in formats and at price points that specifically targeted scholarly users. As the following discussion will show, except for *TCAT* all of these tools and services have now been shut down or severely affected by changes to *Facebook*'s and *Twitter*'s API frameworks; this 'APIcalypse' is likely to severely affect further scholarly research on these platforms.

This considerable innovation in research methods and techniques that these tools represent also produced further research initiatives at increasingly ambitious scales, and often these initiatives specifically targeted the major gaps remaining in social media scholarship. For instance, much API-driven *Facebook* research remained limited to the platform's public spaces (such as *Facebook* pages), for obvious ethical, privacy, and practical reasons, and the Danish *Digital Footprints* project (2018) addressed this by inviting Facebook users to donate access to their private networks by connecting with the project's Facebook app (Bechmann & Vahlstrup, 2015). On *Twitter*, the bulk of the research focussed on easily accessible datasets centring on hashtags and keywords (a limitation highlighted *inter alia* by Burgess & Bruns, 2015); the Australian *TrISMA* project (Bruns et al., 2016) addressed this shortcoming by identifying and following the public activities of all 3.7 million Australian *Twitter* accounts. Across both platforms (and beyond), there was a need to generate more reliable, long-term, comparative metrics for user activities, especially around major world events, and the *Illuminating 2016* (Stromer-Galley et al., 2016) project addressed this task in the context of the 2016 US presidential elections, for example.

Finally, such work has also been increasingly supported by scholarly infrastructure. Journals such as *Information, Communication & Society* have opened their pages to a growing number of social media research articles (Snelson, 2016, p. 7); the International Conference on Weblogs and Social Media (ICWSM) grew out of earlier Web- and blog-related events in 2007; the annual Social Media & Society conference was launched in 2010; and the (unrelated) open-access journal *Social Media + Society* followed in 2015. More established conferences such as those of the Association of Internet Researchers (AoIR) or the International Communication Association (ICA) have also featured a substantial number of papers building on social media scholarship.

The platforms themselves have long had an ambivalent relationship with such research, however. Early on, and especially in the face of accusations that social media were merely used for 'pointless babble' (Pear Analytics, 2009) and other 'banal' purposes (Rogers, 2014), they utilised scholarly research from time to time to demonstrate their own relevance and convince prospective commercial and government institutions to sign on to their platforms (see e.g., *Twitter Blog* posts such as Baker, 2015; Rogers, 2013). Over the years, the platforms have also hired a substantial number of university graduates – in instrumental fields such as computer science, unsurprisingly, but importantly also from more critical disciplines such as media, communication, and cultural studies – to bolster their workforce in key areas of operation; on occasion, they have also collaborated with external research teams (e.g., Kramer, Guillory, & Hancock, 2014; Su, Sharma, & Goel, 2016). And from time to time, the platforms have offered 'data grants' and similar competitive schemes that explicitly invited scholars to apply for funding and data access for particular research initiatives. Indeed, for all its faults, even *Twitter*'s ill-fated 'gift' of the entire *Twitter* archives since 2006 to the US Library of Congress (Alaimo, 2017; Stone, 2010) could be charitably regarded as a recognition both of the historical value of *Twitter* archives as a 'first draft of the present' (Bruns & Weller, 2016), and of the possible benefits of an in-depth scholarly investigation of their contents.

Yet the relationship between researchers and platforms was never entirely harmonious. For example, while *Twitter* offered elevated API access to researchers and developers in the early days of the platform (Bucher, 2013), in order to build its ecosystem and generate publicity, such access was eventually rescinded as the platform began to exploit the value of its data through commercial access frameworks like the data reseller GNIP (which eventually became its wholly-owned subsidiary). This shift in attitude towards the third-party researcher and developer ecosystem was summed up by one developer as 'thanks for getting so many people interested in Twitter. Now get lost', as a study by Bucher (2013) reports.

A notable early sign of this reorientation was that in 2011, *Twitter* forced the closure of the popular *TwapperKeeper.com* service, which had operated an on-demand keyword and hashtag gathering service and had made the resulting datasets publicly available to its users (O'Brien, 2011); this also meant that the sharing of datasets between researchers was increasingly conducted through non-public, grey channels (Weller & Kinder-Kurlanda, 2015). *Facebook*'s relationship with scholars, too, soured considerably, especially after the substantial global controversy around the 2014 'emotional contagion' study it conducted in collaboration with researchers at Cornell University (Kramer et al., 2014), which was widely criticised for insufficiently addressing the ethical dimensions of a research approach that did not seek informed consent from the nearly 700,000 *Facebook* users whose newsfeeds were manipulated (Flick, 2016).

Indeed, this controversy may be seen as an early example of the significantly more intense criticism that has been levelled at *Facebook*, *Twitter*, and other social media platforms since 2016 for their treatment of users and their data, for their insufficient responses to platform issues ranging from hate speech and abuse through breaches of privacy to the dissemination of mis- and disinformation, and for their systematic evasion of critical and independent oversight. Such critiques, and the platforms' responses to them, were prompted especially by the widely publicised controversy around the dubious data analytics company Cambridge Analytica (Constine & Hatmaker, 2018), but in reality, that specific case is merely emblematic of a longer and more gradual process of disconnect between platforms and scholars, even if it was used by both sides as a justification for their subsequent actions.

Drawing substantially on the public statements of *Facebook* and other platforms, as published through their own corporate sites and reported in the mainstream media, and on the responses from the scholarly community that they prompted, this article explores the radical changes to API access, especially for *Facebook*, that have followed the Cambridge Analytica moment. It offers a critical evaluation, from the scholarly perspective, of the justifications provided for these changes, and considers the implications of this 'APIcalypse' for critical, independent, public-interest scholarship. It also critiques the alternative data access models now proposed and implemented by platforms like *Facebook* and *Twitter* and shows how these initiatives appear designed more to generate positive media coverage than support meaningful scholarship. It closes with an overview of the possible pathways for researchers affected by this sudden crippling of social media data access, and a call to action for scholars to resist the platforms' duplicitous changes to their API policies.

In doing so this article takes a decidedly 'data activist' perspective (Kazansky, Torres, van der Velden, Wissenbach, & Milan, 2019), prompted by a growing consensus amongst social media scholars that these increasing restrictions are problematic not only for the research itself, but also for the society and societies in whose interest such critical, independent, publicly-funded research is conducted. These concerns have been expressed most prominently in a series of open letters to *Facebook* and other platforms by scholars and the foundations and non-government organisations that support their research (e.g., Bruns, 2018; Knight First Amendment Institute, 2018; Mozilla, 2019a, 2019b), as well as in public interventions from former *Facebook* insiders (e.g., Stamos qtd. in Hughes, 2019; Mac & Warzel, 2018). This article also draws on these contributions to outline the platforms' key strategies in responding to such criticism, and to identify four possible pathways for social media researchers trying to grapple with the rapidly changing environment for their work.

Cambridge Analytica and its aftermath

The Cambridge Analytica scandal broke in earnest with the publication of Carole Cadwalladr's investigative article in *The Guardian* on 17 March 2018. In addition to more conventional, offline techniques, the media coverage revealed Cambridge Analytica's apparent data analytics and psychographic voter targeting capabilities, building especially on social media data obtained from *Facebook* with the help of a 'personality test' app that gathered information from up to 87 million users (Constine & Hatmaker, 2018). This highlighted *Facebook*'s commodification of user data in general, and its lax user privacy protection measures in relation to third-party *Facebook* apps in particular.

Key to this aspect of the controversy was the role played by researcher and developer Aleksandr Kogan, who was singled out in *Facebook*'s initial statement on its suspension of Cambridge Analytica and parent company Strategic Communication Laboratories from the platform:

> In 2015, we learned that a psychology professor at the University of Cambridge named Dr Aleksandr Kogan lied to us and violated our Platform Policies by passing data from an app that was using Facebook Login to SCL/Cambridge Analytica, a firm that does political, government and military work around the globe. (Grewal, 2018)

For his part, Kogan acknowledges that he developed the app used by Cambridge Analytica, but also claims that he did so in the employ of Cambridge Analytica rather than as a University of Cambridge scholar. From this perspective, then, Kogan suggests that

> [what] Cambridge Analytica has allegedly done, [to] use people's Facebook data for micro-targeting, is the primary use case for most data on these platforms. Facebook and Twitter and other platforms make their money through advertising and so there's an agreement between the user of 'hey, you will get this amazing product that costs billions of dollars to run and in return we can sell you to advertisers for micro-targeting'. (Qtd. in Weaver, 2018)

This article is not the appropriate vehicle to judge the truth of these conflicting claims; rather, for our present purposes it is important to highlight the immediate emphasis on inappropriate data sharing practices between research and industry in *Facebook*'s public response. This diverts attention from far more fundamental questions about the ethical and privacy implications of its commodification of user data. After all, even *Facebook* itself admits that Kogan 'gained access to this information in a legitimate way and through the proper channels that governed all developers on Facebook at that time', and only 'subsequently' failed to 'abide by our rules', by sharing the data with Cambridge Analytica (Grewal, 2018). Indeed, this point is strengthened further in a next-day update to the press release, in response to media reports that the scandal constituted a data breach:

> Aleksandr Kogan requested and gained access to information from users who chose to sign up to his app, and everyone involved gave their consent. People knowingly provided their information, no systems were infiltrated, and no passwords or sensitive pieces of information were stolen or hacked. (Grewal, 2018)

An uncharitable reading of *Facebook*'s response to the Cambridge Analytica controversy, then, might conclude that by carefully highlighting Kogan's alleged role in the data gathering process the company's public relations department deliberately sought to obscure the fact that the platform's fundamental business model had ostensibly enabled the emergence of Cambridge Analytica and similar political and advertising microtargeting services. This should not immediately be understood as part of a long-term strategy to discredit scholarly social media researchers, however – more likely, as Kogan himself also alludes to (Weaver, 2018), his unquestionable involvement in Cambridge Analytica's data gathering efforts simply positioned him as an obvious and convenient scapegoat that enabled *Facebook* to divert attention from its own business practices.

Facebook's reaction to the Cambridge Analytica controversy, and its and other platforms' subsequent actions in related contexts, reveal a number of interweaving corporate strategies that claim to improve data security and user privacy, but by accident or design also severely undermine critical, independent, public-interest research. Based on the platforms' own announcements, the following discussion documents three key elements of these strategies; subsequently, the article also outlines various possible pathways for scholarly responses to these interventions.

Suspension and shutdown: new restrictions to APIs and terms of service

The immediate response to the Cambridge Analytica controversy was to disable data access for potentially problematic API clients, and to exclude potential future users by tightening the APIs' terms of service. In addition to cancelling the API data access of Cambridge Analytica itself, *Facebook* reviewed the practices of several other social media data analytics services, in specific political as well as more general commercial fields, and reportedly suspended some 200 third-party apps (Pasternack, 2018). In July 2018, it even briefly banned one of the industry leaders, Crimson Hexagon, over allegations of improper data use. In relation to that suspension, *Facebook*'s Vice-President of Product Partnerships stated, somewhat implausibly, that 'we don't allow developers to build surveillance tools using information from Facebook or Instagram' (ABC News, 2018).

In the wake of the immediate scandal, *Facebook* soon announced further changes to the data access regimes for its public API services. Without warning third-party developers and researchers, it advanced the previously planned shutdown of subsidiary platform *Instagram*'s public API from 31 July to 4 April 2018 (Constine, 2018); on the same day, it also announced substantial reductions to the functionality of *Facebook*'s Events, Groups, and Pages APIs – that is, to the key APIs providing data on public activity on the platform – that similarly came into effect immediately, 'starting today' (Schroepfer, 2018). The announcement also foreshadowed further API adjustments as well as reviews of data access permissions for existing apps 'over the coming months'.

Although some of these changes may be welcome in principle where they genuinely improve data protection and user privacy, the lack of consultation about and speed of implementation of these adjustments also meant that a considerable number of third-party apps and services, including key research tools, were now failing to operate correctly, or were threatened by future changes. One key casualty was the widely used *Facebook* research tool *Netvizz*, which was required to undergo a new app review process for 'suspicious applications' and failed to regain approval, for reasons that *Facebook* has not clarified. As developer Bernhard Rieder, a scholar in the Digital Methods Initiative at the University of Amsterdam, has written, this means that to date 'Netvizz still functions ... and may very well continue to live a zombie existence in the future', but *Facebook*'s inherently non-specific feedback to app approval requests also means that scholars are increasingly unlikely to try to maintain such research tools 'in this structurally opaque and unhelpful environment'. For his part, Rieder himself has already decided to 'take a step back from Netvizz' (Rieder, 2018), and he is unlikely to be the only app developer – in both the scholarly and commercial fields – to have responded in this way.

Facebook and its subsidiaries are not the only platforms to have reacted in this way to the Cambridge Analytica controversy: in July 2018, *Twitter*, too, announced changes to the way it manages its API. Here, the initial changes were predominantly administrative rather than technical: while previously, it was comparatively straightforward to register as a *Twitter* developer and request one or more authentication keys required for *Twitter* apps (including key scholarly data gathering tools like *TCAT*) that access the public *Twitter* API, the company is now implementing a new registration process requiring developers 'to provide detailed information about how they use or intend to use Twitter's APIs so that we can better ensure compliance with our policies' (Roth & Johnson, 2018). However, as a *Bloomberg* article on these changes has pointed out,

> users who sign up to use the developer platform also have to agree to Twitter's policies. One of these imposes restrictions on studying a range of subjects, including political beliefs and racial and religious topics. ... It's disturbing that the company requires researchers using their API to agree to policies that include restrictions on studying topics like identity politics. (Alaimo, 2018)

Facebook's terms of service similarly restrict the conduct of legitimate scholarly and journalistic research into problematic uses of the platform (Knight First Amendment Institute, 2018, p. 2f.)

Subsequent changes to the *Twitter* API itself appear to have been targeted especially at third-party clients used by power users; this has curtailed the functionality of popular tools such as *Twitterific* or *Hootsuite*, which can now no longer offer automatically refreshing

Twitter timelines or push notifications. While less critical for most scholarly purposes, these changes reveal a growing desire for *Twitter* to position its own apps and Website as the only legitimate point of access to *Twitter* content (Perez, 2018), in what the company itself calls a 'more focused approach' (Johnson, 2018). In addition to such end-user tools, however, another target of this 'more focused approach' was also the commercial data service *Texifter*, which had previously provided historical *Twitter* data and analytics to scholarly users under a long-standing licence arrangement with the platform. According to *Texifter* CEO Stu Shulman, 'Twitter rejected its application to renew its contract to use Twitter data for academic purposes and said that only use of Twitter data for businesses would be acceptable. … Twitter made the pricing prohibitive' (qtd. in Alaimo, 2018), too, and *Texifter* was eventually decommissioned on 30 September 2018 (Texifter, 2018).

It should be noted here, of course, that other commercial social media analytics services still exist, and continue to offer metrics for *Twitter* and other platforms; additionally, *Twitter* itself also offers premium, paid data access models. However, their price points, data offers, and analytics services are generally ill-suited to typical scholarly research needs: the costs associated with such services are usually unaffordable for scholars with limited funding; data access – especially with respect to export for analysis in scholarly content or network analysis software – is often shallow and limited; and analytics functions are generally geared to basic market research questions rather than more complex scholarly investigations. Amongst the commercial data providers, *Texifter* was the only service that explicitly addressed scholarly customers, and its loss leaves a considerable gap in the social media research landscape.

For increasingly beleaguered major platforms such as *Facebook* or *Twitter*, it is easy to see independent, critical scholarly research as a potential threat to their corporate identity, and to treat it accordingly; as Stanford University's Justin Littman has put it, 'research by academic institutions is clearly perceived as a liability post-Cambridge Analytica. … While there's clearly a huge societal benefit to this research, it's not necessarily research that benefits social media companies directly. It's easier to say no than to figure out how to handle it properly' (qtd. in Alaimo, 2018). From this perspective, the rapid reduction of data access through the platform APIs in the wake of Cambridge Analytica may not simply be a genuine countermeasure to stop similar rogue operators: these would presumably have the resources to buy data from commercial social media data resellers, or the wherewithal to engage in data acquisition through large-scale scraping or other unauthorised means. Rather, it is also a convenient step towards disabling and evading unwanted independent, critical, public-interest scholarly scrutiny.

Indeed, such efforts to evade scrutiny transcend API-based access methods. In early 2019, *Facebook* also took explicit steps to disable the functionality of a browser plugin promoted by the investigative journalism initiative *ProPublica* that would capture the *Facebook* ads encountered by plugin users, as well as a number of similar other tools. Using direct Web scraping methods that did not rely on API access, the plugin sought to generate independent, publicly accessible observational data especially on political advertising practices in the United States and elsewhere; citing a need 'to keep people's information safe', *Facebook* responded by deliberately obfuscating the HTML code served by its Website in such a way that ads could no longer be immediately recognised as distinct elements of a *Facebook* page (Merrill & Tobin, 2019). Subsequent updates and counter-updates to the plugin and HTML code have sought to re-enable and re-disable the tool's functionality, respectively. It should be noted here that *Facebook* also provides a searchable *Facebook* Ad Library that is meant to offer some transparent information on what ads are scheduled on the platform, and by whom – but a lack of comprehensive search functionality and limited international coverage have resulted in widespread criticism of this initiative, and public calls for a more research-focussed redesign (Mozilla, 2019a, 2019b).

Corporate data philanthropy: a 'new paradigm' for data access?

Partly in an effort to address the significant data access gaps caused by such shutdowns, and partly also to ward off the negative publicity resulting from the growing scholarly criticism of their heavy-handed new enforcement tactics, several major social media platforms have sought to replace their previously indiscriminately available APIs with more targeted, bespoke schemes for scholarly data access; the *Facebook* Ad Library is one example for such initiatives. Indeed, even before Cambridge Analytica broke, and partly in response to persistent criticism of its insufficient response to rampant abuse, hate speech, and fascist propaganda on its platform, *Twitter* had launched a somewhat vague call for research proposals that would help it 'measure the health of Twitter' (Twitter, Inc., 2018); in July, it revealed that two of more than 230 proposals had been selected for funding and data access (Gadde & Gasca, 2018). This approach broadly mirrors the company's never repeated 'Twitter #DataGrants pilot program' of 2013, which awarded data access to six out of 1,300 submitted applications (Kirkorian, 2014) – in each case, the success rate for applications was considerably lower than even for most of the competitive funding schemes operated by the various national and international research councils, and it is therefore perhaps more appropriate to describe these initiatives as data *lotteries* than as data grants (Burgess & Bruns, 2015).

Facebook has chosen to follow a broadly similar path, but to avoid a fully in-house applications assessment process. Instead, it empowered two researchers from Harvard and Stanford to set up a new entity, 'Social Science One', that also partnered with seven US-based non-profit foundations and the non-profit Social Science Research Council to facilitate its own applications process for funding and *Facebook* data access. The mission of this new entity is outlined in an unpublished manuscript authored by the founders, Gary King and Nate Persily, and made available via Social Science One's site: 'we propose here a new model of industry-academic partnerships designed to span the divide between the needs of internet technology firms, academic researchers, and the public, even in highly politicized environments' (King & Persily, 2018, p. 2). On Social Science One's Website, however, it is also made clear that this partnership is not envisaged as one between equals: 'it enables firms to enlist the scientific community to help them produce social good, while protecting their competitive positions' (Social Science One, 2018a). This form of corporate data philanthropy appears designed predominantly to benefit the corporation, therefore.

The 'King-Persily paper' presents the needs of social media research in a way that makes the organisational model for Social Science One appear as the logical 'new paradigm for industry-academic partnerships' (Social Science One, 2018b). To justify Social Science One's model of data philanthropy, King & Persily present the reader with only two stark, 'antipodean' choices for how the relationship between scholars and platforms could be organised: on the one hand, data provision to 'fully independent' scholars, which is unlikely to serve the interests of the platform, and on the other hand, academic research 'inside companies' and under 'nondisclosure and other legal agreements' (King & Persily, 2018, p. 3). Both of these models are flawed, they suggest: 'academic independence with inadequate information generates little value. Full information with dependence on the firm for pre-publication approval poses actual or apparent conflicts of interest' (2018, p. 4). The obvious answer to this dilemma is the Social Science One paradigm, naturally, rather than any of the fundamentally different approaches we might also envisage: a model that 'ensures that the company's interests are protected, the data is kept secure and private, and the researchers publishing maintain independence' (2018, p. 4).

The proposed price of such harmony, however, is to limit scholarly inquiry to issues and topics that are unlikely to put pressure on the platform providing the data: 'the optimal way forward ... is to find research questions that are of intellectual interest to the scientific community and either provide valuable knowledge to inform product, programmatic, and policy decisions, or are orthogonal to company interests' (King & Persily, 2018, p. 12). This reads as a very thinly veiled call to researchers to restrain their criticism if they hope to work under the Social Science One paradigm: in the case of platforms like *Facebook* or *Twitter*, this approach to finding research questions would presumably rule out research that seeks to address key current issues such as abuse, hate speech, or disinformation (which are certainly not 'orthogonal' to these platforms' interests), if there was any likelihood that the research might find the platforms' own affordances or policies culpable in facilitating such phenomena. King & Persily allow that 'some bad news for the company will sometimes unavoidably surface', but warn that 'few companies would participate in facilitating research designed solely to evaluate [their] own actions' (2018, p. 12).

In line with the 'new paradigm' outlined in the King-Persily paper, therefore, Social Science One set a number of strict limitations for the first (and thus far only) call for project proposals it has published. The call

> invites proposals that examine the impact of social media and related digital technologies on democracy and elections, generate insights to inform policy at the intersection of media, technology, and democracy, and advance new avenues for future research (Social Science One, 2018b),

yet requires that researchers 'should not be investigating internal corporate policies, decisions, or product development' and should do so only 'for scientific purposes, not for purposes of advocacy, journalism, investigation of individuals, or research for competitors' (*ibid.*). It is not immediately clear how these restrictions are compatible with the Social Science One model's stated aim that 'researchers publishing maintain independence' (King & Persily, 2018, p. 4).

Presumably, in fact, these restrictions would rule out identifying the individual accounts (i.e., *individuals*) responsible for the spread of mis- and disinformation, hate speech, trolling, and other misuses of the platform that might disrupt democratic processes and change election outcomes, and would prevent researchers from working with mainstream media to disseminate their findings to a general audience (*journalism*), or from developing proposals to policymakers and regulators for how to address such election interference more effectively (*advocacy*). This leaves precious little room for actual, meaningful, socially responsible, and impactful research, especially at a time when there are growing calls for scholars to embrace a more 'data-activist research agenda' (Kazansky et al., 2019, p. 244) in order to combat pressing societal problems.

After all, in the wake of the UK's Brexit referendum and the US presidential election and the widely publicised role that interference campaigns on social media platforms by various political, commercial, and state actors played in their outcomes (e.g., Grinberg, Joseph, Friedland, Swire-Thompson, & Lazer, 2019; NATO Strategic Communications Centre of Excellence, 2017; Woolley & Howard, 2017), but also in light of broader concerns about user profiling, spam, abuse, hate speech, trolling, and extreme polarisation in social media, much of the current research agenda for social media scholars is far from 'orthogonal' to the platforms' interests. Instead, it is explicitly designed to assess the extent of the problem, to evaluate the role of platform affordances, policies, and actions in creating or mitigating it, and to develop technological, social, legislative, regulatory, or educational responses to it (e.g., Bounegru, Gray, Venturini, & Mauri, 2017; Wardle & Derakhshan, 2017). In other words, in sharp contrast to an earlier period when social media researchers contributed to the 'debanalisation' (Rogers, 2014) of social media platforms by documenting their increasingly important informational, social, or commercial roles, and thereby also facilitated these platforms' gradual societal acceptance, the subject matter of much current research is a great deal darker: as they focus on the most prominent contemporary social media phenomena, scholars are now dealing with a great deal more dysfunction and deliberate disruption than was the case some five or ten years ago. Therefore, they may well be seen by platform providers as contributing to a growing chorus of public criticism.

Finally, the Social Science One call also provides some additional detail about the proposal review process. In addition to a peer review effort overseen by the Social Science Research Council, and an additional ethics and privacy review by a separate panel, in a final stage

> the co-chairs at Social Science One, acting like editors at a scholarly journal, take input from both prior steps, along with their knowledge as a trusted third party following the structure of this initiative, and make final **substantive decisions** about which proposals to support. Examples of the private knowledge the co-chairs have include ongoing litigation that would subject researchers addressing certain topics to legal discovery; proprietary information that change[s] the likely importance of certain research topics; and complex privacy constraints that would be violated in certain types of data. (Social Science One, 2018b; emphasis in original)

Hidden within this language is the fact that this third step provides the Social Science One chairs with the exclusive power to veto proposals even where they have successfully passed the first two hurdles, in a way that seems entirely *unlike* the decisions commonly made by journal editors once peer review has recommended an article for publication. Further, as this power to make 'substantive decisions' at this final stage is largely based on proprietary 'private knowledge' stemming from their privileged relationship with *Facebook*, such decisions are inherently intransparent, and there appears to be no opportunity for researchers to appeal against them. Surely, a removal of this third, final step – leaving only peer review and ethics and privacy review as the two hurdles that proposals must pass – would ensure a much more accountable, transparent, and independent selection process.

Deflection and spin: generating positive PR, not critical research

To be very clear: this critical reading of the Social Science One model is not meant as an attack on the foundations that support it, nor on the scholars from around the world who have chosen to serve on its peer review and other committees; there is every indication that they are genuinely interested in exploring new models to provide access to *Facebook* data for research purposes. The same cannot be said so easily about *Facebook* itself, however: in addition to its efforts to control the flow of data to researchers more explicitly, the company has also engaged in some highly problematic attempts to spin the public debate in its favour.

As noted, *Facebook* seems to be making its API and Website changes at least in part to disable and exclude critical scholarly social media research, while using far more circumscribed and deeply flawed alternative data access schemes like Social Science One or the *Facebook* Ad Library for cover. These corporate 'data philanthropy' initiatives – and others before them, like *Twitter*'s 'gift' of its complete archive to the Library of Congress (Stone, 2010) or the *Twitter* Data Grants and Health Metrics initiatives – certainly also generate substantial positive publicity for the platforms and enable them to be seen to do something that demonstrates their corporate social responsibility. If, in the end, these initiatives come to nothing – if the Library of Congress fails to develop appropriate frameworks for providing access to the data (Alaimo, 2017), if the data grants support only a vanishingly small percentage of proposals, or if Social Science One excludes any non-orthogonal research projects – then the companies can still point to their initial support for these initiatives and say 'well, we tried'.

This openly cynical reading of these initiatives might be dismissed as mere conspiracy theory, were it not for the fact that companies like *Facebook* have undeniable form in acting in such duplicitous ways. In late 2018, a major *New York Times* investigation revealed that rather than, or at the very least in addition to, addressing its extensive problem with Russian interference campaigns during and after the 2016 US presidential election, *Facebook* embarked on

> an aggressive lobbying campaign to combat Facebook's critics, shift public anger toward rival companies and ward off damaging regulation. Facebook employed a Republican opposition-research firm to discredit activist protesters, in part by linking them to the liberal financier George Soros. (Frenkel, Confessore, Kang, Rosenberg, & Nicas, 2018)

As journalists covering the story were quick to point out, the attempt to embroil Soros in this debate demonstrates particularly bad faith, given the persistent attacks on Soros by elements of the domestic and international far right, neo-fascists, anti-Semites, and Russian-controlled disinformation operatives:

> no company in the world is in a better position than Facebook to know what a toxic dog-whistle this is: Soros has been the bogeyman of far-right and nationalist movements across the world, and has become a transparent means for people trying to keep a veneer of respectability to spread anti-Semitism. (Ball, 2018)

In response to the *New York Times* report, *Facebook* acknowledged that it had been working with Definers Public Affairs, a lobbying firm that is itself associated at least indirectly with far-right influence campaigns in the United States, but played down its efforts to control and reshape the narrative (Facebook Newsroom, 2018). Such feeble efforts to justify the company's actions were met with widespread derision and dismay. For instance, Kate Starbird, a leading scholar of social media disinformation campaigns at the University of Washington, tweeted:

> This is turning my stomach. Around the same time I was invited to Facebook to give a presentation on online disinformation, FB's leadership was hiring an influence firm to use disinfo to attack its critics (invoking one of the same tropes that we'd seen Russia use for years). (2018a)

> I know a lot of amazing people who work for Facebook and I know there are people who care working hard to improve how the platform deals with mis/disinformation. But I'm having a hard time reconciling that with this most recent revelation about their own information operations. (2018b)

Facebook's emphasis on the role of Aleksandr Kogan as the purported source of Cambridge Analytica's data should be read in this context, too. It is notable that the King-Persily paper also follows *Facebook*'s line of argument, repeating this accusation as a justification for its very hands-on *Facebook* partnership model:

> after all, the notorious recent 'Cambridge Analytica' scandal began with a breach by an academic (acting as a developer) of a developer's agreement with Facebook, which barred his sale of the data to a for-profit company. That scandal is an academic scandal as well. (King & Persily, 2018, p. 13)

However, if Kogan was indeed 'acting as a developer' rather than academic, then most likely he did not breach *Facebook*'s developer agreement, as even *Facebook*'s own statements have acknowledged (Grewal, 2018). Again, the point of the present article is not to pass judgment on Kogan's culpability as an actor in Cambridge Analytica – but to paint Cambridge Analytica as an 'academic scandal' in any significant way seems to deflect from the fact that the fundamental corporate responsibility must surely rest with *Facebook* and Cambridge Analytica as corporate actors, rather than with individual employees.

Attempts by major corporations to smear rather than engage perceived enemies are far from new, of course. They resemble the efforts of the tobacco, pharma, or fossil fuel industries to discredit their critics (e.g., for the tobacco industry: Yach & Bialous, 2001; for fossil fuels: Nasiritousi, 2017) – attempts that have often been successful in delaying meaningful societal debate and action by decades (e.g., Chapman & Carter, 2003). Scholars with longer memories may also recall the concerted efforts by Microsoft and other stakeholders in the commercial software industry in the mid-1990s to ward off the perceived threat from open-source development projects by orchestrating a publicity campaign that highlighted the supposed unreliability and insecurity of collaboratively and communally developed open-source operating systems and other critical software, in comparison to their proprietary, closed-source solutions. Such calculated smear campaigns became so persistent during this time that they even acquired their own acronym: FUD, for the 'fear, uncertainty, and doubt' that open-source advocates suspected them of trying to spread (Pfaffenberger, 2000; Raymond, 2001).

That said, as Starbird's tweets indicate, it should be acknowledged here that the platform providers and their workforces themselves are likely to be genuinely conflicted about how to deal with new scholarly and especially methodological advances: to the extent that new methods enable them to more effectively combat the spam, abuse, and disinformation that drive users away from engaging in social media, for example, relevant teams within these corporations have a vested interest in employing these methods themselves, *internally*, in order to improve user experience and retention; at the same time, however, the use of these methods by independent researchers, *externally*, could also result in the generation of public outcomes that would alert policymakers, regulators, law enforcement, and ordinary users to the true extent of these and other problems, and at least at the corporate leadership level platform providers have an equally strong interest in preventing such embarrassment. This is not simply an abstract conflict, but one that may be fought quite literally between a platform's tech and PR departments – it is important not to envisage transnational social media corporations as monolithic entities without their own internal politics.

Investigative reports are increasingly, if often without direct attribution, referring to internal conflicts within social media companies about their appropriate corporate stance towards such issues, and some former staff have also provided insights into the complex political battles being fought between them. Most prominently, in an internal memo to staff published by *BuzzFeed*, *Facebook*'s departing Chief Security Officer Alex Stamos outlined a number of corporate policies and processes requiring 'a bottom-up change in culture' (qtd. in Mac & Warzel, 2018: n.p.); in his open letter in the *New York Times*, *Facebook* co-founder Chris Hughes expressed his concerns that all-powerful CEO Mark Zuckerberg 'has surrounded himself with a team that reinforces his beliefs instead of challenging them' (2019: n.p.), and calls for the company to be broken up.

Again, such intra-organisational conflicts are also known from the tobacco, pharma, and fossil fuel industries. If the *Times*' allegation that *Facebook* engaged in a deliberate, multi-year effort to attack and undermine the company's critics is correct, it might thus be appropriate to speak of 'Big Social' – in addition to other unscrupulous transnational industries misusing their corporate power to evade parliamentary, regulatory, journalistic, and societal scrutiny. It also becomes a great deal easier to believe that *Facebook* would be prepared to avert further critical investigation of its platform by other means – for instance by locking out independent, scholarly, public-interest researchers and partnering instead with select partners to set up Social Science One as an incentive for scholars to redirect their efforts to more 'orthogonal' matters instead.

The path ahead: four options for scholarly researchers in a hostile environment

As social media platforms are crippling the functionality of their public APIs to the point that they no longer enable anything but the most basic forms of investigation; as they single out scholarly researchers as convenient scapegoats in order to demonstrate action against data abuse, and conduct cynical fear, uncertainty, and doubt campaigns against them; and as they largely continue business as usual in building their emerging data analytics industries, in spite of occasional action against commercial operators that are implicated in the inappropriate use of such data: what opportunities remain for critical, independent, public-interest scholarly research? Four major pathways are becoming increasingly clear.

Walk away

First, researchers frustrated with the diminishing functionality of platform APIs, the disingenuous attacks on their work, and the ill-constructed alternative data lotteries orchestrated by the platforms and affiliated entities may be tempted simply to walk away. Such frustration is evident in Starbird's statement that *Facebook*'s FUD campaign 'is turning my stomach' (2018a); it has already led to *Texifter*'s discontinuation of its scholarly *Twitter* data access service. Similarly, *Netvizz* developer and Digital Methods Initiative scholar Bernhard Rieder stated in a post about the future of his crucial *Facebook* data gathering tool that

> I enjoy programming like few other things in life … , but the increasing hostility toward independent research is creating demands that can only be tackled through more sustainable institutional forms. … At least in my immediate environment, I do not see such forms emerge. (Rieder, 2018)

Researchers acting on such frustration might leave the field altogether, or focus on digital platforms and user practices where data access remains considerably more straightforward; historically, such differences in data access have already facilitated the considerably more advanced development of scholarship on *Twitter* in comparison to *Facebook*. As *Twitter* data access is now similarly curtailed, scholars may move on to studying platforms like *Reddit* or *Wikipedia*, where full datasets of public user activity remain readily available. But while further research into those platforms is welcome, because of their widespread take-up *Twitter* and especially *Facebook* remain the most critical social media spaces at the present moments, and newer platforms such as *WhatsApp* are rapidly becoming more important – research that focusses only on the 'easy data' (Burgess & Bruns, 2015) of more obscure spaces while ignoring these mass platforms must be seen as insufficient. In the absence of other meaningful scrutiny of these spaces, to give up on *Facebook*, *Twitter*, and other platforms is to leave their users to fend for themselves; it also prevents scholars from providing policymakers and regulators with the independent advice that they need so urgently as they seek to address social media's dysfunctions. After all, it is unlikely that the perpetrators of abuse and hate speech, the trolls, the bots, and the domestic and foreign operators of influence campaigns are similarly going to walk away from these platforms.

Lobby for change

If giving up is not an option, then, a second approach is to keep pushing for different and better data access frameworks for scholarly research. The open letters to *Facebook* and other platform providers by the Internet research community and affiliated research, journalistic, and technology foundations (Bruns, 2018; Knight First Amendment Institute, 2018; Mozilla, 2019a, 2019b), and the media coverage they have generated, are one step in this. Such calls are naturally aligned with the emerging field of critical digital studies, which investigates centrally the political economy of these platforms (Poletti & Gray, 2019). More recently, additional calls for intervention have also been made from outside of the scholarly community: as noted, in an op-ed in the *New York Times*, *Facebook* co-founder Chris Hughes has called for the break-up of the corporation (Hughes, 2019). But such calls also demonstrate the limitations of public advocacy: *Facebook* has the corporate resources and political power to fight such unwanted interference, and its employment of Definers, as a public relations company linked with alt-right disinformation campaigns, provides a troubling indication of how it intends to respond to calls to exercise corporate social responsibility.

Importantly, the platforms' creation of alternative data access frameworks, from the intransparent and unaccountable paradigm of Social Science One to the data lottery of the *Twitter* Health Metrics, cannot be regarded as sufficiently addressing calls for better scholarly data access: on current evidence, they are constructed primarily to generate positive publicity for the companies, and – if they do so at all – provide access to data only for a vanishingly small minority of research projects that are carefully and explicitly selected to be 'orthogonal' to the platform's corporate interests. As one open letter from the scholarly community has argued, genuinely meaningful data access for scholarly research would be best provided through a separate research API that is transparently accessible to all scholars at tertiary institutions whose work has received appropriate ethics clearance (Bruns, 2018), *without* further powers of veto for the platform providers themselves, or for their partners in initiatives such as Social Science One.

It seems evident from their track record to date that the major platforms are unlikely to offer such research-specific API access on their own initiative; scholarly lobbying efforts on this matter must therefore be redirected from the platforms themselves to the policymakers and regulators that could force the platforms' hands. Sadly, however, the political will to compel the platforms to enable better independent scrutiny by scholarly researchers acting in the public interest is poorly developed to date: in spite of genuine, bipartisan frustration with the platforms' response to revelations about the role of nefarious influence operations in affecting the outcomes of the Brexit referendum, the 2016 US presidential elections, and other political processes, various calculations about how action against the platforms might affect the next elections have quickly kicked in and prevented effective regulation.

Further, the sheer commercial and thus political power of the platforms as multi-billion-dollar transnational industry leaders has meant that most national parliaments and governments can only exercise distinctly limited leverage over them. Congress might be best able to introduce effective regulation, given the key companies' US heritage, but the terminal dysfunction of the American political system makes this exceptionally unlikely for the foreseeable future; the EU Parliament might have the greatest domain knowledge and political will to act, yet has little actual leverage over the platforms. A concerted effort between both may have the best chance of generating real change, but is unlikely as the current US administration continues to undermine the country's status as a trustworthy partner. Recent national and transnational regulatory initiatives, including the European Union's General Data Protection Regulation (GDPR) or the US$5 billion fine expected to be imposed on *Facebook* by the US Federal Trade Commission (FTC) for the platform's handling of user data (Overly & Scola, 2019), do indicate a growing preparedness by regulators to take on the social media platforms – but as yet these have not substantively addressed the need to support critical, independent, public-interest scholarly inquiry.

Accommodate and acquiesce

In the absence of, and with no hope for, meaningful changes to data access regimes any time soon, then, a third option for researchers is to take a pragmatic approach and find ways to work within the *Realpolitik* of social media data access in the post-Cambridge Analytica era. This means maximising what data can still be gathered through the increasingly crippled public APIs offered by the platforms, applying for elevated access through Social Science One and/or the platforms' various data lotteries, and even – where sufficient funding is available – buying additional data from commercial data services, and thus finding ways of still doing meaningful scholarly work by drawing on a combination of these disparate, incomplete, imperfect datasets.

However, this approach is likely to be frustrated on the one hand by that very disparity: public APIs are increasingly limited in what they provide; new data access frameworks offered by the platforms and their partners are often centred on very specific, tightly circumscribed research topics; and commercial data services tend to focus only on comparatively simplistic market research questions. As we have seen, some of the commercial data services are also themselves negatively affected by the new data access regimes: like *Texifter* or Crimson Hexagon, they have themselves seen their data streams permanently or at least temporarily suspended.

The increased cost and complexity of working with such disparate sources, especially as compared to previous widely used open-source tools like *TCAT* or *Netvizz*, is also likely to require researchers to work more often in large-scale consortia that are able to share the financial and operational load of data acquisition, processing, and analysis. In addition to overall organisational challenges, this also places them in uncertain territory with respect to the platforms' terms of service, which frequently include prohibitions against data sharing (Weller & Kinder-Kurlanda, 2015). While platforms have generally refrained from prosecuting data sharing *within* institutional research teams, it has yet to be tested whether they would condone data on-sharing *across* a multi-institutional consortium of researchers.

Indeed, a further step beyond the formation of such consortia would be the establishment of formal data repositories, mirroring similar efforts that have proven critical to major fields of research such as genomics or climate science (Weller & Kinder-Kurlanda, 2016). There as well as here, such repositories are especially critical to longitudinal and comparative research efforts and also enable the more rigorous replication and verification of research results; in other fields of science, they are operated by trusted, independent institutions and are governed by strict access rules that protect the privacy and integrity of the data while facilitating further research. In the field of social media, however, they are likely to be in explicit violation of platform rules; *Twitter*'s forced closure of *TwapperKeeper.com*, the only major attempt to build a public repository for *Twitter* archives in a standardised format, as early as 2011 (O'Brien, 2011) created a chilling effect that has discouraged follow-up attempts to this day.

Break the rules

Finally, however, the very immutability of the platforms' terms of service, combined with the mounting evidence of their failure to act in good faith not only in their dealings with scholars, but indeed also with their overall userbase as such, is now also emboldening a growing chorus of voices in the scholarly community and beyond that are placing public over platform interest and are advocating the deliberate breach of platform rules (cf. Freelon, 2018; Rogers, 2018; Venturini & Rogers, 2019). On the one hand, a purely legal argument may be mounted that in some circumstances the benefits to society from breaching the terms of service outweigh the detriments to the platform itself, or to specific users; a case currently before US courts tests this in a very specific context (Sandvig, 2017). On the other hand, this is also the legal expression of a much broader moral argument that points to the need for independent, critical, public-interest scrutiny of social media spaces that are now critical to public communication across many societies. The latter argument even points to the freedom of research as a recognised human right (United Nations, 1976) that supersedes the commercial interests of the platform providers.

In the absence of better API access, researchers pursuing this argument therefore also argue for data acquisition from the platforms through explicitly unsanctioned means. The leader of the University of Amsterdam's Digital Methods Initiative, Richard Rogers, has hinted at the need for a return to Web scraping, for example (Rogers, 2018), and a growing number of practical tools for scraping data from *Facebook*, *Twitter*, and other platforms are now becoming available. As many of its proponents readily admit, this approach is inherently problematic (see e.g., van Schie, Westra, & Schäfer, 2017): in addition to its dubious legal status, it is ethically questionable as – for a platform like *Facebook* – it would require researchers to create a 'fake' account and simulate that account's login to and browsing of the platform in order to scrape the content it encounters; this might thus also include simulated interactions with, and therefore the explicit deception of, genuine users. From a practical perspective, too, scraping poses challenges: since platforms like *Facebook* shape the content seen by users based on what their algorithms appear to know about the users' interests, the content scraped from the platform will be affected by how it understands the 'fake' user created by the researchers, rather than the perhaps more neutral content selection provided by an API.

Further, increased attempts by scholars to scrape data from social media platforms, if detected by the platforms, are also likely to kickstart an unsustainable arms race of scraping tools and countermeasures between researchers and platform providers, as *Facebook*'s efforts to frustrate *ProPublica*'s ad scraper plugin have already shown (Merrill & Tobin, 2019). Platforms might develop better means of detecting and banning 'fake' accounts, or of obfuscating the HTML structure of their pages, requiring researchers to constantly adjust their scraping strategies – this makes scraping-based approaches precarious and unreliable especially for larger-scale and longer-term projects. Scraping is also useful mainly for platforms that are accessed through Web-based interfaces – it would be considerably more difficult to scrape the content encountered within proprietary apps on mobile devices. Given the considerably asymmetrical distribution of resources and control over platform affordances between providers and scholars, it is therefore difficult to see this as a race that can possibly be won by researchers, even if the legal, moral, and ethical justifications for entering into it can be found.

Conclusion: ceterum censeo

In the immediate future, it is likely that we will continue to see researchers proceeding down all four of these possible paths, often at the same time. Already, key scholars and scholarly support services have withdrawn from the field, as we have seen; at the same time, other researchers have also engaged in increased public advocacy, with little measurable success to date; they have explored available commercial data access services and alternative data grants; and they have stepped up their efforts to develop the next generation of data scraping tools. Such exploration and experimentation in response to the 'APIcalypse' is welcome in principle and demonstrates the overall resilience of the field of social media research, but these immediate tactical responses to the disruption wrought by the Cambridge Analytica scandal and the platforms' instrumentalisation of it have yet to translate into a sustainable longer-term strategy for the field.

As noted throughout this article, it is unlikely that social media scholars alone are able to facilitate the circumstances under which such a strategy can emerge; this effort must also involve other key stakeholders including research institutions, policymakers, and the platform providers themselves. Critically, as Rieder (2018: n.p.) has noted, 'if any successful resistance to these developments can be mobilized, it will require substantial support from organizations capable of investing resources that may not lead to immediate deliverables or quantifiable publications' – this includes universities themselves, national research councils, and charitable foundations providing research funding.

It is crucial in this context to keep up the pressure on policymakers and platform providers, too. As scholars, we must highlight the deleterious consequences of current API access regimes for independent, critical, public-interest research at any opportunity, in order to maintain and increase public awareness of how poorly the platforms have responded to challenges ranging from abuse and hate speech to the deliberate dissemination of disinformation so far, and in order to forcefully counteract their FUD campaigns. Indeed, we might do well to learn from a classical example here: in his relentless campaign to commence a Third Punic War between Rome and Carthage, Roman Senator Cato the Elder concluded all of his speeches, independent of their substantive topic, with the phrase '*ceterum censeo Carthaginem esse delendam*': 'furthermore, I propose that Carthage is to be destroyed'. Today, social media researchers might similarly need to take to concluding their articles, papers, and presentations with a consistent call to action, such as the following:

> Furthermore, we demand that social media platforms provide transparent data access to critical, independent, public-interest research.

It is important to emphasise, however, that we do so not simply because we have become dependent on 'big social data' for our research, or out of self-interest in furthering our own careers. Rather, it is now obvious that social media have become critical to many of the most pressing challenges for societies around the world: they are implicated, for example, in the disruption of democratic processes by deliberate disinformation campaigns; in the growing polarisation of public debate; and in the re-emergence of naked fascism even within the most powerful democratic nation in the world. Therefore, Bernhard Rieder is typically understated when he points out that 'the idea that independent research of a 2+ billion user platform just got a lot harder should make us at least a little uneasy' (2018: n.p.) – in reality, we should be profoundly concerned about being locked out of studying in detail what happens on social media platforms at this critical point in world history, and we must hold to account those who have locked us out, and expose their reasons for doing so.

Acknowledgments

This research is supported by the Australian Research Council Future Fellowship project *Understanding Intermedia Information Flows in the Australian Online Public Sphere* and LIEF project *TrISMA: Tracking Infrastructure for Social Media in Australia*.

Disclosure statement

No potential conflict of interest was reported by the author.

Funding

This work was supported by Australian Research Council: [Grant Number FT130100703, LE140100148].

References

ABC News. (2018). Facebook suspends and investigates data analytics firm Crimson Hexagon. Retrieved from https://www.abc.net.au/news/2018-07-21/facebook-suspends-data-analytics-firm-crimson-hexagon/10021378

Alaimo, K. (2017). All tweets belong in the Library of Congress. *CNN*. Retrieved from https://www.cnn.com/2017/12/27/opinions/library-of-congress-should-keep-all-tweets-opinion-alaimo/index.html

Alaimo, K. (2018). Twitter's misguided barriers for researchers. *Bloomberg*. Retrieved from https://www.bloomberg.com/opinion/articles/2018-10-16/twitter-s-barriers-for-academic-researchers-are-misguided

Baker, B. (2015). Twitter data for research: From understanding relationships to spotting the Aurora Borealis. *Twitter Blog*. Retrieved from https://blog.twitter.com/en_us/a/2015/twitter-data-research.html

Ball, J. (2018). Is Facebook's leadership incompetent, or malicious? *New Statesman*. Retrieved from https://www.newstatesman.com/science-tech/social-media/2018/11/facebook-s-leadership-incompetent-or-malicious

Baran, K. S., & Ghaffari, H. (2017). The manifold research fields of Facebook: A bibliometric analysis. *Journal of Information Science Theory and Practice*, *5*(2), 33–47. doi:10.1633/JISTAP.2017.5.2.3

Bechmann, A., & Vahlstrup, P. B. (2015). Studying Facebook and Instagram data: The Digital Footprints software. *First Monday*, *20*(12), doi:10.5210/fm.v20i12.5968

Borra, E., & Rieder, B. (2014). Programmed method: Developing a toolset for capturing and analyzing tweets. *Aslib Journal of Information Management*, *66*(3), 262–278. doi:10.1108/AJIM-09-2013-0094

Bounegru, L., Gray, J., Venturini, T., & Mauri, M. (2017). *A field guide to fake news: A collection of recipes for those who love to cook with digital methods*. Amsterdam: Public Data Lab. Retrieved from http://fakenews.publicdatalab.org/

Bruns, A. (2018). Facebook shuts the gate after the horse has bolted, and hurts real research in the process. *Internet Policy Review*. Retrieved from https://policyreview.info/articles/news/facebook-shuts-gate-after-horse-has-bolted-and-hurts-real-research-process/786

Bruns, A., Burgess, J., Banks, J., Tjondronegoro, D., Dreiling, A., Hartley, J., … Sadkowsky, T. (2016). *TrISMA: Tracking Infrastructure for Social Media Analysis*. Retrieved from http://trisma.org/

Bruns, A., & Weller, K. (2016). Twitter as a first draft of the present – and the challenges of preserving it for the future. In W. Nejdl, W. Hall, P. Parigi, & S. Staab (Eds.), *Proceedings of the 8th ACM conference on Web Science* (pp. 183–189). Hannover: ACM Press. doi:10.1145/2908131.2908174.

Bucher, T. (2013). Objects of intense feeling: The case of the Twitter API. *Computational Culture: A Journal of Software Studies*, (3), Retrieved from http://computationalculture.net/article/objects-of-intense-feeling-the-case-of-the-twitter-api

Burgess, J., & Bruns, A. (2015). Easy data, hard data: The politics and pragmatics of Twitter research after the computational turn. In G. Langlois, J. Redden, & G. Elmer (Eds.), *Compromised data: From social media to big data* (pp. 93–111). New York: Bloomsbury Academic.

Cadwalladr, C. (2018). 'I made Steve Bannon's psychological warfare tool': Meet the data war whistleblower. *The Guardian*. Retrieved from https://www.theguardian.com/news/2018/mar/17/data-war-whistleblower-christopher-wylie-faceook-nix-bannon-trump

Chapman, S., & Carter, S. M. (2003). "Avoid health warnings on all tobacco products for just as long as we can": A history of Australian tobacco industry efforts to avoid, delay and dilute health warnings on cigarettes. *Tobacco Control*, *12*(suppl 3), iii13–iii22. doi:10.1136/tc.12.suppl_3.iii13

Constine, J. (2018). Facebook restricts APIs, axes old Instagram platform amidst scandals. *TechCrunch*. Retrieved from http://social.techcrunch.com/2018/04/04/facebook-instagram-api-shut-down/

Constine, J., & Hatmaker, T. (2018). Facebook admits Cambridge Analytica hijacked data on up to 87 m users. *TechCrunch*. Retrieved from https://techcrunch.com/2018/04/04/cambridge-analytica-87-million/

Digital Footprints. (2018). Retrieved from https://digitalfootprints.dk/

Facebook Newsroom. (2018). Elliot Schrage on Definers. Retrieved from https://newsroom.fb.com/news/2018/11/elliot-schrage-on-definers/

Flick, C. (2016). Informed consent and the Facebook emotional manipulation study. *Research Ethics*, *12*(1), 14–28. doi:10.1177/1747016115599568

Freelon, D. (2018). Computational research in the post-API age. *Political Communication*, *35*(4), 665–668. doi:10.1080/10584609.2018.1477506

Frenkel, S., Confessore, N., Kang, C., Rosenberg, M., & Nicas, J. (2018). Delay, deny and deflect: How Facebook's leaders fought through crisis. *New York Times*. Retrieved from https://www.nytimes.com/2018/11/14/technology/facebook-data-russia-election-racism.html

Gadde, V., & Gasca, D. (2018). Measuring healthy conversation. Retrieved from https://blog.twitter.com/official/en_us/topics/company/2018/measuring_healthy_conversation.html

Grewal, P. (2018). Suspending Cambridge Analytica and SCL Group from Facebook. Retrieved from https://newsroom.fb.com/news/2018/03/suspending-cambridge-analytica/

Grinberg, N., Joseph, K., Friedland, L., Swire-Thompson, B., & Lazer, D. (2019). Fake news on Twitter during the 2016 U.S. Presidential election. *Science*, *363*(6425), 374–378. doi:10.1126/science.aau2706

Hughes, C. (2019). It's time to break up Facebook. *New York Times*. Retrieved from https://www.nytimes.com/2019/05/09/opinion/sunday/chris-hughes-facebook-zuckerberg.html

Johnson, R. (2018). Investing in the best Twitter experience for you. *Twitter Blog*. Retrieved from https://blog.twitter.com/official/en_us/topics/product/2018/investing-in-the-best-twitter-experience-for-you.html

Kazansky, B., Torres, G., van der Velden, L., Wissenbach, K., & Milan, S. (2019). Data for the social good: Toward a data-activist research agenda. In A. Daly, S. K. Devitt, & M. Mann (Eds.), *Good data* (pp. 244–259). Amsterdam: Institute of Network Cultures. Retrieved from http://networkcultures.org/wp-content/uploads/2019/01/Good_Data.pdf

King, G., & Persily, N. (2018). *A New Model for Industry-Academic Partnerships*. Retrieved from https://gking.harvard.edu/partnerships

Kirkorian, R. (2014). Twitter #DataGrants selections. Retrieved from https://blog.twitter.com/engineering/en_us/a/2014/twitter-datagrants-selections.html

Knight First Amendment Institute at Columbia University. (2018). *Knight Institute Calls on Facebook to Lift Restrictions on Digital Journalism and Research* [open letter]. Retrieved from https://knightcolumbia.org/sites/default/files/content/Facebook_Letter.pdf

Kramer, A. D. I., Guillory, J. E., & Hancock, J. T. (2014). Experimental evidence of massive-scale emotional contagion through social networks. *Proceedings of the National Academy of Sciences, 111*(24), 8788–8790. doi:10.1073/pnas.1320040111

Mac, R., & Warzel, C. (2018). Top Facebook security officer's departing memo: 'We need to be willing to pick sides'. *BuzzFeed News*. Retrieved from https://www.buzzfeednews.com/article/ryanmac/facebook-alex-stamos-memo-cambridge-analytica-pick-sides

Merrill, J. B., & Tobin, A. (2019). Facebook moves to block ad transparency tools — including ours. *ProPublica*. Retrieved from https://www.propublica.org/article/facebook-blocks-ad-transparency-tools

Mozilla. (2019a). Open letter: Facebook, do your part against disinformation. Retrieved from https://blog.mozilla.org/blog/2019/02/11/open-letter-facebook-do-your-part-against-disinformation

Mozilla. (2019b). Facebook and Google: This is what an effective Ad Archive API looks like. Retrieved from https://blog.mozilla.org/blog/2019/03/27/facebook-and-google-this-is-what-an-effective-ad-archive-api-looks-like

Nasiritousi, N. (2017). Fossil fuel emitters and climate change: Unpacking the governance activities of large oil and gas companies. *Environmental Politics, 26*(4), 621–647. doi:10.1080/09644016.2017.1320832

NATO Strategic Communications Centre of Excellence. (2017). *Digital hydra: Security implications of false information online*. Riga: NATO Strategic Communications Centre of Excellence. Retrieved from https://www.stratcomcoe.org/digital-hydra-security-implications-false-information-online

O'Brien, J. (2011). Removal of export and download / API capabilities. Retrieved from https://twapperkeeper.wordpress.com/2011/02/22/removal-of-export-and-download-api-capabilities/

Overly, S., & Scola, N. (2019). Facebook expects up to $5B FTC fine. *Politico*. Retrieved from https://www.politico.com/story/2019/04/24/facebook-ftc-fine-1289564

Pasternack, A. (2018). Facebook reinstates data firm it suspended for alleged misuse, but surveillance questions linger. *Fast Company*. Retrieved from https://www.fastcompany.com/90219826/why-did-facebook-re-friend-a-data-firm-that-raised-spying-concerns

Pear Analytics. (2009). *Twitter Study – August* 2009. San Antonio, TX: Pear Analytics. Retrieved from http://pearanalytics.com/wp-content/uploads/2012/12/Twitter-Study-August-2009.pdf

Perez, S. (2018). Twitter company email addresses why it's #BreakingMyTwitter. *TechCrunch*. Retrieved from http://social.techcrunch.com/2018/08/16/twitter-company-email-addresses-why-its-breakingmytwitter/

Pfaffenberger, B. (2000). The rhetoric of dread: Fear, uncertainty, and doubt (FUD) in information technology marketing. *Knowledge, Technology & Policy, 13*(3), 78–92. doi:10.1007/s12130-000-1022-x

Poletti, C., & Gray, D. (2019). Good data is critical data: An appeal for critical digital studies. In A. Daly, S. K. Devitt, & M. Mann (Eds.), *Good data* (pp. 260–276). Amsterdam: Institute of Network Cultures. Retrieved from http://networkcultures.org/wp-content/uploads/2019/01/Good_Data.pdf

Raymond, E. S. (2001). Why Microsoft smears – and fears – open source. *IEEE Spectrum, 38*(8), 14–15. doi:10.1109/6.938720

Rieder, B. (2013). Studying Facebook via data extraction: The Netvizz application. In *Proceedings of the 5th Annual ACM Web Science Conference* (pp. 346-355). New York, NY, USA: ACM. doi:10.1145/2464464.2464475.

Rieder, B. (2018). Facebook's app review and how independent research just got a lot harder. Retrieved from http://thepoliticsofsystems.net/2018/08/facebooks-app-review-and-how-independent-research-just-got-a-lot-harder/

Rogers, R. (2014). Foreword: Debanalising Twitter: The transformation of an object of study. In K. Weller, A. Bruns, J. Burgess, M. Mahrt, & C. Puschmann (Eds.), *Twitter and society* (pp. ix-xxvi). New York: Peter Lang.

Rogers, R. (2018). Social media research after the fake news debacle. *Partecipazione e Conflitto: The Open Journal of Sociopolitical Studies, 11*(2), 557–570. doi:10.1285/i20356609v11i2p557

Rogers, S. (2013). Tweet marks the spot. *Twitter Blog*. Retrieved from https://blog.twitter.com/en_us/a/2013/tweet-marks-the-spot.html

Roth, Y., & Johnson, R. (2018). New developer requirements to protect our platform. Retrieved from https://blog.twitter.com/developer/en_us/topics/tools/2018/new-developer-requirements-to-protect-our-platform.html

Sandvig, C. (2017). Heading to the courthouse for Sandvig v. Sessions. Retrieved from https://socialmediacollective.org/2017/10/19/heading-to-the-courthouse-for-sandvig-v-sessions/

Schroepfer, M. (2018). An update on our plans to restrict data access on Facebook. Retrieved from https://newsroom.fb.com/news/2018/04/restricting-data-access/

Snelson, C. L. (2016). Qualitative and mixed methods social media research: A review of the literature. *International Journal of Qualitative Methods, 15*(1), 1–15. doi:10.1177/1609406915624574

Social Science One. (2018a). Retrieved from https://socialscience.one/

Social Science One. (2018b). Requests for proposals: Social media and democracy research grants. Retrieved from https://socialscience.one/rfps

Starbird, K. (2018a). This is turning my stomach. Around the same time I was invited to Facebook to give a presentation on online disinformation, FB's leadership was hiring an influence firm to use disinfo to attack its critics (invoking one of the same tropes that we'd seen Russia use for years). https://twitter.com/passantino/status/1065366769454338048 … [Tweet]. Retrieved from https://twitter.com/katestarbird/status/1065654767773409281

Starbird, K. (2018b). I know a lot of amazing people who work for Facebook and I know there are people who care working hard to improve how the platform deals with mis/disinformation. But I'm having a hard time reconciling that with this most recent revelation about their own information operations. [Tweet]. Retrieved from https://twitter.com/katestarbird/status/1065658223397560320

Stone, B. (2010). Tweet preservation. Retrieved from https://blog.twitter.com/official/en_us/a/2010/tweet-preservation.html

Stromer-Galley, J., Hemsley, J., Tanupabrungsun, S., Zhang, F., Rossini, P., Bryant, L., … Robinson, J. (2016). *Illuminating 2016 Project*. Retrieved from http://illuminating.ischool.syr.edu

Su, J., Sharma, A., & Goel, S. (2016). The effect of recommendations on network structure. In *Proceedings of the 25th International Conference on World Wide Web - WWW '16*, 1157-67. Montréal: ACM Press. doi:10.1145/2872427.2883040

Texifter. (2018). Retrieved from https://sifter.texifter.com/

Twitter, Inc. (2018). Twitter health metrics proposal submission. Retrieved from https://blog.twitter.com/official/en_us/topics/company/2018/twitter-health-metrics-proposal-submission.html

United Nations. (1976). *International Covenant on Economic, Social and Cultural Rights*. Retrieved from https://www.ohchr.org/EN/ProfessionalInterest/Pages/CESCR.aspx

Van Osch, W., & Coursaris, C. K. (2014). Social media research: An assessment of the domain's productivity and intellectual evolution. *Communication Monographs, 81*(3), 285–309. doi:10.1080/03637751.2014.921720

Van Schie, G., Westra, I., & Schäfer, M. T. (2017). Get your hands dirty: Emerging data practices as challenge for research integrity. In M. T. Schäfer & K. van Es (Eds.), *The datafied society: Studying culture through data* (pp. 183–200). Amsterdam: Amsterdam University Press.

Venturini, T., & Rogers, R. (2019). "API-based research" or How can digital sociology and journalism studies learn from the Facebook and Cambridge Analytica data breach. *Digital Journalism*, 1–9. doi:10.1080/21670811.2019.1591927

Wardle, C., & Derakhshan, H. (2017). *Information Disorder: Toward an Interdisciplinary Framework for research and policy making (DGI(2017)09)*. Strasbourg: Council of Europe. Retrieved from https://shorensteincenter.org/wp-content/uploads/2017/10/Information-Disorder-Toward-an-interdisciplinary-framework.pdf

Weaver, M. (2018). Facebook scandal: I am being used as scapegoat – academic who mined data. *The Guardian*. Retrieved from https://www.theguardian.com/uk-news/2018/mar/21/facebook-row-i-am-being-used-as-scapegoat-says-academic-aleksandr-kogan-cambridge-analytica

Weller, K., & Kinder-Kurlanda, K. (2015). Uncovering the challenges in collection, sharing and documentation: The hidden data of social media research? In *Proceedings of the Ninth International AAAI Conference on Web and Social Media* (pp. 28-37). Oxford: AAAI Press. Retrieved from https://www.aaai.org/ocs/index.php/ICWSM/ICWSM15/paper/view/10657/10552

Weller, K., & Kinder-Kurlanda, K. E. (2016). A Manifesto for Data Sharing in Social Media Research. In *Proceedings of the 8th ACM Conference on Web Science* (pp. 166-172). New York: ACM Press. Retrieved from http://doi.acm.org/10.1145/2908131.2908172

Woolley, S. C., & Howard, P. N. (2017). *Computational Propaganda Worldwide: Executive Summary* (Working Paper 2017.11). Oxford: Computational Propaganda Research Project. Retrieved from http://comprop.oii.ox.ac.uk/wp-content/uploads/sites/89/2017/06/Casestudies-ExecutiveSummary.pdf

Yach, D., & Bialous, S. A. (2001). Junking science to promote tobacco. *American Journal of Public Health*, *91*(11), 1745–1748. doi:10.2105/AJPH.91.11.1745

YourTwapperKeeper. (2013). Retrieved from https://github.com/540co/yourTwapperKeeper

Zimmer, M., & Proferes, N. J. (2014). A topology of Twitter research: Disciplines, methods, and ethics. *Aslib Journal of Information Management*, *66*(3), 250–261. doi:10.1108/AJIM-09-2013-0083

An end to the wild west of social media research: a response to Axel Bruns

Cornelius Puschmann

ABSTRACT
Current models of data access in social media research offer clear benefits, but are also fraught in a number of ways, including by posing risks to user privacy, being constrained in terms of reliability and reproducibility of results, and incentivizing questionable and in some cases unethical research practices. I argue that partnerships between academics and industry represent one potential option for improving this situation. While no panacea, such arrangements may be able to contribute to a more rules-based and less anarchic situation in social media research, placing greater emphasis on preserving user privacy and the reproducibility of results, rather than mainly on compiling large data sets. Due to a number of recent shifts, not just in research, but in the public discourse surrounding social media platforms and user data, we are entering an era of increased institutionalization and standardization in the study of online communication. This new environment appears poised to replace the 'Wild West of social media research' that we have witnessed in the past, in which academics compile huge troughs of data with few constraints, not always acting in the public's best interest.

Introduction: the mess we are in

In the wake of the Cambridge Analytica scandal, researchers are increasingly finding themselves locked out of the developer APIs that have in the past given them cheap, fast and relatively reliable access to a treasure trove of social media data. In his essay, Axel Bruns (2019) provides an account of the research ecosystem that has sprung up over the last decade around data APIs such as those offered by Twitter, Facebook and Google. He describes the bottom-up development of tools and practices surrounding APIs and how academic projects such as the University of Amsterdam's Digital Methods Initiatives (DMI) have contributed considerably to making social media data widely available not only for academics, but also to journalists and activists, in order to study a dazzling array of issues. Following this account, which pitches bold academic initiatives against increasingly restrictive company policies, Bruns describes projects such as Social Science One, which aim to foster alternatives to developer APIs, in very critical terms, calling them a form of 'corporate data philanthropy'. He points out the dilemma of any industry partnership: that outright policies or inadvertent chilling effects may lead researchers to refrain from publishing results that pose a threat to their corporate partners, lest they want to risk biting the hand that is feeding them data. I will return to this point in the course of this essay, but the risks associated with enabling critical research that is truly unimpeded by such effects with a functioning partnership are non-trivial, and this segment of Bruns' essay clearly contains valid arguments. When suggesting, for example, that Social Science One's governance should leave 'only peer review and ethics and privacy review as the two hurdles that proposals must pass [..] [this] would ensure a much more accountable, transparent, and independent selection process', Bruns points to a shortcoming of the present model, albeit one deemed necessary at Social Science One's inception to increase its chances of success.[1] Finally, Bruns proposes that researchers are faced with one of four choices: give up, lobby for change, accommodate and acquiesce, and break the rules. He closes by arguing that, perhaps surprisingly, we should not look to broadly similar moments to this one in the history of the social sciences (say, the genesis of public opinion polling in the 1930s or early television research in the 1970s), but to ancient Rome. Like Cato, researchers should stoically end each of their statements with the line 'Furthermore, we demand that social media platforms provide transparent data access to critical, independent, public-interest research'. My own suggestion, in short, is for the research community to do bits of all of these things, but while adding a fifth option: to engage constructively will all stakeholders, including internet companies, but also with regulators and political actors, in order to improve the current situation. It is a European stance in that it places significant trust in the power of regulation and political pressure to bring about openness for academic research while safeguarding user privacy.

Corporate data philanthropy or equal partnership?

Axel Bruns deserves credit for clearly describing the challenges that researchers face in the current moment, and for articulating a number of contentions to the model of consortia like Social Science One. As a commission member and member of a funded ERC team, I have been engaged in a number of discussions over the last year with colleagues who have contributed to this special issue and are authorities in the field, many of whom have articulated similar doubts. What is more is that to my knowledge, nobody, including the initiators of Social Science One, Nate Persily and Gary King, pretend to know with certainty that the current model is a perfect approach that will unequivocally succeed, or that there is no chance of complete breakdown of the model in the face of another Cambridge Analytica scandal (one potentially caused by a Social Science One grantee). The concern that research with the potential to expose industry malpractice will be suppressed – whether by fiat or inadvertently, by industry 'data philanthropy' leading to conformist behavior – or that academic research will be treated as cost-effective helpers that solve problems that would otherwise be addressed within companies, or that research partnerships will be treated as a mere fig leaf to score PR points are *exactly* the same concerns that people actively involved in Social Science One have also voiced. Then why are we staking our reputation on this approach?

From all I have seen, what unites the Commission, the Social Science Research Council and the ERC grantees is that we are scholars who want to solve a problem. We want to find an acceptable alternative to the data acquisition practices that have been predominantly used to date, from developer APIs and web scraping to one-off collaborations in which researchers sign a company NDA. We are working under the assumption that existing approaches are severely limited and are likely to become yet more limited in the future as a result of data privacy concerns. Facebook, we think, has the means of solving the data access problem for academic researchers and an interest in working with academics in a way that can potentially benefit academic research, the public at large, and thereby also the company. This group is neither starry-eyed regarding the legitimate commercial interests of Facebook or any other company, nor do we believe the approach taken to be a panacea. But for reasons described in what follows, I am convinced that the current approach is both no longer viable and, perhaps more importantly, that it was flawed to begin with. I also believe that a workable model must consider the interests of the public, academics and companies (in roughly that order), meaning it must balance user privacy with the freedom of research and (yes, I dare say it) the legitimate business interests of companies, provided that the latter do not abuse their considerable market power and act within the law, in order for such a model to be workable. I also firmly believe that scholars should not do the job of regulators, and that scientific research is distinguishable from activism or journalism, though in some cases the lines may admittedly blur.

Cambridge Analytica was the real 'APIcalypse'

In my reading, Bruns' characterization is at once confrontational (good!) and pessimistic (not so good). Speaking of an 'APIcalypse' and alleging that social media platforms are engaged in a 'fight against critical scholarly research' suggests several things: that academics are virtuous and corporations are evil, that both are uniform entities acting in purely strategic ways, rather than improvising as they go along, and that critical academic research is a thorn in the side of the Googles, Facebooks and Twitters of the world, who are closing down their APIs largely because of our critical revelations. While Bruns is clear on who the good actors are, he also finds it 'difficult to see this as a race that can possibly be won by researchers, even if the legal, moral, and ethical justifications for entering into it can be found'. This is both a depressing premise and at the same time the defiant tone seems eerily reminiscent of the social media discourses that many of us study, in which a beleaguered but morally superior minority takes on shadowy conspiracies with a scant chance of success. The privacy scandals of recent years have clearly resulted from a combination of laxity and a prioritization of the interests of advertizers over the privacy concerns of users on the side of companies, with the interests of academic research largely ignored by both parties. There is a lot to be fed up with from the perspective of politicians, regulators and consumers, not just academics. But I doubt that moral outrage will serve the research community terribly well in the present situation. Unless one expects the internet majors to simply disappear overnight, why not aim for a solution that works for all relevant parties, while acknowledging that privacy concerns and the freedom of research need to be balanced with one another? Clearly, this is something that will not be easy to achieve, and it is unlikely to happen in the blink of an eye. But it seems worth trying, rather than ruling out the possibility that it might work from the onset. And needless to say, making a serious attempt at such a solution should not prevent us from walking away if said approach turns out to be a dead end.

I am slightly more optimistic than Axel Bruns, and decidedly *not* because I believe in the virtuousness of publicly listed companies, but because I believe that the considerable political, regulatory and cultural pressure they are under will have a significant practical impact on how social media data is handled in the future. This is probably a very European (read 'regulation optimistic') perspective relative to the views articulated by Axel Bruns and Alex Halavais (2019) in this issue, who are decidedly more fatalistic (Bruns) or believe that academics should side-step companies to communicate directly with users to ask them for their data (Halavais). The pressure from governments, regulators and NGOs is reshaping the debate around user privacy and the right to data self-determination not just for corporations who must face legal and PR risks to their business (and should therefore change their behavior purely out of self-preservation), but for academics as well. As Bruns would surely agree, the past decade has seen several gross cases of academic misconduct of which the Cambridge Analytica scandal – in which Facebook data collected for academic research was eventually used for commercial political micro-targeting during the 2016 US elections – is merely one instance. It is simply disingenuous for academics to pin serious privacy breaches on the companies and pretend that they are without blame. Anyone of us who is certain to be without sin – think GDPR compliance – is welcome to cast the first stone. If one really wants to consider Alexandr Kogan, a protagonist of the scandal, a victim, it is of his own ambition, paired with an utter disregard for ethical standards.

The flaws of the present system go back to the beginnings described by Bruns. As he points out, developer APIs were an early means for social media platforms to incentivize programmers to extend the platform. This model proved to be a boon to Twitter and certainly spurred its growth. But supporting empirical research was never the aim of this approach. And while there are no doubt tools developed by researchers that are widely used by activists, journalists and companies, the reverse is equally true: that researchers benefitted from developers in the early social media era, many of whom had commercial interests or activist causes in mind, rather than academic research, with considerable implications for data quality. That developer APIs (which is what they are called, after all) were never intended to support empirical social science is more than just a footnote. The type of Twitter research that Bruns describes is plagued by non-trivial issues of validity and reproducibility (Gerlitz & Rieder, 2013; Liang & Fu, 2015), not all of which can be laid down at the doorstep of corporations, but which are a natural result of repurposing an instrument for software development for research and, simply put, doubtful research practices that incentivize gathering data without any real idea what to do with said data, while frequently disregarding privacy laws and ethical standards. The suspicion that developer APIs may no longer be viable is also voiced by Freelon (2018), who argues that we already live in 'the post-API age' and that many of the approaches used to date are in the process of becoming obsolete. The bottom line here is that we need a combination of data access options that are widely available to anyone with no restrictions, but that only cover very limited offerings, and more comprehensive options that allow more in-depth research, but with more specific preconditions. Such offerings must safeguard user privacy and the researchers operating within it must do so under the same strict regime of peer review, legal and ethical controls and transparent reporting of the research process as any large-scale human-subjects research project would do. They must be accountable both to a neutral academic third party which carries out peer review and to the company that provides the data (and is therefore legally responsible for safeguarding its users' data). How else should such an approach ever work? Only if one assumes that privacy is merely a convenient excuse to stifle critical research can this problem be ignored. Whether or not Social Science One will fully live up to these aims is to be seen, and it may well turn out to be a failure. But this is what it should strive to achieve.

Twitter as a doubtful model for social media research

Despite the comprehensive scope of his description, Bruns' criticism focuses on Facebook, a platform which, arguably, has a very different relationship to user privacy by nature of its design than does Twitter. Users engage in a dazzling array of practices on Twitter, but public or semi-public communication is clearly the aim for most. There is limited profile information and with the exception of protected accounts and direct messages, it is hard to see what confidential information on Twitter could lead to a major privacy scandal. Now switch to Facebook. Its user base is much larger, more diverse, global and representative than that of Twitter. Its users provide in-depth profile information and conduct countless activities through the platform, much of them personal or even intimate. What is more, Facebook has obviously become extremely relevant to politics globally, from activist causes that use it for mobilization to parties and candidates that use it to target political ads. The same is not true of Twitter, which is of lesser importance in many countries.

The Cambridge Analytica scandal has permanently redrawn the map of what social media data may be accessed, how and by whom. It has raised awareness among lawmakers, regulators and the general public about how leaky social media platforms are in terms of how much data can be retrieved from them. And it has prompted a rethink (or if you prefer, the pretense of a rethink) among companies who now see modes of data access that previously served their commercial interests – developer APIs – as a security risk. This risk in turn poses a threat to the business model that overrides other priorities once it is regarded as being sufficiently severe. Bruns describes some of the rushed decisions taken in this context, such as expediting the termination of the Instagram API. It hardly matters whether companies change tack out of heartfelt concern for users, or because they are under legal and political pressure to do so. This does not mean stopping to profile users in order to target them algorithmically, it means restricting data sharing with third parties. And third parties necessarily include researchers, who are hardly a group that is homogeneous and clearly defined in institutional terms and is therefore hard to deal with for companies.

In Axel Bruns' telling, it is largely the companies who are to blame for scandals such as Cambridge Analytica, and their reason to close down developer APIs is to frustrate critical research. Their malpractice has made breaches of data privacy possible, while the researchers exploiting them are without blame. Yet Bruns also argues researchers should 'demand' open APIs every time they open their mouths. I apparently lack the imagination to conceive of an API that would be open in the way that Bruns demands and that would at the same time honor user privacy, *for any service other than Twitter*. Instead, the argument seems to be that platforms should both openly provide data and take the blame for the resulting abuses when they occur. At the very least, the academic community should contend with the rebuke that this is attitude is self-serving and interest-driven, rather than critical.

Damned if you don't

Should scientists who study online communication engage in partnerships with internet companies? Should we as academics at public universities and research institutes work with corporate behemoths such as Facebook and Google, if we believe that gaining direct access to their troves of user data can substantially advance our research and benefit society? Or are we naively lending our credibility to a concerted PR initiative ('FUD', in Bruns' words), initiated by some of the world's most valuable corporations, entities that would like nothing more than for the specter of the Cambridge Analytica scandal to disappear again? Responding with a 'Yes' to this question seems somewhat like entering into a Faustian pact, in which we can either sign away our souls in exchange for data access or refrain from doing so because we think the price too high.

Axel Bruns has therefore answered this question with an emphatic 'No' and has provided clear and pricipled arguments for this choice in his essay, but he has also left us with few alternative options. My own response is a hedged 'Yes, but' that attaches conditions to such a partnership, and I think that this reflects the views of many Commission members, ERC grantees and other scholars involved in Social Science One. These conditions include being given access to the relevant data through tools that match those generally used in social media research and being provided with documentation and support to conduct analyses, including those that touch on (to the companies) sensitive issues, such as the spread of fake news and hate speech, and the responsibility of companies in them. They necessarily include being unimpeded by restrictions on what questions can be asked and forbid any direct interference in the research agenda.

Ever since the proverbial horse – in the ominous shape of the Cambridge Analytica scandal that has drawn considerable public attention since 2017 – has bolted from its stable, internet companies in general and Facebook in particular have tried to nail the door shut again, and have conducted concerted outreach efforts to prove it (Bruns, 2018). They have tried both to tighten security and restrict access to user data where once all manner of publicly available information could easily be retrieved through open developer APIs. They have also embraced academia, whether out of a genuine belief that this can contribute to tackling some of social media's most serious problems, or because they see it as a convenient way of signaling they understand the severity of these problems – or, most likely, both. Research collaborations had previously occupied a quite marginal place outside a handful of elite US universities with direct personal ties to the companies. Nobody working in the field will have missed the dramatic increase in initiatives, programs, grant opportunities and calls for collaboration from major players over the last years. Facebook in particular has become much more active, launching a plethora of collaborative initiatives with academia. Whether these will eventually constitute a practical alternative remains to be seen, and there are good reasons for skepticism.

Why should we then consider such partnerships despite their apparent risks? For three reasons. First, the ability to study how people communicate and interact on social media is of vital importance for social science, and arguably for society as a whole. Social media have become an integral part of everyday life, both for billions of individuals who use them every day to connect, express and inform themselves, but also for society's vital systems of politics, business and culture. While Western markets have for the most part reached saturation, globally there is both a tangible strong growth in social media usage and a less tangible increased influence of social media communicators in all areas of society. Arguably it is a profound constraint when we as scholars are unable to study these dynamics. A host of problems including the influence of misinformation campaigns and the root causes of aggressive online behavior could be studied and possibly addressed more effectively if scholars had access to social media data in a manner that satisfies scientific standards, which the use of developer APIs and scraping both do not.

Second, there is currently no suitable alternative model in place able to provide platform data to academics in a fashion that both ensures high standards of representativeness and reproducibility, and at the same time respects user privacy. The assumption that commercial APIs aimed at software developers as they presently exist can provide such a point of access is misplaced. Developer APIs represent a tacit agreement between companies and software developers that was assumed to be of mutual benefit when companies were small and growth could be accelerated by allowing developers to build tools that processed platform data – a model that has clearly run its course. Academics presently piggyback on this model but were never its intended target audience. Accordingly, commercial API data is biased, incomplete, and subject to a range of awkward technical and contractual restrictions that impede its usefulness for empirical research. If anything, new mechanisms for controlled access to data for research purposes could in the future serve as a model for developer APIs, rather than the other way around. Furthermore, open APIs that anyone can readily use will in many cases prove incompatible with stringent legal requirements for privacy and data security.

Third, only by interacting with the companies directly can we learn how they function internally and what constraints their data is under – and, if need be, contribute to holding them accountable. We can determine what works and what does not, but in order to do this, a process designed specifically to support academic research is needed. Such a process is likely to be realized through some kind of API, but it is unlikely to be open to anyone who self-identifies as an academic. This undoubtedly represents an additional barrier to access that risks disadvantaging individual researchers, scholars at small institutions, and academics in non-Western countries, while aiding large conglomerates, prestigious institutions and entrenched scientists. However, the present model that requires in-depth technical expertise but no regard for ethical or scientific standards is only superficially better.

To summarize, it is unclear whether partnerships between academics and industry represent a viable solution to the current challenges faced by the academic community. This essay has argued that the risks such approaches represent are worth taking, in part because there are no clear alternatives. At this point in the evolution of the Internet, it is impossible to tell whether such an approach will prove short-sighted or that to companies it only represents a convenient way of buying time and escaping a regulatory crackdown. We will not know if this latter assessment or a more positive outcome are more likely unless we try. Engaging with all relevant stakeholders – including companies – to resolve these important challenges therefore seems like a sensible approach. Partnerships with industry naturally engender risks and may well fail, but it is difficult to imagine any scientific endeavor worth pursuing that does not. For now, I see good reasons to engage, rather than to rush to the barricades.

Note

1. For example, the global nature of the social media research community, was considered particularly important when Social Science One was set up, but because the initiative was still too young to have any extensive governance structure at this stage of its development, it was decided that some level of veto power by the initiators would best serve to safeguard a global representation of the research community.

Disclosure statement

No potential conflict of interest was reported by the author.

ORCID

Cornelius Puschmann http://orcid.org/0000-0002-3189-0662

References

Bruns, A. (2018). Facebook shuts the gate after the horse has bolted, and hurts real research in the process. *Internet Policy Review*. https://policyreview.info/articles/news/facebook-shuts-gate-after-horse-has-bolted-and-hurts-real-research-process/786

Bruns, A. (2019). After the 'APIcalypse': Social media platforms and their fight against critical scholarly research. *Information, Communication & Society*.

Freelon, D. (2018). Computational research in the Post-API age. *Political Communication*. *35*(4), 665–668. https://doi.org/10.1080/10584609.2018.1477506

Gerlitz, C., & Rieder, B. (2013). Mining one percent of twitter: Collections, baselines, sampling. *M/C Journal*, *16*(2). Retrieved from http://www.journal.media-culture.org.au/index.php/mcjournal/article/viewArticle/620

Halavais, A. (2019). Overcoming Terms of Service: a proposal for ethical distributed research. *Information, Communication & Society*.

Liang, H., & Fu, K. (2015). Testing propositions derived from twitter studies: generalization and replication in computational social science. *PLOS ONE*, *10*(8), e0134270. https://doi.org/10.1371/journal.pone.0134270

Overcoming terms of service: a proposal for ethical distributed research

Alexander Halavais

ABSTRACT
The last two years has marked a turning point in access to large-scale social media data for many researchers, as platforms hobbled their APIs and made recording, archiving, and analyzing social life online far more difficult. Particularly in the context of the United States, where violating the rules put in place by social platforms has the potential to lead to criminal charges, the balance of power between the extremely financially successful social media industry on one side, and the users and researchers of these platforms on the other, has become dangerously skewed. This article argues for a pragmatic partnering with the users to do research, rather than with the platform owners, and suggests some ways in which this might be accomplished.

The end of big social data?

In October of 2018, the United States president went to Twitter to criticize the platform, saying in part, 'it was a Rocket Ship, now it is a Blimp!' (Trump, 2018). Though characteristically polysemic, his complaint seemed to be that opaque changes to the policies of the platform were negatively affecting its utility for him. Like many social media participants, researchers might have sympathized, as what once seemed an inexhaustible source of social data felt a bit like a deflating dirigible thanks to new policies that made effectively extracting data from the platform exponentially more difficult.

And it was not just Twitter; Facebook was faced with a series of scandals. Cambridge Analytica became symbolic of a broader threat: the relentless collection and analysis of user data by the 'silent listeners'– advertisers, state actors, political campaigners, and the platforms themselves (Stutzman, Gross, & Acquisti, 2013). The result was increased restrictions on access to data; especially inexpensive data, as its monetization is core to most platforms' business models.

The rise of social media over the last three decades briefly opened a window to observe social interaction that was unprecedented. The scale of social interactions online allowed for the observation not just of individual conversations, but of public discourse more broadly. Especially as blogging became popular, researchers suddenly had access to the thoughts not just of the influential or powerful, but of a broad cross-section of the population in countries with high internet penetration. This opens up new ways of studying mass shifts in opinion and in social organization, including changes in the structure of everyday life that may remain invisible to those of us who are part of those changes. Ethnography and other smaller-scale qualitative research have also been affected relatively modestly, but large-scale, unobtrusive measures of public conversation and interaction allow for substantial methodological innovation and new insights.

Unfortunately, 2018 marked the year in which many watched with dismay as this new window began to close rapidly. Not every researcher was affected by this in the same way. Those with money to buy data, with relationships with the platforms, or who had access to government resources continue to enjoy a bonanza of social data. This represents a disappointing loss for those researchers who are left in the cold and who suddenly find themselves without the means of researching large-scale interaction afforded to their better-resourced colleagues. Axel Bruns noted in 2013 that already 'scholars at conventional research institutions [were] likely to be further marginalized from this growing field, due to their inability to marshal the funds required to access the comprehensive or large-scale datasets which such resellers now offer'. As a result, the research endeavor as a whole is harmed: a reduction in the range of perspectives, approaches, and backgrounds of those engaged in such work reduces the opportunity for innovative work and establishes the platforms themselves as more substantial gatekeepers of social research. More troubling, as that window closes, it also drives a wedge between the observers and the studied. There is always a danger of a binary division between the researcher and researched, especially when the interests of the former too nearly align with existing structures of power and control. When researchers who are more likely to be able to participants as well as researchers are systematically locked out of access to data, it damages the practice of social science, and its potential utility to the groups and individuals studied.

It would be irresponsible to allow this sunset of mass interaction research to occur without plotting an appropriate path forward. To do so requires understanding the barriers to doing large-scale analysis of social media data and striking a new balance that respects users' agency in the process of discovery, limits the ever-growing ability of platforms to dictate the nature of those investigations, and provides for a diversity of research that reflects the diversity of interaction online.

A brief history of collecting (big) social data

The beginning of online mass data collection looked in many ways like it does today. In the early days of the internet, hosts had access to log files and other collections that revealed the behavior of their users. Researchers who could establish relationships with the companies and individuals who had access to that data were able to engage in research that would have been otherwise impossible. This included some of the earliest proto-platforms on the web, like Slashdot. While the site explicitly allowed for scraping, large-scale analysis like that done by Lampe and Resnick (2004) was facilitated mainly thanks to the provision of log data by the administrators of the platforms themselves.

Around the same time search engines were beginning to crawl the web, researchers began to do the same. In some cases, the two went hand-in-hand, as when Marlow (2004) used his Blogdex project as a source of hyperlink data to analyze how blogs tended to influence one another. Initially, if you wanted to collect large-scale web data, you had to put together programs to do this on your own, and much of the earlier hyperlink analysis did just this (Park & Thelwall, 2003), though some widely-used tools eventually emerged (Rogers, 2010). Researchers sometimes shared the data they had collected, but then, as now, this was the exception rather than the rule.

Collection from blogs became somewhat easier with syndication via RSS. For a while, RSS found its way into a range of services – tracking information for package delivery, reports from the International Space Station, and other serial sources. Over time, it has moved away from the limelight, though it still undergirds things like podcast syndication. The need for both authentication and the ability to respond to more detailed requests brought about the growing use of Application Programming Interfaces (APIs), and a new phase in large-scale social media analysis.

Overall, this meant it became easier for researchers to gain access to information from social platforms. Some knowledge of programming was required, but as APIs and tools that made use of them began to be widely available, the technical barrier was lowered. However, as these APIs provided access to 'walled gardens' like Facebook, they often came with growing obligations for those who wished to use them. In the early days, when data was collected by scrapers, there was a general sense that tools collecting data should be 'polite' – a term that was often left undefined, but generally referred to respecting the wishes of the site owners: making sure to avoid collecting pages that were marked as off limits to robots, crawling during less busy hours, and limiting the rate of requests. But as access to complex, password-protected data increased – and as the marketing value of accessing such data became more apparent – platforms limited programmatic access. In some cases, these were sensible restrictions intended to protect the rights of users. In others, they were simply an effort to charge for automated access to material that would otherwise be freely available to manual access. And by separating the role of 'users' as suppliers of social data from a different class of, often, customers who made use of the APIs, the new era of programmatic access helped to end to the more participatory phase of the social internet (Halavais 2016).

The situation today echoes some elements of that past, at least from the perspective of the scholar. Those researchers who are employed by the platforms, who can establish data sharing arrangements, or who can afford to buy large collections of data, represent the 'Big Data rich' (boyd & Crawford, 2012). Recent efforts to provide access to select groups of scholars ensure that the slammed door is opened to a small pool, but only under strict restrictions by the platforms. The data partnership between the Social Science Research Council and Facebook, for example, allows for access only on specially encrypted and locked down laptops which cannot leave a secure room, invoking the kinds of conditions under which highly classified information is viewed (Gonzalez, 2018). Naturally, most researchers who have an interest will never see this data. Nor will the users who contributed to it. In this, such efforts represent largely a formalization of the existing informal system of patronage that has existed from the earliest days of the web. The restrictive and constantly-shifting terms of service being applied to researchers mean attenuation of not just online social science research, but of the potential of the platforms themselves (Bruns & Burgess, 2016).

Platforms could move in just the opposite direction, providing direct downloads of archives of the data they have collected from users. Efforts to provide a public Twitter archive like this through the United States Library of Congress faltered for the better part of a decade

(Zimmer, 2015). There are significant challenges to making such data available, but these are far from insurmountable. Other archives of public data – those produced and made available to researchers and the public alike – exist for several platforms, including Wikipedia, Reddit, and StackOverflow. Each has seen the value of making this material freely available as more important than the value of monetizing its availability. But they are remarkable in their exception. The majority of online social platforms are advertising-driven, and the advantage they have to offer to advertisers is the availability of research tools that help to narrowly identify those users who will be most easily converted into customers.

Contexts of control

Terms of service represent the ways in which users are legally constrained when using a platform: what actions may be taken, how the information found on the site may be used, and how it may be manipulated by the user. Failure to adhere to these terms, as in any contract, may result in termination or exclusion from the site. However, given that most social platforms are free of charge to the user, and the difficulty in positively identifying users, the threat of exclusion is a relatively light one.

Terms of service provide other legal remedies should they be violated. There have been efforts at creating international regimes for enforcing, for example, trademark and copyright laws. The United States, in particular, has worked through the World Intellectual Property Organization to make many of the provisions of the Digital Millennium Copyright Act enforceable via synchronized laws around the world. But in practice, the legal and policy regimes that exert influence on a given platform represent a complex overlapping set of contexts. Many of the most popular platforms may have been founded in the United States but are bound to adhere to the laws where they most directly interact with users. Social media companies must decide whether they will create separate policies and terms of service for a given legal context, as several have in China, or if they will apply the restrictions of one region across their platform as a whole, as they seem to be doing in the case of the General Data Protection Regulation.

Researchers in China, or within the European Union, or the United States, face somewhat different challenges as they go about their work, making a general analysis of both the legal and ethical aspects of access difficult (Beurskens, 2014; Buchanan & Ess, 2008). This becomes all the more apparent when research groups work across regulatory contexts. And unlike companies, which might be mobile enough to engage in 'regulatory arbitrage', researchers are generally bound to the national context of their institutions and funders. What follows is couched in the context of doing research within the United States, but researchers in other contexts will likely find useful parallels.

Within the context of the United States, researchers are faced with platform terms of service that are often highly restrictive. Researchers are bound to follow these terms of service in three ways: state enforcement, enforcement by institutional ethics panels, and embodiment of these rules in the technical infrastructure of the platforms themselves.

A right to data

The most obvious way terms of service may be binding on researchers is the threat of civil suit. Courts in the United States have broadly accepted that terms of service are binding on users, and often to those users' disadvantage (Braman & Roberts, 2003). But there have yet to be clear cases where those collecting data for research or other non-profit uses have met with significant consequences thanks to a lawsuit.

There is the potential for criminal charges as well. The Computer Fraud and Abuse Act (CFAA) was enacted in 1986, as part of a continuing effort to come to terms with computer crimes. Along with a range of other prohibitions, it makes it a federal crime 'to access a computer with authorization and to use such access to obtain or alter information in the computer that the accesser is not entitled so to obtain or alter'. In other words, it made a crime of violating Terms of Service (Jarrett & Bailie, 2015, pp. 8–9). This law has been interpreted in various ways by the courts, but it was the arrest of Aaron Swartz in 2011 that made clear how ripe it was for abuse. Swartz was accused of programmatically downloading large numbers of academic articles from the JSTOR database. He had permission to download these articles as a person, but because he used a program to do it, he was accused of violating the CFAA. He committed suicide preceding the trial, but if convicted he could have been sentenced to 35 years in prison and been forced to pay up to a million dollars in fines.

The parallel was not lost on social media researchers. The kind of crawling and scraping that Aaron Swartz had been arrested for was similar in many ways to the data collection methods of internet researchers in the US and elsewhere. There had already been some discussion regarding the contexts and conditions under which violating the terms of service of a social platform was ethically justified. As Gillespie (2018, p. 208) argues, when these platforms become such a crucial part of public discourse, they enter into an 'implicit contract' that can differ from the terms of service users (including researchers) click through. But from a practical perspective, the threat of significant jail time means that terms of service, no matter how vague or impractical, have the force of federal prosecution behind them.

In the aftermath, there have been a number of efforts to reign in the CFAA, including a proposed 'Aaron's Law', that would not consider terms of service in determining access that 'exceeds authorization', but the bill languished in committee (Brewster, 2014; Constant, 2013). More recently, the American Civil Liberties Union brought a case forward on behalf of Christian Sandvig and other researchers of social media platforms. Their claim was that their research relating to racial disparities and other inequalities required them to violate the terms of service of the platforms they would scrape, and criminal penalties for doing so represented an unconstitutional curtailment of their civil rights (Williams, 2018).

There is an affirmative defence in the case of copyright violation in the US, an established right to fair use. It allows copyrighted materials to be used in a transformative way: to create new knowledge and cultural goods (Jaszi & Aufderheide, 2010). Were this right not available to scholars, it would make large parts of what we do impossible. The equivalent right does not exist for access to publicly available data. There was a failed early effort to legislate data fair use (Fisher & Fortmann, 2010), but there may still be the possibility of at arriving at such a protection – one that should exist for many of the reasons the Fair Use Doctrine itself exists. The degree to which terms of service may be enforced against researchers in the future remains unclear, but the potential that these website rules might have the force of criminal law represents a significant barrier for researchers.

Institutional review boards

Even if researchers were comfortable with violating terms of service, especially in the United States, Institutional Review Boards have been reluctant to permit researchers to conduct research that does so. Their primary role is in ensuring that research is respectful of the research subjects, and that does, generally, mean turning down proposals that violate federal law. Usually, ensuring that research does not violate contracts, at least in as far as the activities do not interfere with the rights of subjects, is not the purview of the IRB, but given the ambiguity surrounding the degree to which terms of service enforceable under the CFAA, some IRBs are likely to continue to insist they are adhered to. Even without the connection to the CFAA, many IRBs have suffered a 'mission creep', and seek to limit the legal liability of the university (Dougherty & Kramer, 2005).

There are good reasons for IRBs to attend to terms of service. For more than two decades now, there has been an understanding that terms of service can help to shape user expectations around the privacy of online spaces (Jones, 1994). This is likely how it has become a shibboleth for most IRBs. The Rutgers University IRB website, for example, notes that 'users must follow the guidelines that users agree to when accepting the EULA [End User License Agreement], TOS, and/or site or platform rules' (Rutgers University, 2018). In the long process of public comment relating to the new Common Rule – the set of legal requirements that govern IRBs decision making – that comes into full effect in 2019, the terms of service question came to the fore. Leaving aside the thornier issue of whether subjects read and understand the terms of service or privacy policies of the platforms they use (frequently they do not; Obar & Oeldorf-Hirsch, 2018) and the convoluted space between public and private, the broader question of whether terms of service should be determinant in IRB approval remains.

The potential danger of treating these rules as an ethical bright line is already being reflected in the professional guidelines of scholarly organizations. Aside from a brief mention of the tendency in the United States to place questions of privacy in the framework of contracts, the 2002 version of the Association of Internet Researchers' ethics guide made no mention of terms of service (Ess & Jones, 2002). In revisiting and updating these guidelines a decade later, Markham and Buchanan (2012) make mention of 'terms of service' three times, each within the context of asking what those terms might tell us about the broader questions of privacy (and of copyright, etc.) that they might inform. In other words, they are treated not as an absolute, but as a potential point of reference to be weighed against others. As members of the SIGCHI Research Ethics Committee (2017) indicate, questions surrounding the ethics of violating terms of service are the ones they hear most frequently. If there is any emerging consensus, it is that the current situation is untenable. Many argue that Association of Computing Machinery should be active in lobbying for clearer and more consistent application of the CFAA. Others feel that there are conditions under which the terms of service may be violated, but those conditions must be accompanied by a very clear explanation of why it is the ethical decision.

And it is not just the case that terms of service and ethical choices are not always congruent; in many cases they collide directly. Like others (Coughlan & Perryman, 2015), I have taught classes on social media platforms. When I taught on Facebook, I encouraged students, for their own privacy and safety, to create an alternative account to use for the course. This is a violation of Facebook's terms of service, but it was a reasonable way of mitigating risk to my students. Simply equating those terms with users' rights is unreasonable. Clearly, corporations are not humans, and IRBs are not charged with their protection.

Many of the issues surrounding IRBs and big social data revolve around the scale, complexity, and the speed with which this field of research evolves. But just as challenging is a lack of consistency among the boards at different universities. In many ways, the problems of 'data rich' and 'data poor' are multiplied by universities with particularly restrictive or non-responsive IRBs when it comes to issues of access to social media data. As with other challenges presented here, at least one potential aid is the introduction of greater transparency and public discussion. At present, IRBs act largely as a gateway: a hurdle researcher must overcome in order to move forward with their work. This often devalues a process in which ethical examination should be present throughout. By requiring researchers to share publicly their IRB-approved protocols, along with any ethical observations beyond these protocols, journals would provide an important service to the scholarly community (Halavais, 2011). Not only would this foreground the ethical questions that scholar should be grappling with, it would provide members of IRBs with a view to what other boards have found to be an acceptable balancing of risks. This need not lead to rapid consensus, but it may open up a process that right now suffers thanks to its secrecy and support a broader set of ethical discussions and debates, well beyond the question of platforms' data restrictions.

Practical limitations to scraping

The third and final lever of control social platforms have in shaping data collection relates to technological checks on collection. APIs have made it much easier to collect data, but they have also made it easier for platforms to police that process. For APIs that require a token or key, any perceived or actual violation of the rules can result in the token being revoked. The decision of whether to issue a key, to whom, and under what conditions it is revoked is entirely in the hands of the platform.

Of course, there has always been another option: 'scraping' the data directly from the web. APIs provided at least two advantages over scraping. The first is that they made it easier to get at the data. Rather than effectively 'unbaking' the HTML-formatted data and user interface, the API allowed for an ordered and predictable transmission of information. The second is that the API often provided information that was not visible to the public through the web. This is true, obviously, for a semi-private platform like Facebook, where gaining access to the user's posts (and at one point, their friends' posts) and other information required the permission of the user, and an API to extract the data. Even for platforms that support a much greater amount of publicly available data, the API provides more than could be gleaned from what appears on the web page. The encoded data the API would provide for a single tweet, for example, is often an order of magnitude larger than the diminutive text that shows up on the web (Russell, 2013, p. 22; Twitter, n.d.), and includes metadata about the tweet itself (like the location where the tweet was sent, or the application used to craft it) as well as the user who posted it. These 'enhancements' change the lens through which we are interpreting the data, giving the API itself a role in being a data-creator (Vis, 2013), and despite the convenience of using APIs and the addition of metadata, there is an argument to be made for viewing and capturing information directly from the 'live' web just as users do (Marres & Weltevrede, 2013).

But as APIs have become ever more restrictive, there is renewed interest among researchers related to effectively collecting data in what Deen Freelon has termed the 'Post-API Age' (2018). Freelon's answer is straightforward: they should familiarize themselves with scraping and understand the consequences of violating the terms of service when they do so. While collecting data via scraping is often technically somewhat more difficult than doing so through the services' APIs, the emergence of several scraping libraries has made it easier than it might have been during the pre-API age. Moreover, the scholars who scrape from the web have a closer relationship with what is collected. Though automated, it largely replicates the role of a person sitting in front of a computer and collecting data as it is presented there. Especially as previously-available data is systematically excised from API calls, there is also the danger that scholars will tailor their questions to those that can be answered using the kinds of data platforms find most palatable. Where the API itself is not the object of study, scholars must decide whether seeing the platform through the peep hole of the API is providing what is needed to understand user behavior and the influence of the platform on it.

Scholarly researchers come late to the rush of bots and scrapers. Advertisers and those wishing to influence discourse online have long been required to use methods outside of the APIs. As a result, most platforms take measures to detect and eliminate non-human users of their services. A badly designed bot can ask for far more information far more quickly than any human could. Indeed, without limits on the requests, a badly-behaved bot is indistinguishable from a denial of service attack.

Beyond protecting the integrity of service by identifying resource hogs, the process becomes something of a distributed Turing test for the platform, seeking out anomalies that will betray the inhumanity of a user (Cai, Li, & Zeng, 2017). This may include requests that come a bit too quickly, chains of requests that seem to continue on indefinitely, or requests by multiple users from the same IP address. Regular rhythms of requests can likewise alert watchful services (Chu, Gianvecchio, Koehl, Wang, & Jajodia, 2013), and so bots must walk without rhythm, so as to avoid attracting attention. In other words, it is not enough to merely learn to use a scraping library like BeautifulSoup, and track on the interface changes for each platform in order to adapt the scraping routines to changes; it seems inevitable that working around the rules of the platform will yield an ever-increasing arms race. We may need to rethink our weapon of choice.

Partnering with users to collect big data

There is an obvious way of avoiding IP blocks; one that comes with a much more important advantage. Obtaining server-side logs often requires partnering with the platforms or the carriers, as noted above. This brings with it the potential for undue influence, an inequality of researcher access, and the false assumption that users have understood the terms of service and that these represent some weak form of informed consent. Ethical client-side data collection requires the explicit informed consent of the user and provides a range of advantages. Users of these platforms have largely lost the ability to interact effectively with the data that they create and partnering with those users would shift that balance away from governments and large corporations and provide the end users with both agency in the process of data collection and tools to effectively collect and share their own data (Puschmann & Burgess, 2014). Naturally, the ethics of participants being engaged in the research process is nothing new to those who do smaller scale and qualitative work (see, *inter alia*: Dwyer & Davies, 2010; Foth, 2006; Gray, 2012; Kelley, 2016; Morrow, Hawkings, & Kern, 2015), but is not usually a feature of research using big social data.

One path of engagement is to allow users to knowingly provide a bit of their computing power when they are idle, following on crowdsourced efforts like the SETI@home or Folding@home projects, and help to create a botnet for data collection. But asking users to knowingly assume the risks of violating terms of service is far different from having researchers to do the same; it is, in other words, untenable.

Another workable model might be to allow users to contribute downloads of their data to a shared repository for research use – donating their corpus of social media to science. Moves toward data portability (encouraged, in no small part, by the requirements in article 20 of the GDPR) mean that users might be instructed in how to download and contribute their social media data from a given platform, or from multiple platforms. Archiving data in this way has already been suggested in other contexts, such as in order to maintain records in preparation for electronic discovery in legal cases (McPeak, 2017; Stevenson, 2017). How these egocentric collections could aid in archiving the social lives of public officials has also been considered (Acker & Kriesberg, 2017; Rogers, 2019). Many users already engage in some form of self-archiving, either using export functions or copying materials directly (Sinn & Syn, 2014), and might be willing to donate it. But the process here is cumbersome, and potentially introduces a substantial delay, would be limited in scope to particular platforms, and would present complicated privacy issues.

Although the questions of maintaining subjects' privacy are retained, a logistically simpler approach is to record users as they go about their social lives online. This has the distinct advantage of recording the ways in which people move across the web, often bisecting multiple platforms and drawing them together into an assemblage of data traces. Directly scraping data from the users' access of these platforms leaves out a variety of metadata provided by some APIs, but it may provide a less distorted view of the users' perspective of these sites than the APIs or third-party aggregators do (Driscoll & Walker, 2014). For study of big data to be valid, it is vital that we avoid being limited solely to the views provided by the 'Big Institutions' of government and corporations (Halavais, 2015). Though such collection has not happened in a decentralized way for large collections of social data up until now, we have decades of experience of doing such collection on a smaller scale. In some cases, users' activities have been routed through proxy servers (Menchen-Trevino & Karr, 2012), though this does little to allay the problem of requests to platforms from a small number of IP addresses. In other cases, particularly in educational settings, students have been given access to devices with the understanding that their activities on them are logged (e.g., Underwood, Ehrenreich, More, Solis, & Brinkley, 2015).

The most straightforward way to collect data both about users' social behavior online and the content that they are exposed to is through a browser plugin. Zhang, Blum, and Karger (2016) describe a prototype of such a system, which they call Eyebrowse. The intention of Eyebrowse is to allow for open sharing of (some) web activity. Such an open recording of the streams and content of the sites visited would bypass the current choke-point represented by platforms' control of users' data. The approach potentially overcomes the three barriers to large-scale data collection already noted. It also allows for direct control of the collection process – and with appropriate design – the archiving and sharing procedures.

While terms of service might be adjusted to stop users from archiving and sharing their own work, it is difficult to imagine the courts seeing such activities as an 'abuse' under the CFAA and similar legislation. Social media sites are largely created and sustained by users, and while they may – in an oft-repeated aphorism – be the product rather than the customer, few platforms can risk entirely alienating their user base. Users should have the right to record and share their own data.

It also represents a clearer case to a human subject's board by providing for much more appropriate, explicit, and ongoing forms of informed consent. Many have avoided the issues around informed consent, particularly given the difficulties of obtaining it and API frameworks that tend to obscure it. As Lomborg and Bechmann (2014) argue, an informed consent process 'is a viable ethical procedure for small-sample, qualitative studies using APIs, where researchers may keep close contact with the research participants but is hardly an option for large-scale research with thousands of users involved'. That may be true when using APIs, which can mask interaction with participants in the research, but when implemented as a browser plug-in, a more effective effort may be made to inform the user of potential risks and engage the user more directly with the research. There remain, as with all social data, issues around the privacy rights of those the users interact with. Likewise, addressing problems of anonymization and maintaining the security of collected data would be paramount. Nonetheless, this represents a significant improvement over the current practices of quietly observing or, as in the case of the emotional contagion study (Kramer, Guillory, & Hancock, 2014), manipulation of users, largely behind a veil of panoptic secrecy.

Finally, it represents a partial solution to platforms' efforts to curtail researcher access to scraping. Requests come to the various platforms not from a small group of IP addresses, but from the users themselves. Some bandwidth would be asked of those users individually, but from the perspective of the platforms, this process would reduce the amount of bandwidth required when compared with existing API traffic. (We might consider this the other side of a DDoS: A Distributed Provision of Service.) Especially in an era when more and more social platforms are accessed not by browsers but through proprietary apps, there remains the potential for blocking such distributed self-archiving. For the moment, though, the browser still dominates (Perez, 2018).

Transparency and participatory research

An approach that brings users in as partners in the data collection process does more than overcome some of the legal, ethical, and technical boundaries to data collection. It opens the door to much more participatory processes in the research itself. It does so primarily by increasing the transparency of data collection. It would be naïve to assume that transparency alone will make 'users' and 'subjects' into co-researchers, but it is a prerequisite. If we are to become 'citizens as well as researchers' (Luka & Millette, 2018) it requires that we evolve methods that draw those roles together.

Analogues of the proposed solution have already been implemented at a small scale, and one could imagine that even a small pool of users collecting social data would represent a significant opportunity for learning about social behavior online. But to move beyond this model of social media 'New Nielsen Families' (Lynch, 2017) we would want relatively large-scale adoption. Big Data would require big participation. Certainly, this need not be all or even most users; significant discoveries could be made on the basis of forensic traces of any large proportion of a platform's users. Naturally, there remains a sampling issue, but this a problem that social scientists regularly address, and not absent from API access.

One of the greatest barriers to such participation is a lack of trust. So far, advertisers, political operatives, state actors, businesses, ISPs, telecoms, and the platforms themselves have been cavalier about how they handle users' data, and in several well-publicized cases, academic researchers have been willing to cozy up with each. The model proposed here, of a plug-in that records a person's online activities and sends them along to a third party, may sound familiar to many. It is not just the platform-based apps – like the Cambridge Analytica Facebook app that was presented as a scholarly effort – that have deceived users. The idea that apps on your phone or browser plugins may be 'leaking' your data is well-established. In a particularly egregious example, a Chrome plug-in called 'Web of Trust' that provided ratings of trustworthiness for visited sites to an enormous database, readily handed that data over to what they thought was an advertising agency when offered a bit of money (Humphries, 2016).

The above-mentioned prototype, Eyebrowser, was an experiment in collaborative sharing of browsing data. It produced a public feed that presented any interested party with a path of web usage, within the bounds set by the user. Participants were willing to share that information because they knew what they were sharing (it was *revealed*), were able to control what was in it (it was *restricted*), and they received the value of community connections by doing so (it was *reciprocal*). When presented with the advantages of sharing this information with their peers, despite a number of concerns, they were willing to do so. As one of Zhang et alia's respondents remarked, they would prefer sharing this data with social scientists to it ending up in the hands of the platforms. This should not be news. Critics have been telling online businesses for years that being transparent about what data they collect and what they do with it increases trust among customers (Morey, Forbath, & Schoop, 2015). Social scientists have too long relied on institutional authority to project a trustworthy aura. Given some spectacular violations of that trust, we need to rebuild it by acting more ethically as a group. The Eyebrowser work also represents the first of what should be a larger set of empirical contributions to understanding the expectations and attitudes of research participants to data observation. Too often, researchers and ethics boards draw on their own preconceived notions of participants' relationship to their data traces rather than drawing on research that can better reveal those relationships.

Many researchers see informed consent as a gateway – something to be 'taken care of' so that the work can begin. This is hardly unique to social media research (Hayden, 2012). Meanwhile, we have seen a general shift in how people are expected to engage with consent in the case of sexual relationships. Planned Parenthood in 2016 presented the acronym 'FRIES' to help people recall the required elements: consent is 'Freely Given, Reversible, Informed, Enthusiastic, and Specific' (Feinn, 2016). Consent as a form to be signed – or worse, as inferred from terms of service – appears especially impoverished by comparison. Yes, we should be sharing the results of our research with our subjects; but they should also be involved (or be able to reverse that involvement) at each stage, from seeing the raw data as they are collected to understanding the ways in which those data were used to draw conclusions.

There is a larger story here: one about decentralization and returning control of the social internet to the people who make it. The issue with Twitter or Facebook restricting access to researchers is that we are also the users of the web – we should all have access to what we produce. At the edges, there has been a growing movement toward re-decentralizing the web. You see it in distributed search engines like YaCy, that draw on participants' own computers to populate a web index without any centralized control (Mislove, Gummadi, & Druschel, 2006). Or in Berners-Lee's (2018) new project to build decentralized platform for storage and sharing. And it is crying out from Swartz's (2008) 'Guerrilla Open Access Manifesto', which reminds us that there is no justice in following unjust laws. Partnering with the people we study also gives us the opportunity to place tools in their hands that will allow them to control and share their own data, reshaping 'the *I* and the *We*' through a critical engagement with the corporate and institutional paradigms of data management (Renzi & Langlois, 2015).

'Routing around' the restrictions that are being put in place by platform owners is both a pragmatic and a just solution to the problem of observing online behavior. At the same time, it gives us the opportunity to rethink our relationship to the public we serve, and to help encourage more sociable forms of social media research, teaching, and practice. Certainly, some of the approaches suggested here raise questions as much as they provide answers, but many of these are questions are ones we should already be asking.

Disclosure statement

No potential conflict of interest was reported by the author.

ORCID

Alexander Halavais http://orcid.org/0000-0002-7164-9208

References

Acker, A., & Kriesberg, A. (2017). Tweets may be archived: Civic engagement, digital preservation and Obama White House social media data. *Proceedings of the Association for Information Science and Technology*, *54*(1), 1–9. doi:10.1002/pra2.2017.14505401001

Berners-Lee, T. (2018, September 29). One small step for the web .... Retrieved from https://medium.com/@timberners_lee/one-small-step-for-the-web-87f92217d085

Beurskens, M. (2014). Legal questions of Twitter research. In K. Weller, A. Bruns, J. Burgess, M. Mahrt, & C. Puschmann (Eds.), *Twitter and society* (pp. 123–133). New York: Peter Lang.

boyd, d., & Crawford, K. (2012). Critical questions for big data. *Information, Communication & Society*, *15*(5), 662–679. doi:10.1080/1369118X.2012.678878

Braman, S., & Roberts, S. (2003). Advantage ISP: Terms of Service as media law. *New Media & Society*, *5*(3), 422–448. doi:10.1177/14614448030053007

Brewster, T. (2014, August 6). Aaron's Law is doomed leaving US hacking law 'broken'. *Forbes*. Retrieved from https://www.forbes.com/sites/thomasbrewster/2014/08/06/aarons-law-is-doomed-leaving-us-hacking-law-broken/

Bruns, A. (2013). Faster than the speed of print: Reconciling 'big data' social media analysis and academic scholarship. *First Monday*, *18*(10). doi:10.5210/fm.v18i10.4879

Bruns, A., & Burgess, J. (2016). Methodological innovation in precarious spaces: The case of Twitter. In H. Snee, C. Hine, Y. Morey, S. Roberts, & H. Watson (Eds.), *Digital methods for social science* (pp. 17–33). London: Palgrave Macmillan.

Buchanan, E. A., & Ess, C. (2008). Internet research ethics: The field and its critical issues. In K. E. Himma & H. T. Tavani (Eds.), *The handbook of information and computer ethics* (pp. 245–272). Hoboken, NJ: Wiley.

Cai, C., Li, L., & Zeng, D. (2017). *Detecting social bots by jointly modeling deep behavior and content information*. In *proceedings of the 2017 ACM on conference on Information and knowledge Management* (pp. 1995–1998), New York, NY, USA: ACM. doi:10.1145/3132847.3133050

Chu, Z., Gianvecchio, S., Koehl, A., Wang, H., & Jajodia, S. (2013). Blog or block: Detecting blog bots through behavioral biometrics. *Computer Networks*, *57*(3), 634–646. doi:10.1016/j.comnet.2012.10.005

Constant, S. A. (2013). The Computer Fraud and Abuse Act: A prosecutor's dream and a hacker's worst nightmare: The case against Aaron Swartz and the need to reform the CFAA. *Tulane Journal of Technology and Intellectual Property*, *16*, 231–313.

Coughlan, T., & Perryman, L.-A. (2015). A murky business: Navigating the ethics of educational research in Facebook groups. *European Journal of Open, Distance and e-Learning*, 146–169. http://www.eurodl.org/materials/special/2015/Coughlan_Perryman.pdf

Dougherty, D. S., & Kramer, M. W. (2005). A rationale for scholarly examination of Institutional Review boards: A case study. *Journal of Applied Communication Research*, *33*(3), 183–188. doi:10.1080/00909880500149270

Driscoll, K., & Walker, S. (2014). Working within a black box: Transparency in the collection and production of big Twitter data. *International Journal of Communication*, *8*, 1745–1764. https://ijoc.org/index.php/ijoc/article/view/2171

Dwyer, C., & Davies, G. (2010). Qualitative methods III: Animating archives, artful interventions and online environments. *Progress in Human Geography*, *34*(1), 88–97. doi:10.1177/0309132508105005

Ess, C., & Jones, S. (2002). *Ethical decision-making and internet research*. Association of Internet Researchers. Retrieved from https://aoir.org/reports/ethics.pdf

Feinn, L. (2016). *How french fries can be used to explain consent*. Retrieved from https://www.bustle.com/articles/178198-planned-parenthood-graphic-uses-fries-to-explain-consent-in-a-way-anyone-can-understand

Fisher, J. B., & Fortmann, L. (2010). Governing the data commons: Policy, practice, and the advancement of science. *Information & Management*, *47*(4), 237–245. doi:10.1016/j.im.2010.04.001

Foth, M. (2006). Network action research. *Action Research*, *4*(2), 205–226. doi:10.1177/1476750306063992

Freelon, D. (2018). Computational research in the post-API age. *Political Communication*. Advance Online Publication. doi:10.1080/10584609.2018.1477506

Gillespie, T. (2018). *Custodians of the internet: Platforms, content moderation, and the hidden decisions that shape social media*. New Haven: Yale University Press.

Gonzalez, R. (2018, May 28). Facebook is giving scientists its data to fight misinformation. *Wired*. Retrieved from https://www.wired.com/story/facebook-is-giving-scientists-its-data-to-fight-misinformation/

Gray, K. L. (2012). Deviant bodies, stigmatized identities, and racist acts: Examining the experiences of African-American gamers in Xbox live. *New Review of Hypermedia and Multimedia, 18*(4), 261–276. doi:10.1080/13614568.2012.746740

Halavais, A. (2011). Social science: Open up online research. *Nature, 480*, 174–175. doi:10.1038/480174a

Halavais, A. (2015). Bigger sociological imaginations: Framing big social data theory and methods. *Information, Communication & Society, 18*(5), 583–594.

Halavais, A. (2016). The blogosphere and its problems: Web 2.0 undermining civic Webspaces. *First Monday, 21*(6). https://doi.org/10.5210/fm.v21i6.6788

Hayden, E. C. (2012). Informed consent: A broken contract. *Nature, 486*(7403), 312–314. doi:10.1038/486312a

Humphries, M. (2016). 'Web of Trust' browser extension cannot be trusted. *PCMAG.* Retrieved from https://www.pcmag.com/news/349328/web-of-trust-browser-extension-cannot-be-trusted

Jarrett, H. M., & Bailie, M. W. (2015). *Prosecuting computer crimes.* Washington, DC: Office of Legal Education, Executive Office for United States Attorneys. Retrieved from https://www.justice.gov/sites/default/files/criminal-ccips/legacy/2015/01/14/ccmanual.pdf

Jaszi, P., & Aufderheide, P. (2010). *Code of best practices in fair use for scholarly research in communication.* International Communication Association. Retrieved from http://cmsimpact.org/code/code-best-practices-fair-use-scholarly-research-communication/

Jones, R. A. (1994). The ethics of research in cyberspace. *Internet Research, 4*(3), 30–35. doi:10.1108/10662249410798894

Kelley, B. (2016). Toward a goodwill ethics of online research methods. *Tranformative Works and Cultures, 22.* doi:10.3983/twc.2016.0891

Kramer, A. D. I., Guillory, J. E., & Hancock, J. T. (2014). Experimental evidence of massive-scale emotional contagion through social networks. *Proceedings of the National Academy of Sciences, 111*(24), 8788–8790. doi:10.1073/pnas.1320040111

Lampe, C., & Resnick, P. (2004). Slash(dot) and burn: Distributed moderation in a large online conversation space. CHI 2004, April 24-29, Vienna.

Lomborg, S., & Bechmann, A. (2014). Using APIs for data collection on social media. *The Information Society, 30*(4), 256–265. doi:10.1080/01972243.2014.915276

Luka, M. E., & Millette, M. (2018). (Re)framing big data: Activating situated knowledges and a feminist ethics of care in social media research. *Social Media + Society, 4*(2), 205630511876829. https://doi.org/10.1177/2056305118768297

Lynch, C. (2017). Stewardship in the 'Age of Algorithms'. *First Monday, 22*(12), doi:10.5210/fm.v22i12.8097

Markham, A., & Buchanan, E. (2012). Ethical decision-making and internet research: Recommendations from the AoIR Ethics Working Committee (version 2.0). Association of Internet Researchers. Retrieved from https://aoir.org/reports/ethics2.pdf

Marlow, C. (2004). *Audience, structure and authority in the weblog community.* Presented at the International Communications Association, New Orleans, LA.

Marres, N., & Weltevrede, E. (2013). Scraping the social? *Journal of Cultural Economy, 6*(3), 313–335. doi:10.1080/17530350.2013.772070

McPeak, A. (2017). Social data discovery and proportional privacy. *Cleveland State Law Review, 65*, 17.

Menchen-Trevino, E., & Karr, C. (2012). Researching real-world web use with Roxy: Collecting observational web data with informed consent. *Journal of Information Technology & Politics, 9*(3), 254–268. doi:10.1080/19331681.2012.664966

Mislove, A., Gummadi, K. P., & Druschel, P. (2006). Exploiting social networks for internet search. In *5th workshop on hot topics in networks (hotnets06)* (p. 79). Irvine, CA.

Morey, T., Forbath, T., & Schoop, A. (2015, May 1). Customer data: Designing for transparency and trust. *Harvard Business Review.* Retrieved from https://hbr.org/2015/05/customer-data-designing-for-transparency-and-trust

Morrow, O., Hawkings, R., & Kern, L. (2015). Feminist research in online spaces. *Gender, Place & Culture, 22*(4), 526–543. doi:10.1080/0966369X.2013.879108

Obar, J. A., & Oeldorf-Hirsch, A. (2018). The biggest lie on the Internet: Ignoring the privacy policies and terms of service policies of social networking services. *Information, Communication & Society*. Published online 3 July 2018. doi:10.1080/1369118X.2018.1486870

Park, H. W., & Thelwall, M. (2003). Hyperlink analysis of the world wide web: A review. *Journal of Computer-Mediated Communication*, *8*(4), JCMC843.

Perez, S. (2018). Facebook is now a major mobile browser in U.S., with 10%+ market share in many states. *TechCrunch*. Retrieved from http://social.techcrunch.com/2018/08/06/facebook-is-now-a-major-mobile-browser-in-u-s-with-10-market-share-in-many-states/

Puschmann, C., & Burgess, J. (2014). The politics of twitter data. In K. Weller, A. Bruns, J. Burgess, M. Mahrt, & C. Puschmann (Eds.), *Twitter and society* (pp. 43–54). New York: Peter Lang.

Renzi, A., & Langlois, G. (2015). Data activism. In G. Langlois, J. Redden, & G. Elmer (Eds.), *Compromised data: From social media to big data* (pp. 202–225). New York: Bloomsbury.

Rogers, R. (2010). Internet research: The question of method. *Journal of Information Technology & Politics*, *7*, 241–260.

Rogers, R. (2019). Periodizing web archiving: Biographical, event-based, national and autobiographical traditions. In N. Brügger & I. Milligan (Eds.), *The SAGE handbook of web history* (pp. 42–56). London: Sage Publishing.

Russell, M. A. (2013). *Mining the social web: Data mining Facebook, Twitter, LinkedIn, Google+, GitHub, and more* (2nd ed). Beijing: O'Reilly Media.

Rutgers University. (2018). *Internet research*. Retrieved from https://orra.rutgers.edu/internet-research

SIGCHI Research Ethics Committee. (2017, December 1). *Do researchers need to follow TOS?* Retrieved from https://medium.com/sigchi-ethics-committee/do-researchers-need-to-follow-tos-f3bde1950d3c

Sinn, D., & Syn, S. Y. (2014). Personal documentation on a social network site: Facebook, a collection of moments from your life? *Archival Science*, *14*(2), 95–124. Retrieved from http://dx.doi.org.ezproxy1.lib.asu.edu/10.1007/s10502-013-9208-7

Stevenson, L. E. (2017). Social media and eDiscovery: Practice Tips and Case Law Developments. *Computer and Internet Lawyer; Frederick*, *34*(9), 1–8.

Stutzman, F., Gross, R., & Acquisti, A. (2013). Silent listeners: The evolution of privacy and disclosure on Facebook. *Journal of Privacy and Confidentiality*, *4*(2), 7–41. doi:10.29012/jpc.v4i2

Swartz, A. (2008). Guerrilla open access manifesto. Retrieved from http://archive.org/details/GuerillaOpenAccessManifesto

Trump, D. J. (2018, October 26). 'Twitter has removed so many … ' [Tweet]. Retrieved from https://twitter.com/realDonaldTrump/status/1055822810940129283

Twitter. (n.d.). *Tweet object*. Retrieved from https://developer.twitter.com/en/docs/tweets/data-dictionary/overview/tweet-object.html

Underwood, M. K., Ehrenreich, S. E., More, D., Solis, J. S., & Brinkley, D. Y. (2015). The BlackBerry project: The hidden world of adolescents' text messaging and relations with internalizing symptoms. *Journal of Research on Adolescence*, *25*(1), 101–117. doi:10.1111/jora.12101

Vis, F. (2013). A critical reflection on big data: Considering APIs, researchers and tools as data makers. *First Monday*, *18*(10). doi:10.5210/fm.v18i10.4878

Williams, J. (2018, April 12). D.C. Court: Accessing public information is not a computer crime. Retrieved from https://www.eff.org/deeplinks/2018/04/dc-court-accessing-public-information-not-computer-crime

Zhang, A. X., Blum, J., & Karger, D. R. (2016). *Opportunities and challenges around a tool for social and public web activity tracking*. In *Proceedings of the 19th ACM conference on Computer-Supported Cooperative Work & Social Computing - CSCW '16* (pp. 911–923), San Francisco, California, USA: ACM Press. doi:10.1145/2818048.2819949

Zimmer, M. (2015). The Twitter Archive at the Library of Congress: Challenges for information practice and information policy. *First Monday*, *20*(7). doi:10.5210/fm.v20i7.5619

Data craft: a theory/methods package for critical internet studies

Amelia Acker and Joan Donovan

ABSTRACT

Disinformation campaigns continue to thrive online, despite social media companies' efforts at identifying and culling manipulation on their platforms. Framing these manipulation tactics as 'coordinated inauthentic behavior,' major platforms have banned culprits and deleted the evidence of their actions from social activity streams, making independent assessment and auditing impossible. While researchers, journalists, and civil society groups use multiple methods for discovering and tracking disinformation, platforms began to publish highly curated data archives of disinformation in 2016. When platform companies reframe manipulation campaigns, however, they downplay the importance of their products in spreading disinformation. We propose to treat social media metadata as a boundary object that supports research across platforms and use metadata as an entry point for investigating manipulation campaigns.

We illustrate how platform companies' responses to disinformation campaigns are at odds with the interests of researchers, civil society, policy-makers, and journalists, limiting the capacity to audit the role that platforms play in political discourse. To show how platforms' data archives of 'coordinated inauthentic behavior' prevent researchers from examining the contexts of manipulation, we present two case studies of disinformation campaigns related to the Black Lives Matter Movement. We demonstrate how data craft – the exploitation of metrics, metadata, and recommendation engines – played a prominent role attracting audiences to these disinformation campaigns. Additionally, we offer some investigative techniques for researchers to employ data craft in their own research of the disinformation. We conclude by proposing new avenues for research for the field of Critical Internet Studies.

1. Introduction

'New data shows that Russian propaganda may have been shared billions of times on Facebook' read an 6 October 2017 headline on Business Insider (Bertrand, 2017a). Nearly a year after Trump's unexpected victory in the 2016 US presidential election, researchers were still trying to unearth and unpack related data from platform companies, who were unwilling to take public responsibility their role in spreading political disinformation. Later that month, Facebook, Twitter, and Google sent representatives to sit before a Senate Intelligence Committee to answer questions about 'foreign meddling' in US elections (Kang & Frenkel, 2018). These corporations gave few direct answers at this hearing, and instead showed some strangely packaged data in the form of printed PDFs and poster board displays.

In this paper, we recount this recent history to show how platform companies responded to the US Congress and UK Parliament investigative hearings by defining election meddling and other cyber threats as coordinated inauthentic behavior. Nathan Gleicher, Facebook's Head of Cyber Security defines coordinated inauthentic behavior as 'creating networks of accounts to mislead others about who they were and what they were doing' (Gleicher, 2018). These official inquiries, alongside pressure from investigative journalists, resulted in platform companies shifting the blame to individual bad actors and rolling back platform APIs, limiting data access to outside parties.[1] In the Senate Intelligence Committee hearing, it was apparent that platform companies were only finding what they were explicitly looking for, clashing with the advice of internal public relations advisors who urged them not to look at all (Frenkel, Confessore, Kang, Rosenberg, & Nicas, 2018).

Technologists at platform companies complained that the public, politicians, and researchers did not understand that their internal platform systems were designed to prohibit wide-net browsing across the entire social graph. This limited search capacity was developed in response to prior public and government concerns about surveillance and privacy. In effect, platform representatives claimed that even if they wanted to carry out dragnets for manipulation campaigns, the platforms themselves were designed to prevent this research and external inquiry (Driscoll & Walker, 2014; Walker, 2017). As a result, the public, governments, civil rights activists, journalists, and researchers have no way of knowing how thoroughly platform companies are searching their systems for evidence of foreign meddling, manipulation, or intentional disinformation campaigns (Bertrand, 2017b). Moreover, these unknown methods of detection are not auditable by anyone outside of these companies.

In 2018 after relentless pressure from journalists, Facebook and Twitter gave access to some evidence of election meddling, but with serious limitations. Both Facebook and Twitter provided curated datasets on manipulation by the Internet Research Agency (hereafter, the IRA), a Russian 'troll farm' located in Saint Petersburg that was allegedly operating at the instruction of the Kremlin (Barrett, Horwitz, & Helderman, 2016). According to technologists, creating custom datasets takes time and requires anonymization to protect users. This customization accounts for the lag in time from the 2016 election to the release date to the public after the Senate Intelligence Committee hearing. Anonymization, however, meant that the most meaningful metadata documenting the tactics and their impact was not included in these curated datasets. Taken together, lag and anonymization ensured that researchers would not be able to recreate the full context of distribution for the IRA manipulation campaign.

As researchers, we assert that these prepackaged datasets act as boundary objects, which are things that take on

> different meanings in different social worlds but their structure is common enough to more than one world to make them recognizable, a means of translation. The creation and management of boundary objects is key in developing and maintaining coherence across intersecting social worlds. (Star & Griesemer, 1989, p. 393)

Boundary objects are ideas and things that can be understood differently by different groups. The election meddling datasets were and continue to be understood differently by platforms, Congressional representatives, social media researchers, journalists, civil society organizations, and individual social media users.

Yet, these election datasets were a result of the formation of a 'tacit coalition' of journalists, government and policy makers, technologists, and civil society groups (Epstein, 2007). Unlike social movements or advocacy organizations that coordinate and sustain campaigns, tacit coalitions are very loosely networked groups or elites and lay people who share a certain unity of purpose (p. 53–54). Key to the success of a tacit coalition is the establishment of a precedent that can then be called for again and again by other groups. As such, these datasets are now the fodder for continued research, investigative journalism, government inquiry, and audits by civil rights organizations. Yet for a number of reasons we discuss later, meaningful access to these and other archives of disinformation remains a challenge that is worth continued and sustained coalition building for critical internet scholars, political communication researchers, journalists and policymakers alike. Consequently, the social worlds of these different professional sectors have become bound up with each other as an arena of practice (Clarke & Star, 2008). Clarke and Star (2008:, p. 117) demonstrate that methods should not be construed as acting in service of theory, instead theories and methods are co-constructed, they write, 'The concept of theory/methods package assumes that ontology and epistemology are both co-constitutive (make each other up) and manifest in actual practices.'

As boundary objects, these datasets reveal how bad actors disrupt the field of trustworthy information online by amplifying polarizing issues and manipulating online communication and advertising tools. We argue that the metadata provided in these datasets can also act as boundary objects for researchers, allowing for cross-platform analysis. Databases from across different social media platforms can be connected by linking together similar screen names, geo locations, structured content, images, advertising, targeted audiences, and other traces. By understanding social media platforms' datasets and their metadata as boundary objects, we can see how social categories of use and users are entrenched, hidden, and exploited. Users are increasingly positioned both as customers and producers of activity data, as profitability supplants the early promise of social networks..

Platform companies such as Facebook and Twitter have developed paid advertising as the core capacity for spreading messages and assuaging shareholders (Benkler, Faris, & Roberts, 2018). Ongoing design changes to these platforms are intended to increase user engagement, creating increasingly robust data sets useful for targeted advertising. As a result, political communication online has shifted into a complex assemblage of organic content, advertising, and disinformation driven by algorithmic personalization (Nadler, Crain, & Donovan, 2018). The US is not alone in seeing the impact of advertisement and media manipulation during campaigns. Since 2016, election observations throughout the world have revealed that it is no longer possible to run political campaigns online without interference from a range of motivated individuals and groups, including foreign agents, oppositional parties, social movements, and manipulation efforts in the forms of bots and coordinated trolling (Howard, Woolley, & Calo, 2018; Woolley & Howard, 2016).

As a result of platforms being weaponized by manipulators for political gain, profit, or just for fun, there are many disincentives for corporations to open up the Pandora's box of data. Acker (2018, p. 4) writes, 'Political disinformation campaigns attempt to influence civil discourse, erode democracy with mistrust, meddle with elections, and even attack the public sphere by hijacking the platforms where more than half of Americans get their news.' According to Benkler et al. (2018), this is a new era of 'networked propaganda,' which refers to 'the ways in which the architecture of a media ecosystem makes it more or less susceptible to disseminating these kinds of manipulations and lies' (Benkler et al., 2018, p. 24). The 2016 election revealed how these digital dirty tricks could emerge in the form of imposter accounts, attack ads, and 'fake news' (Benkler et al., 2018). Datasets that have been curated by platforms through APIs or other data access regimes typically provide limited metadata, stripped of valuable organic context or the ability to view it in context is a strategy and an attempt to mitigate reputational harms of corporate, for-profit platforms.

The distinction between 'users' and third party 'customers' is helpful for critiquing how authentic and inauthentic behavior are operationalized by platforms. For our theory/methods package of mapping disinformation across platforms, *users* are account holders, while *customers* pay to spread beyond the 'organic' reach of the user by using either off the shelf advertising tools, imposter accounts, or search engine optimization strategies. In instances where users are achieving coordination authentically, it happens through interrelated and direct connections that are mapped on the social graph at each platform company. Coordinated inauthentic behavior is harder to decipher because it requires the detection of imposter accounts, bots, or some other manipulation tactic that requires different contextual information. Further, there is no entity responsible for surveying how these disinformation campaigns leverage the data and capacities available on one platform to manipulate another. For example, the IRA organized a multi-platform disinformation campaign by optimizing the pay-to-play features and APIs of each platform to exaggerate their coordination capacity, and ultimately increased the audience for their cross-platform disinformation campaign.

These API updates to platforms' data access regimes have impacted researchers, digital archivists, and cultural heritage institutions, and will undoubtedly shape archives of digital culture in the near future. *We contend that the analysis of 'coordinated inauthentic behavior' is better described as a particular kind of disinformation campaign, where the spread of disinformation is enhanced by platform companies' own products, such as advertising infrastructure and data access through APIs, and the sale of user data for reuse.* We analyze the corporate framing of the issue to illustrate that platform companies' responses to disinformation campaigns is opposed to the interests of those, such as researchers and journalists, who seek the capacity to audit and assess the role that platforms play in political discourse and the spread of disinformation. We conclude by providing our own theory/methods package for assessing disinformation campaigns as data craft, a collection of practices that create, rely on, or even play with computational and algorithmic mechanisms of organization and classification. While the two cases of metadata manipulation we identify below are examples of data craft, we aim to offer some investigative techniques for researchers to employ data craft in the field of critical Internet studies.

2. Theorizing metadata as boundary object

We propose to treat social media metadata as boundary object that supports research across platforms as well as data that has been extracted from platforms. Metadata or 'data about data' are those standards that are created by any system as a result of designers keeping track of users' actions. Metadata are always created with some intended future use, even if those future metadata applications may be unknown to system designers (Greenberg, 2005). In social platforms, metadata ranges from the posts a user has tagged with geolocation labels, to the types of new stories a user has read, clicked, posted or watched. While 'traces of human behavior that are recorded as metadata are often hidden from users of digital information infrastructures' they are increasingly leveraged in social platform development and advertising technology that underwrites the personalization of web experiences like online shopping, search, and news consumption across social media (Mayernik & Acker, 2018, p. 178).

Metadata has always been driven by the classification of ideas, actions, and things into categories of meaning. The acts of classifying phenomena, or applying metadata and different meanings, inherently advances particular kinds of world views onto the things it is used to describe. When technologists design information systems like platforms, metadata structures not only allow for access and use, but they influence identities, categories of experience, even build and enact authority. As Morville argues, 'Product taxonomies, brand architectures, and enterprise vocabularies are intimately connected to strategy and competitive advantage' (2005, p. 125).

Metadata generated from social media activity is increasingly being leveraged as a boundary object in different ways by platforms, manipulators, and researchers. In this section, we layout how metadata are the raw materials used by platform companies to power their technology and provide services (i.e., without metadata there would be no social media), but it is also the human data capital that generates revenue for the corporation (i.e., the business model of platform companies requires the packaging and selling data for reuse).

Increasingly, metadata from networked engagement is becoming a core offering of the experience and services of social media platforms. For example, Facebook's Newsfeed algorithm and Twitter's personalized timeline both leverage popular or current events over chronological posts. Platforms like Facebook, YouTube, Instagram, and Twitter publicly display engagement activity, data signals that provide measurements for understanding the user (who they are following), and the networks that they influence (who is following them). These metadata can also provide information about the credibility, reliability, or trustworthiness of the information and content that a user may circulate. Research has shown how metadata features can also be manipulated with fake data intended to appear real (Stewart, Ahmer, Starbird, 2018; Benkler et al., 2018; Rainie, Anderson, & Albright, 2017). Manipulators exploit platform metadata categories by gaming engagement metrics, obscuring provenance, and generating noise or 'junk metadata' that can easily be taken up and reproduced in social activity streams.

Metadata from social networking sites as a research phenomenon has been a concern to security researchers, privacy scholars, and information scientists for more than a decade. These researchers have found that digital metadata traces are powerful identification tools, curiously resistant to deanonymization techniques even at large scales of aggregated collections (Perez, Musolesi, & Stringhini, 2018). Social media researchers have identified the long term 'changingness' and decay of social media metadata after it's been collected from platform APIs (Walker, 2017; Zubiaga, 2018), revealing a massive vulnerability in the persistence of evidence for tracking these happenings, especially for historical, investigative, or preservation purposes.

More recently, social media researchers began studying the spread of rumors, hoaxes, and disinformation through engagement metadata and embedded content metadata (Shu, Sliva, Wang, Tang, & Liu, 2017; Starbird, Dailey, Mohamed, Lee, & Spiro, 2018). Because digital platforms accumulate power and capital through user-generated metadata on connectivity and engagement, media manipulators see metadata as a vulnerability to be exploited for financial and political ends. As API access is increasingly limited for researchers and developers, disinformation campaigns continue to leverage a variety of platform metadata to spread content, gain traction, and influence public discourse in an effort to sow discord (Meserole & Polyakova, 2018).

New platform affordances provide effective ways of amplifying legitimate, noisy or fake content to expanded audiences through monetized advertisement. However these audiences are unaware of how this content is delivered or arranged for their consumption (Rainie et al., 2017; Shearer & Gottfried, 2017). Twitter's feed and Facebook newsfeed are both social activity streams that tend to flatten streams of content by stripping the context of distribution (Marwick, 2012). The context of distribution includes who shared the content and how, be it by other users, bots, foreign actors, oppositional actors, or advertizers and through automated, human centered, or mixed approaches to delivery. Flattening the context of distribution makes it easier for users to consume different genres of content faster, but it also incentivizes outrageous content, which tends to receive more engagement and thus circulate faster. As such, motivated actors see the manipulation of metadata as a core feature for ensuring the success of a campaign. This context collapse found in social activity streams is not only a problem for users, it is a blind spot for platforms themselves in their efforts to address manipulation campaigns with automated moderation tools.

Media manipulation researchers have found that common disinformation campaign tactics travel across platforms, with traceable information moving from web to platform and back again. These techniques hopscotch across social and news media, relying on provenance laundering, stripping context, and assume context collapse between platforms to build durability, strategies for distribution, leveraging organic reach with what we call 'data craft' (Acker, 2018). But because researchers access platform data as third parties (just like advertizers), they are locked out of the complete, platform perspective of these manipulation campaigns. Other data access techniques, like web scraping, violate the Terms of Service of most platforms. As a result, when the API access is rolled back, researchers are unable to continue their studies (Bertrand, 2017b).

In effect, access to platform data are shifting rapidly, not only for journalists and researchers, but also users who create and consume it (Bastos & Walker, 2018). Despite user data being available to third parties, users themselves do not have ready access to personalization algorithms that structure the content in feeds. Moreover these algorithmic recipes are not auditable in their personalization (Pasquale, 2016), and are often characterized as corporate trade secrets (Burrell, 2016). While policies and regulation such as the GDPR introduced new challenges to platform companies, where explicit opting-in is a requirement for use, there has been little public education as to what rights and responsibilities are for the consumer or companies alike in participating in this data access regime. Controversies around data harvesting, use, and reuse by companies, like Cambridge Analytica and Crimson Hexagon, have presented new challenges for corporations seeking to purchase and use third party data with platforms.

Lack of platform transparency has given rise to a new field of data journalists, social scientists, and for-profit digital identity management firms assuming the role of detectives by identifying and assessing disinformation campaigns in the public sphere online. While this tacit coalition pressures platforms to provide open data about disinformation campaigns, overall these companies have been reluctant, and the response has been slow and haphazard. In fact, the UK Parliament and US Congress have largely been unsatisfied with testimony given by platform companies. In December 2018, The UK Parliament published internal company documents and records from Facebook in order to retroactively audit the corporation for improperly handling users' data and selling it to third party customers (Lanxon & Frier, 2018).

3. Collecting, curating, and archiving disinformation for what?

Contemporary archival theory and practice attempts to make the original order, provenance, conditions of access, and appraisal decisions known to users, researchers, and creators who donate their materials (Gilliland, 2017). Many of these practices are difficult to apply to dynamic, born digital environments, particularly in platforms with social activity feeds that contain multi-media objects such as hyperlinks, text, video, and images. Extracting data from platforms for access and digital preservation remains a technical challenge because social media data contain many layers of contextual information, including multimedia objects, hyperlinks to other web resources and engagement metadata. One outcome of disinformation campaigns US and UK investigations has been platforms' early (and in some cases, first) attempts at documenting and sharing evidence outside of the platform beyond existing APIs. While platform companies use the language of archives to describe providing access to collected data about disinformation campaigns, they do not meet the standards of contemporary theory and practice such as documenting curation and assembling processes (Acker & Kriesberg, 2017). These collections represent 'kinds' of archives of disinformation in that they show how manipulation occurs, and in many cases, how the platform features perpetuated or allowed techniques to go unnoticed. As archives, prepackaged platform data about disinformation are incomplete without documentation of their pre-processing and transformation.

The first robust and accessible archive of social media disinformation campaigns was not published by a platform, but instead the result of a community driven effort to create a searchable database of collected ads submitted to Congress as part of the 2017 intelligence hearing on election meddling. Facebook provided the House Committee on Intelligence a series of PDFs of ads bought by the IRA as evidence of Russia's meddling in the 2016 US Presidential election (US House of Representatives, 2016). By publishing the data as a PDF, it was difficult to reuse and circulate these documents. Thus, the labor of making it usable and searchable became the duty of a concerned citizen archivist and open source developers. Archivist and developer, Ed Summers parsed these long PDFs, extracting structured and descriptive metadata to create a machine readable dataset (Summers, 2018).

Then, web developer Simon Willison created an open source, searchable database of the data and metadata parsed from the digitized PDFs from Facebook (Willison, 2018a, 2018b). The IRA ads database illustrates the problem of formatting and assembly of decontextualized social media data and the layers of transformation needed to provide access.

In addition to Facebook's IRA ads (US House of Representatives, 2016), there were two were two incomplete archives offered in the following years, the subsequent Facebook Ad Archive API (Leathern, 2018), and Twitter's Election Integrity Data Archive (Elections integrity: Data archive, 2018). These releases deceptively resemble legitimate archives, but severely limit access by stripping away the context of distribution, limiting flagging or moderation motivations, and obfuscating their pre-processing, i.e., the curation and refinement of these datasets for open access.

In response to assertions by the tacit coalition that advertising technology played a role in spreading disinformation, Facebook created the Ads Archive API to search ads that have been flagged, marked as abuse, or removed based on their content. The goal is to increase the transparency about political ads on Facebook, but it has led to criticism that it violates free speech principles by singling out political content. The Ads API has lots of problems with its automated moderation of politically-oriented promoted content and does not necessarily serve researchers or journalists concerned with the impact of political ads on platform discourse. Yet even with the archive in place, manipulators continue to exert data craft using ads and continue to violate terms of service by buying political ads that aren't labeled as such (Turton, 2018). Further, this interface better serves those who want to buy ads because it allows them to search for similar content and view competitors' ads.

Twitter's election integrity efforts are now under the umbrella of their 'healthy conversation initiative' (Gadde & Gasca, 2018). Twitter made eight million tweets from IRA and Iran available for download in easily readable formats – zipped CSV files. Curiously disinformation campaigns from both IRA and Iran are put together but separated by subfolders. The dataset's README is indeed a good faith effort in capturing the metadata contained in the data archive and describes what can be found in the dataset explaining each column header and the formatted data found in each row (Twitter, 2018). The Elections Integrity Data Archive README file also provides some indication of how the data was scrubbed before being made available for access, particularly mentioning engagement metadata from known accounts banned for coordinated inauthentic behavior and terms of use violations.

Each of these examples are characterized as digital collections or web archives of disinformation in social platforms, and they each represent different ways of documenting and providing access to coordinated inauthentic behavior. Yet, many researchers have noted that it is not technically or conceptually an 'archive' just because they are presented as complete collections with well-documented provenance and original order. Indeed, close examination reveals that these have been curated, in some cases heavily edited and appraised for reputation management. Any archive of disinformation faces serious ethical concerns regarding how to balance the preservation warrant of documenting culture to provide access for accountability with the drawbacks of providing manipulators the recipes for sharing and improving these techniques. In each case, more must be done to uncover the context of distribution before research can begin to address how these disinformation campaigns seeded across platforms impacted election outcomes.

What platform archives of disinformation reveal about manipulation campaigns online is important, but they are still only partial knowledge. Similar to the tactics in the dark markets of search engine optimization (Ziewitz, 2016), the observable activities of media manipulators are strategic and routine across platforms. Once manipulators put in place protocols for developing and distributing content, the remaining work was largely maintenance of the social relations by cultivating audiences using data craft. Evidence of data craft is difficult to gather from platform's pseudo-archives because the curation and lack of metadata strips away the rich context of distribution and dynamism of social feeds. Manipulating metadata activity can be seen as skillset, or data craftwork that plays with the features and automated operations of platform. Data craft is akin to what Gabriella Coleman calls the 'interplay between craft and craftiness' of hacking (Coleman, 2016, p. 164). Our research shows that data craft is best observed *in situ*, where unmasking of manipulation campaigns takes place. In the next section, we show how tracing media manipulation campaigns requires analyzing metadata across platforms to reveal how disinformation spreads through a wide network of accounts, platforms and the open web.

4. Methods for analyzing data craft

In order to spot disinformation campaigns across platforms, we created this step by step rubric for detecting data craft across social platforms (see below). Here, we outline how to see metadata embedded within a post without scraping or using an API. By tracking the different metadata signals available across platforms, data trails can be investigated, and inauthentic accounts identified. By reading the metadata categories that are being exploited, gamed, or drift with disinformation campaigns, we build on the digital methods of information studies, science and technology studies, and anthropology to illustrate how metadata can be utilized to map media manipulation in and across platforms.

For example, by closely examining metadata such as the rapidity of account activity, follower/audience counts, post timestamps, media content types, user bios, and location data these platform metadata features can provide activity fingerprints that are clearly spam-like, spotty, formulaic, or suspicious. Each of these signals evidence the existence and spread of disinformation in platforms. These manipulation tactics that leverage platform features, spread disinformation by mimicking human behavior, and create swaths of networked digital traces can be understood as practices of data craft (Acker, 2018) (Table 1).

5. Two examples of data craft

Because search engines on platforms do not look outside of their own domain for search returns, media manipulators use data craft to leverage keywords and content tags so that they appear first in the returns for social, political, or newsworthy issues on each platform. Matching profile information, content tags, and continuously updating content across platforms can be tedious and time consuming. Motivations to game social media are usually economic, and as such, platform companies' Trust and Safety Teams often look for spam and indications of monetary fraud with promoted content. When multi-platform media manipulation campaigns seek to change political opinions and sow division across political wedge issues, though, it can be difficult to detect them, especially when they

Table 1. Detecting data craft across social platforms.

Detecting data craft across social platforms		
Steps	Red flags	To verify
1. Account names	• Double consonants, default avatars, random numbers • Screen name different from user name • Nonverified account • Name contains 'Official' or 'Real'	• Search for user name and screen name on other platforms
2. Recycled banner, bio, profile pics, or content	• Available on Wikipedia, Internet Archive, or other public platforms • Posted to other social media accounts • More reposts than 'original' content • Lots of duplicate content over time	• Search for images with reverse image search tools to discover copied or original image sources • Search distinct phrases with 'quotes' to discover sources of copied content • Compare to profiles from other platforms with similar account names
3. Content tags	• Location check-ins or geotags that contradict the content of posts • Total absence of content or geotags • Absence of other accounts tagging themselves in content • Pervasive use of link shorteners for automated messaging and mass content posting	• Trace content back to the platform of original upload • Use APIs or other tools to verify geotags and client source
4. Followers	• Recent account creation • Followed by large numbers of suspicious accounts • Nonsense comments from followers • Sudden growth in followers or following	• Examine internet archives such as the Wayback Machine's archive of account to determine rate of growth • Reconduct steps 1 and 2 with a sample of followers to ensure authentic behavior with account engagement
5. Authentic interaction	• Inaccurate descriptions of content suggesting mismatches, dubious origins, or false context • Unrelated hashtags Automated responses from other accounts (e.g., 'Thanks for the follow! Check out my webpage!') • Low rates of being liked or shared by other accounts Content promoted by ad purchase	• Search for conversations, interaction, and activity between the account and followers • Assess whether followers interacting with the account's activity are engaging in good faith, meaningful reception, or unique responses • Confirm that replies are not simply automated messages, reshares, or responses with links

appear as imposters using 'cloaked' content (Daniels, 2009). Cloaking refers to creating imposter accounts or websites and generating synthetic content.

However, cloaking does not ensure that content will be seen and optimized for search engines; a strategy for discovery is necessary. Prior to platformization, domain squatting was a way for manipulators to purchase domain names in the hope of selling them or using them in phishing scams. Once a company noticed that their domain was purchased, they could spend thousands to buy it back. However, domains are not keywords in and of themselves. The sociotechnical design of platforms allows for anonymous posting as well as anonymous administration of large groups, a feature that has led to the proliferation of keyword squatting, the strategic domination of keywords and sockpuppet accounts to misrepresent groups or individuals.

When anonymous accounts pose as social movement organizations or among queries for breaking news, celebrities, public figures, and politicians, they are employing data craft. As data craft, keyword squatting relies on social media users' interests in social or political issues and the capacity for social media administrators to be responsive to audiences and malleable as conditions change. Malleability refers to the ability for social media administrators to change or mask their identity, augment account or page names, change or hide content quickly, and remain undetected by Trust and Safety teams as well as content moderators employed by platforms. If cloaking and malleability tactics fail to raise manipulated content in search results, then purchasing advertising is also effective because it ensures targeted audiences will see the content (Nadler et al., 2018).

Here, we show two examples of manipulation campaigns related to the Black Lives Matter Movement, where keyword squatting as data craft played a prominent role in attracting audiences. In the first example, the IRA troll farm, used keyword squatting to hijack online conversations and impersonate social movements by showing up in the search results for numerous political wedge issues (Chen, 2015). The second example involves a Black Lives Matter Facebook page and a related domain that was used to solicit private donations for a white man in Australia unaffiliated with the movement. In each case, the social engineering of the content creators required them to conform to the socio-technical norms of online and offline engagement as part of their data craft to impersonate legitimate activists. Yet when finally confronted, bad faith actors were unsuccessful at hiding all of the extraneous metadata points generated across platforms and the web. That is to say, the metadata was the message.

5.1. The data craft of the Internet research agency

Many journalists and researchers have focused on 3,000 ads purchased by 470 'suspicious and likely fraudulent' Facebook accounts and pages linked back to the IRA, a fact confirmed by Facebook in September 2017 (Schrag, 2017; Stamos, 2018). In October 2017, Facebook admitted that 10 million Facebook users may have seen the ads purchased by these pages (Shinal, 2017). The ads are said to have focused on a number of divisive issues, not just straightforward candidate endorsements and attacks. Moreover, these accounts used the advertising technology built by Facebook to capture new audiences and game the metric cues that signaled their legitimacy.

On 5 October 2017, Jonathan Albright, the Research Director at the Tow Center for Digital Journalism, released a dataset gathered from data on CrowdTangle that monitors platforms, which showed that Russian influence on Facebook likely extended well beyond these paid ads (Albright, 2017). Specifically, the IRA adopted an organic marketing approach of cultivating a following using fraudulent pages, aided in part by directly paying Facebook for ads and promotion. Using data craft, the IRA were able to attract people with highly targeted messages by making appeals to their emotional responses around sociocultural, political, and moral questions. To be discoverable on platform's search engines they optimized certain keywords across polarizing wedge issues, ranging from political and religious affiliation, patriotism, Black activism, conservatism, LGBTQ issues, and more.

Across 'Black Lives Matter' pages and accounts on Facebook, it is difficult to discern which are actively engaged in the movement, which have been abandoned, and which are being operated by a sockpuppet account (Confessore & Wakabayashi, 2017; Frenkel, 2018; Rosenberg, 2018). Two inauthentic pages, 'Blacktivist' and 'Black Matters,' both were IRA operated (Figure 1). At that time, most social media users would not be able to deduce that these were suspicious pages because the content was often shared directly

Figure 1. Screenshot of IRA Facebook page 'Blacktivist' Ad.

from other Black Lives Matter sources and consistently used similar narrative frames about documenting police brutality and government inaction. IRA administrators on these pages posted content, replied to messages, and organized events, all without revealing their identity to subscribers. Moreover, the co-presence of the same accounts across other social media platforms, such as Instagram and Twitter, further substantiated that these cloaked accounts were well-resourced social movement organizations.

The IRA's Blacktivist page also created several Facebook events for rallies and demonstrations (Figure 2). Importantly, Facebook's 'custom audiences' tool allowed advertizers to specifically target people who expressed interest in attending an event, meaning those who clicked 'interested' or 'attending' were once again unintentionally giving up important personal data about themselves. This data could then be used to target these groups with more content, like the ads Facebook confirmed were purchased by the IRA. Here, the reciprocity of generating data as raw materials to power platform services is sold back to the customer as an advertising feature. But for political manipulators, these curated and targeted datasets can be used to inflame tensions and stoke outrage against opponents (Nadler et al., 2018).

Further, because these accounts are malleable and not automated like traditional spam, private message engagement can reveal who or what is motivating use. Metadata with metric cues, such as hundreds or thousands of followers, made these accounts appear legitimate not only to average users, but also to other activists. Even when questioned, the administrators of Blacktivist did not break character, but instead apologized when called out for disrupting local activism (Figure 3).

While BlackMatters and Blacktivist's manipulation campaigns were revealed in the 2017 congressional hearings about social media manipulation in the 2016 election, the IRA's use of social media showed how tech-savvy manipulators could frame a multi-

Figure 2. Screenshot of IRA Facebook 'Blacktivist' event planning.

platform, multi-issue campaign across hundreds of accounts by impersonating social movement organizations through the strategic use of avatars and specific keywords. Even when confronted by local activists, the IRA played it off as a misunderstanding. However, once Facebook investigated the network of accounts using rubles to purchase advertising on their platform, the data revealed a small group of fake accounts administering a larger volume of impersonated groups and pages. In this case, Facebook was the only entity in a position to *confirm* the hoax.

5.2. The data craft of BlackLivesMatter1

Another fraudulent Black Lives Matter page, not tied to the IRA, was confirmed by a CNN investigation (O'Sullivan, 2018). CNN found that the largest Black Lives Matter Facebook

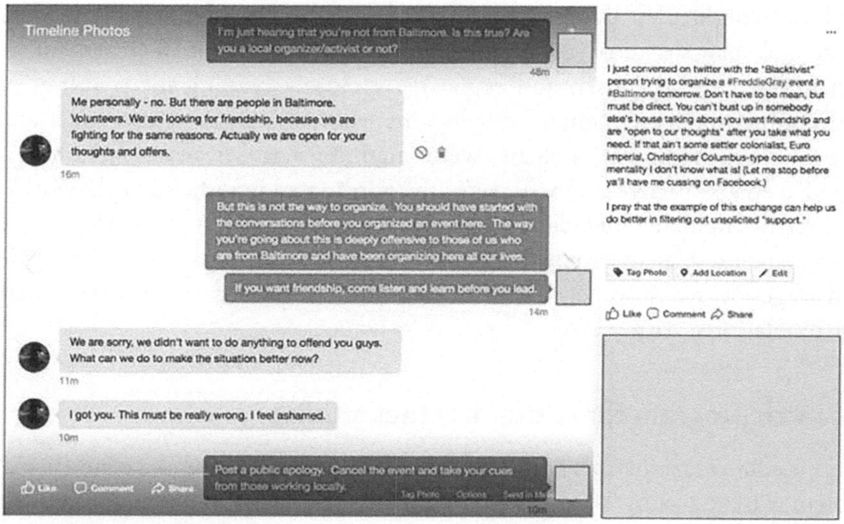

Figure 3. Screenshot of a user's interaction with a moderator about a Blacktivist event (Screenshot originally shared on Twitter).

page, with nearly 700 K likes, was a fraud. Black Lives Matter is a network of activists who routinely communicate with one another through chapters. Activists reported and flagged this page to Facebook numerous times to no avail.

Initial research into the Blacklivesmatter1 Facebook page by a blogger named Jeremy Massler, indicated that the page appeared to be motivated by monetary incentives (Massler, 2017). Massler grew suspicious of the page because it lacked coherence with other Black Lives Matter pages. This Facebook page linked to conservative media sites, shared spam and antagonistic content, and repeatedly asked for donations, while also selling merchandise. Massler debunked the page by searching for content posted to the Facebook page related to the URL metadata 'www.blacklivesmatter.media' in the WHOIS domain database. The WHOIS search revealed the owner to be an Australian man without any apparent ties to the American movement. When Massler reached out to confirm the Facebook page via email and phone, the Facebook page changed, and the donation button was removed. The Australian owner then contacted Massler to say that he did not want his personal information placed online.

Months later, CNN and The Guardian released the Australian owner's information along with many more details of his personal life. Reporters also documented his data craft, which consisted of the exploitation of fundraising campaigns using domain and keyword squatting, interacting with audiences using by posting replies, and co-opting the Black Lives Matter branding to sell t-shirts and mugs (McGowan, 2018). Facebook reacted by taking the account down, but there has not been an accounting of how much damage this person caused to the Black Lives Matter Movement.

In each of these cases of cloaked accounts, metadata was not only the key resource for extending the reach of these sockpuppet accounts, but it was also their undoing. Keyword squatting remains a critical technique for search engine optimization across social media platforms. What these two-case studies reveals is how difficult it is to spot a fake without also searching through the metadata and knowing the context of information sharing.

In both cases of the Blacklivesmatter1 and IRA pages, investigators read the metadata of these Facebook pages against the intended use of the platform features (such as the donation button, events, posts, and replies). By closely reading for spammy or noisy data and comparing these signals with legitimate organizing and user interactions on the platform, these manipulation tactics were caught by activists, researchers, and journalists *before* Facebook discovered these pages as coordinated inauthentic behavior. Without reading these manipulated metadata within the organic context of the platform and alongside other social movement organizing, it is unlikely that the data craft tactics from these exploited pages would have been identified automatically as coordinated inauthentic behavior by platform corporations.

6. A research program for critical internet studies

For social media researchers examining disinformation and manipulation in platforms, the problem with analyzing 'coordinated inauthentic behavior' is that it does not acknowledge the role that the platform's infrastructure plays in masking accounts and metadata, while also providing pay-to-play tool kits for increasing engagement with manipulated content as the Black Matters, Blacktivists, and Blacklivesmatter1 Facebook pages all illustrate. Before the 2016 US election, platform companies were not incentivized to look for problems related to misuse and manipulation, unless it contained pornography, harassment, or terrorism. Instead, platforms' framing of 'coordinated inauthentic behavior' makes the 'misuse' of features the issue, rather than acknowledging the core product of platform tools for audience engagement are vulnerable to manipulation, hacking, or exploitation. Because the infrastructure of platforms motivates and incentivizes certain forms of engagement, users' attention is sold to customers, who are not always virtuous actors. Demarcating authentic from inauthentic behavior is near impossible without corroborating information off the platform.

Most importantly, there is no business incentive to root out manipulation campaigns as it run counter to public relation strategies for reputation management. When Gleicher, Facebook's head of Cybersecurity policy reported on their takedown of Iranian and Russian accounts on Facebook and Instagram, he explained that they received a tip from an outside firm that was then substantiated by looking at website registration information and IP mapping (Gleicher, 2018). Facebook saw that some of these accounts, especially 'The Liberty Front Press,' were run as if they were independent media, but further investigation revealed strong ties to Iranian State media. Over $6,000 was spent on advertising on Facebook to circulate content. Increasingly, we see with platforms' automated efforts at identifying manipulation fail because inauthentic behavior is camouflaged to look like scaled and for-profit authentic content. From social movements, politicians, marketers, journalists, to celebrities, those who can afford to pay-to-play will dominate public conversation and platforms will continue to profit.

Calling disinformation campaigns 'coordinated inauthentic interaction' underplays the seriousness with which foreign and domestic actors exploit the openness of platforms for political gain. By exploiting openness, we mean the capacity to bundle an audience based on certain algorithmically generated categories and serve targeted content intended to polarize or cause wedges among different groups. The *ex post facto* solution to naming these rapidly evolving techniques reveals platform politics in action: platform corporations define the scope of the problem, they have all the data in-house, and therefore, they are best positioned to mete out a solution. This situation is untenable given the significant threat disinformation campaigns pose to civil society and democracy. Cross-sector approaches that share similar theoretical and methodological commitments to fairness, accountability, transparency, and ethical data practices are a crucial step towards building a transdisciplinary research program that places equity *a priori*.

When researchers and journalists use data access tools intended for customers such as platform APIs, we are limited to collecting data and analyzing for activity signals and content patterns. This appears to be the only long-term solution for cross-platform analysis. However, these access tools for platform data are built for marketers and advertizers, not for researchers. As a result of these commercial-driven access tools, expanding the usefulness of data archives will require a much stronger push from a cross-sector tacit coalition to account for the social costs of exploiting public discourse in our present-day information ecologies. We maintain that what one platform reveals about manipulation in their disinformation archive will be useful to technologists and researchers unmasking campaigns elsewhere. The disinformation archives produced by platform companies may understate the scope of the problem, but we remain hopeful they can be retooled to investigate coordinated disinformation campaigns across platforms and the web.

As a field, critical internet scholars are developing methods of reading when, where, and how manipulators leverage metadata to manipulate discourse in platforms. These methods need to account for the possibilities of data craft, which are often skillful, targeted, and organized around common fault lines in platform features. Understanding manipulation campaigns in and across platforms through metadata as a boundary object, is a promising direction. A critique and historicization of platforms in social and cultural contexts must include the naming and ordering data (at rest, in use, or in motion) across social infrastructures. Social media metadata has multiple overlapping entanglements with different sites of access and meaning to different groups.

Researching metadata as an entry point to the phenomena of disinformation has the potential to pressure platforms to open and create more transparent accountability processes. Therefore, any call for platform auditing must be motivated to increase data literacy amongst the users and the publics that platforms serve. Further, reading metadata and interpreting the data craftwork of disinformation can be generalized to other forms of coordinated behavior online. Securing access to accurate data and metadata continues to be a thumb trap for Internet researchers seeking to discover, document, and audit technology's impact on society.

While platforms' archives of disinformation are laudable efforts to document disinformation campaigns, they remain dull tools for auditing. Indeed, auditing for accountability will require the cross-sector tacit coalition that emerged after the 2016 US election to formalize a set of principles and protocols for sustainable access to users' data and metadata and to develop standardized digital preservation solutions for maintaining long-term, impactful scholarly research. In this article, we used disinformation as our case studies, but this also applies to researchers studying a range of issues from inequality, to redlining, to health, foreign affairs, and so on. We are also not arguing for blanket access to all data, but rather we seek knowledge of malice and wrong-doing for informing evidence-based policy.

Finally, as the access to social media data narrows, social media metadata proves to be a valuable entry point for new methods of reading or tracking media manipulation campaigns, but also a pressure point for platform companies' accountability, where the future of technology is bound up with the societal values of democracy, fairness, equality, and justice. However, as our analysis shows, spotting disinformation campaigns requires a more rigorous approach to field-building across sectors. By understanding how metadata acts as a boundary object that brings together a tacit coalition to mount public pressure against disinformation campaigns, we can also see how the archives of disinformation provided by platform companies underestimates the problem and deflects attention from the flaws in their technological design and assembly.

Data craft is skillful, targeted, and organized around common fault lines in platform features. Therefore, it is not just that journalists, researchers, technologists, policy-makers, and civil society organizations need access to complete disinformation archives for the future of detecting malicious uses of platforms by media manipulators, but rather a new independent and interdisciplinary field of critical internet studies must define and assess the scope of the problem without relying on corporations to self-audit. Otherwise, without protocols and principles in place for meaningful access to data, the fox will continue to guard the henhouse.

Note

1. APIs or Application Programming Interfaces are software that specify rules for access and extraction of data. APIs allow third parties such as data brokers, app developers, advertizers, journalists and scholarly researchers access to social media data extracted from platforms.

Disclosure statement

No potential conflict of interest was reported by the authors.

References

Acker, A. (2018). *Data craft: The manipulation of social media metadata* (p. 25). New York, NY: Data & Society. Retrieved from https://datasociety.net/output/data-craft/

Acker, Amelia, & Kriesberg, Adam. (2017). Tweets may be archived: Civic engagement, digital preservation and obama white house social media data. *Proceedings of the Association for Information Science and Technology*, *54*(1), 1–9.

Albright, J. (2017, October 5). Total reach by page, itemized posts and historical engagement. Retrieved from https://public.tableau.com/views/FB4/TotalReachbyPage?%3Aembed=y&%3AshowVizHome=no&%3Adisplay_count=y&%3Adisplay_static_image=y&%3AbootstrapWhenNotified=true

Barrett, D., Horwitz, S., & Helderman, R. S. (2016, February 16). Russian troll farm, 13 suspects indicted in 2016 election interference. Retrieved from https://www.washingtonpost.com/world/national-security/russian-troll-farm-13-suspects-indicted-for-interference-in-us-election/2018/02/16/2504de5e-1342-11e8-9570-29c9830535e5_story.html

Bastos, M., & Walker, S. T. (2018, April 11). Facebook's data lockdown is a disaster for academic researchers. Retrieved from http://theconversation.com/facebooks-data-lockdown-is-a-disaster-for-academic-researchers-94533

Benkler, Y., Faris, R., & Roberts, H. (2018). *Network propaganda: Manipulation, disinformation, and radicalization in American politics*. Oxford, NY: Oxford University Press.

Bertrand, N. (2017a, October 5). New data shows that Russian propaganda may have been shared billions of times on Facebook. Retrieved from https://www.businessinsider.com/reach-of-russian-facebook-propaganda-content-2017-10

Bertrand, N. (2017b, October 12). Facebook scrubbed potentially damning Russia data before researchers could analyze it further. Retrieved from https://www.businessinsider.com/facebook-russia-data-fake-accounts-2017-10

Burrell, J. (2016). How the machine 'thinks': Understanding opacity in machine learning algorithms. *Big Data & Society*, *3*(1), 1–12.

Chen, A. (2015, June 2). The agency. *The New York Times*. Retrieved from https://www.nytimes.com/2015/06/07/magazine/the-agency.html

Clarke, A. & Star, S. L. (2008). The social worlds framework: A theory/methods package. *The Handbook of Science and Technology Studies*, *3*(0), 113–137.

Coleman, G. (2016). Hacker. In B. Peters (Ed.), *Digital keywords: A vocabulary of information society and culture* (pp. 158–172). Princeton University Press.

Confessore, N., & Wakabayashi, D. (2017, October 9). How Russia harvested American rage to reshape U.S. politics. *The New York Times*. Retrieved from https://www.nytimes.com/2017/10/09/technology/russia-election-facebook-ads-rage.html

Daniels, J. (2009). Cloaked websites: Propaganda, cyber-racism and epistemology in the digital era. *New Media & Society*, *11*(5), 659–683. doi:10.1177/1461444809105345

Driscoll, Kevin, & Walker, Shawn. (2014). Big data, big questions| working within a black box: Transparency in the collection and production of big Twitter data. *International Journal of Communication*, *8*(0), 1–20.

Elections integrity: Data archive. (2018, October 17). Retrieved from https://about.twitter.com/en_us/values/elections-integrity.html

Epstein, Steven. (2007). *Inclusion: The politics of difference in medical research*. Chicago: University of Chicago Press.

Frenkel, S. (2018, August 15). How a fake group on Facebook created real protests. *The New York Times*. Retrieved from https://www.nytimes.com/2018/08/14/technology/facebook-disinformation-black-elevation.html

Frenkel, S., Confessore, N., Kang, C., Rosenberg, M., & Nicas, J. (2018, November 16). Delay, deny and deflect: How Facebook's leaders fought through crisis. *The New York Times*. Retrieved from https://www.nytimes.com/2018/11/14/technology/facebook-data-russia-election-racism.html

Gadde, V., & Gasca, D. (2018, July 30). Measuring healthy conversation. Retrieved from https://blog.twitter.com/official/en_us/topics/company/2018/measuring_healthy_conversation.html

Gilliland, Anne J. (2017). *Conceptualizing 21st-Century Archives*. Society of American Archivists.

Gleicher, N. (2018, August 21). Taking down more coordinated inauthentic behavior, what we've found so far. Retrieved from https://newsroom.fb.com/news/2018/08/more-coordinated-inauthentic-behavior/

Greenberg, J. (2005). Understanding metadata and metadata schemes. *Cataloging & Classification Quarterly*, *40*(3–4), 17–36. doi:10.1300/J104v40n03_02

Howard, P. N., Woolley, S., & Calo, R. (2018). Algorithms, bots, and political communication in the US 2016 election: The challenge of automated political communication for election law and administration. *Journal of Information Technology & Politics*, *15*(2), 81–93.

Kang, C., & Frenkel, S. (2018, November 1). Facebook and Twitter have a message for lawmakers: We're trying. *The New York Times*. Retrieved from https://www.nytimes.com/2018/09/04/technology/facebook-and-twitter-have-a-message-for-lawmakers-were-trying.html

Lanxon, N., & Frier, S. (2018, December 5). Facebook wielded data to reward, punish rivals, emails show. *Bloomberg*. Retrieved from https://www.bloomberg.com/news/articles/2018-12-05/seized-facebook-internal-emails-published-by-u-k-lawmakers

Leathern, R. (2018, August 22). Introducing the Ad Archive API. Retrieved from https://newsroom.fb.com/news/2018/08/introducing-the-ad-archive-api/

Marwick, A. (2012). The public domain: Surveillance in Everyday life. *Surveillance & Society*, *9*(4), 378–393. doi:10.24908/ss.v9i4.4342

Massler, J. (2017, December 2). The largest "Black Lives Matter" page on Facebook is probably a sham. Retrieved from https://www.manicnews.com/2017/12/the-largest-black-lives-matter-page-on.html

Mayernik, M. S., & Acker, A. (2018). Tracing the traces: The critical role of metadata within networked communications. *Journal of the Association for Information Science and Technology*, *69*(1), 177–180. doi:10.1002/asi.23927

McGowan, M. (2018, April 10). Fake Black Lives Matter Facebook page run by Australian union official – report. *The Guardian*. Retrieved from https://www.theguardian.com/us-news/2018/apr/10/fake-black-lives-matter-facebook-page-run-by-australian-union-official-report

Meserole, C., & Polyakova, A. (2018, May 25). Disinformation wars. *Foreign Policy*. Retrieved from https://foreignpolicy.com/2018/05/25/disinformation-wars/

Morville, Peter. (2005). *Ambient Findability: What We Find Changes Who We Become* (pp. 1–208).

Nadler, A., Crain, M., & Donovan, J. (2018). *Weaponizing the digital influence machine*. New York, NY: Data & Society. Retrieved from https://datasociety.net/output/weaponizing-the-digital-influence-machine/

O'Sullivan, D. (2018, April 9). CNN investigation: The biggest Black Lives Matter page on Facebook is fake. Retrieved from https://money.cnn.com/2018/04/09/technology/fake-black-lives-matter-facebook-page/index.html

Pasquale, F. (2016). *The black box society: The secret algorithms that control money and information* (Reprint edition). Cambridge, MA; London, England: Harvard University Press.

Perez, B., Musolesi, M., & Stringhini, G. (2018). You are your metadata: Identification and obfuscation of social media users using metadata information. *Association for the Advancement of Artificial Intelligence* , 1–10. Retrieved from http://arxiv.org/abs/1803.10133

Rainie, L., Anderson, J., & Albright, J. (2017). *The future of free speech, trolls, anonymity and fake news online*. Pew Research Center. Retrieved from http://www.pewinternet.org/2017/03/29/the-future-of-free-speech-trolls-anonymity-and-fake-news-online/

Rosenberg, E. (2018, January 19). Twitter to tell 677,000 users they were had by the Russians. Some signs show the problem continues. Retrieved from https://www.washingtonpost.com/news/the-switch/wp/2018/01/19/twitter-to-tell-677000-users-they-were-had-by-the-russians-some-signs-show-the-problem-continues/

Schrag, E. (2017, October 2). Hard questions: Russian ads delivered to congress | Facebook newsroom. Retrieved from https://newsroom.fb.com/news/2017/10/hard-questions-russian-ads-delivered-to-congress/

Shearer, E., & Gottfried, J. (2017, September 7). News use across social media platforms 2017. Retrieved from http://www.journalism.org/2017/09/07/news-use-across-social-media-platforms-2017/

Shinal, J. (2017, October 2). Facebook says 10 million people saw Russian-bought political ads. Retrieved from https://www.cnbc.com/2017/10/02/facebook-says-10-million-people-saw-russian-bought-political-ads.html

Shu, K., Sliva, A., Wang, S., Tang, J., & Liu, H. (2017). Fake news detection on social media: A data mining perspective. *ACM SIGKDD Explorations Newsletter*, *19*(1), 22–36. doi:10.1145/3137597.3137600

Stamos, A. (2018, April 3). Authenticity matters: The IRA has no place on Facebook | Facebook newsroom. Retrieved from https://newsroom.fb.com/news/2018/04/authenticity-matters/

Star, S. L., & Griesemer, J. R. (1989). Institutional ecology, 'translations' and boundary objects: Amateurs and professionals in Berkeley's museum of vertebrate zoology, 1907–39. *Social Studies of Science*, *19*(3), 387–420. doi:10.1177/030631289019003001

Starbird, K., Dailey, D., Mohamed, O., Lee, G., & Spiro, E. S. (2018). Engage early, correct more: How journalists participate in false rumors online during crisis events. In *Proceedings of the 2018 CHI conference on human factors in computing systems* (pp. 1–13). New York, NY, USA: ACM.

Stewart, Leo G., Arif, Amher, & Starbird, Kate. (2018). Examining Trolls and Polarization with a Retweet Network. *MIS2, 2018, Marina Del Rey, CA, USA*, 1–6.

Summers, E. (2018). *Irads: Working with 3,517 Internet Research Agency Facebook ads released by Congress*. Python. Retrieved from https://github.com/edsu/irads (Original work published 2018)

Turton, W. (2018, October 25). Facebook's political ad tool let us buy ads "paid for" by Mike Pence and ISIS. Retrieved from https://news.vice.com/en_us/article/wj9mny/facebooks-political-ad-tool-let-us-buy-ads-paid-for-by-mike-pence-and-isis

Twitter. (2018, October 16). Twitter Elections Integrity Datesets Readme, Version 1.0.1. Twitter. Retrieved from https://storage.googleapis.com/twitter-election-integrity/hashed/Twitter_Elections_Integrity_Datasets_hashed_README.txt

U.S. House of Representatives. (2016). Exposing Russia's Effort to Sow Discord Online: The Internet Research Agency and Advertisements. Retrieved from https://democrats-intelligence.house.gov/social-media-content/

Walker, S. (2017). *The Complexity of Collecting Digital and Social Media Data in Ephemeral Contexts* (Thesis). Retrieved from https://digital.lib.washington.edu:443/researchworks/handle/1773/40612

Willison, S. (2018a, August 6). Analyzing US Election Russian Facebook Ads. Retrieved from http://simonwillison.net/2018/Aug/6/russian-facebook-ads/

Willison, S. (2018b, August 6). Russian Internet Research Agency Facebook ads: Russian-ads datasette. Retrieved from https://russian-ira-facebook-ads.datasettes.com/

Woolley, S. C., & Howard, P. N. (2016). Automation, algorithms, and politics| political communication, computational propaganda, and autonomous agents—introduction. *International Journal of Communication*, *10*(0), 4882–4890.

Ziewitz, M. (2016). Governing algorithms: Myth, mess, and methods. *Science, Technology, & Human Values*, *41*(1), 3–16. doi:10.1177/0162243915608948

Zubiaga, A. (2018). A longitudinal assessment of the persistence of twitter datasets. *Journal of the Association for Information Science and Technology*, *69*(8), 974–984. doi:10.1002/asi.24026

Diverging patterns of interaction around news on social media: insularity and partisanship during the 2018 Italian election campaign

Fabio Giglietto , Augusto Valeriani, Nicola Righetti and Giada Marino

ABSTRACT

The paper considers how social media ecologies are affecting partisan engagement around political news and online attention economies by investigating the case of the 2018 Italian general election. By analyzing Twitter and Facebook interactions around political news in the lead-up to the election, we shed light on levels of insularity characterizing sources preferred by different partisan communities and investigate how specific patterns of active attention emerge around different sources and around stories proposing different framing of specific political actors. Our findings indicate that, on Twitter, sources mainly shared by supporters of populist parties (the Five Star Movement and the League) are characterized by higher levels of insularity compared to those shared by supporters of other parties. We also find that, on Facebook, news items published by highly insular sources receive a higher number of shares per comment. Finally, our analyses show that news presenting a positive framing of the Five Star Movement – the unique 'cyber party' in the system – receives a higher number of shares per comment compared to items presenting the Movement in a negative light, while the opposite is true for stories on all other political parties.

Introduction

In their highly influential study 'Red media, blue media' Iyengar and Hahn (2009) observed how, in the US media market at the beginning of the century, media companies were strategically employing politically biased news to gain audience attention. As a result, ideologically homogeneous and disconnected niches of public, selecting news sources most proximate to their view of the world, were emerging (Hollander, 2008). Stroud (2010) investigated this very phenomenon and defined it as 'partisan selective exposure'. Over the last few years, the radical transformations in communication ecosystems resulting from the increased centrality of social media have strongly contributed to renewed attention to the phenomenon of partisan selective exposure and its implications. The nature of social media affordances which offer their users opportunities to craft their networks of contacts led some authors (e.g., Sunstein, 2017) to argue that, in such a high choice media environment (Prior, 2007), citizens are very likely to develop homophilic information diets and conversational patterns (i.e., consuming only ideologically consistent news and discussing politics only with like-minded partners). According to this view, both as a result of individual choices and of algorithmic filtering (Bakshy, Messing, & Adamic, 2015), social media users would self-entrap themselves into 'echo-chambers' (Sunstein, 2017) of like-minded individuals.

In spite of these indications that technical functioning, as well as social media practices, might foster the emergence of homogeneous digital communities of news consumers, a growing body of research is challenging such a monolithic view. Several empirical studies have shown that echo-chambers might have been 'overstated' (Dubois & Blank, 2018) since their formation is resisted both by the frequent incidental exposure to news on social media (Fletcher & Nielsen, 2018) and by actual news diets of most citizens (Flaxman, Goel, & Rao, 2016). Finally, Dubois and Blank (2018) found that an exclusively supportive social media experience is conditional on specific political attitudes. Self-segregation within homophilic news bubbles should not be understood as a generalized reality but as the experience of segments of citizens having specific characteristics.

Moreover, the emergence and the growing popularity of hyper-partisan digital media outlets (Bhat, 2018) doesn't necessarily imply that their publics avoid other news sources (Garrett, 2009), or that their active social media engagement around political news is limited to the recirculation of such highly homophilic messages. Conversely, within social media environments, partisan users might be incidentally exposed to, or even intentionally flock to adversarial outlets to oppose their narratives through critical comments (Lee, 2012).

The academic debate on how social media ecologies are affecting patterns of active engagement around political news by partisan communities is thus far from univocal. This work joins the conversation by analyzing the case of the Italian general election, held on 4 March 2018. In this sense, by analyzing Twitter and Facebook interactions around political news in the lead-up to the election, we shed light on levels of insularity characterizing sources preferred by different partisan communities and investigate how specific patterns of active attention emerge around different sources and around stories proposing different framings of single political actors. Our findings indicate that, on Twitter, sources mainly shared by supporters of populist parties (the Five Star Movement and the League) are marked by higher levels of insularity compared to those mainly shared by supporters of other parties. We also find that, on Facebook, items published by highly insular sources receive a higher number of shares per comment compared to news stories published by other sources. Finally, our analyses show that news presenting a positive framing of the Five Star Movement receives a higher number of shares per comment compared to items presenting the Movement in a negative light, while the opposite is true for stories on all other political parties.

Some context information is necessary before presenting the theoretical framework and the research questions guiding our study. In March 2018 three main political parties and coalitions competed, unsuccessfully, to reach the threshold of 40% of votes necessary to obtain a majority in Italian Parliament. The centre-right coalition, formed by Silvio Berlusconi's Forza Italia, the League and Brotherhood of Italy (FdI), won the largest share of seats in both chambers with roughly 37% of votes. Within this coalition, only the League substantially increased its percentage of votes (17%), surprisingly outperforming Forza Italia (14%). At the opposite end of the ideological spectrum, the Democratic

Party (PD), the main actor of a centre-left coalition, following a season of infighting, gained an unrewarding 23% of votes. The Five Star Movement (M5S), founded by the comedian and blogger, Beppe Grillo, and the digital evangelist Gianroberto Casaleggio (Bordignon & Ceccarini, 2013), gained 32% of votes, significantly increasing the parliamentary seats secured after the 2013 general election. Finally, Free and Equal (LeU), a left-wing party launched by several popular former PD politicians, competed alone, obtaining just 3% of votes.

While lacking a clear winner, the general election resulted in a precise trend: populist parties (the League and M5S) substantially increased their share of votes, while the traditional parties, PD and Forza Italia were the big losers. This sharp division and altered balance among the political parties resulted in three months of political turmoil, culminating in May 2018 with the agreement signed by the League and the Five Star Movement to form an unprecedented government coalition.

Literature review and research questions

Within the network-step flow of communication (Hilbert, Vásquez, Halpern, Valenzuela, & Arriagada, 2017) characterizing social media ecologies, the role of news communities is crucial in the process of news delivery, multiplying the opportunities of circulation of a news story. In this sense, following Saez-Trumper, Castillo, and Lalmas (2013, p. 2), in this paper we define as 'social media news community' the group of active users who are exposed to the stories of a news outlet and are interested in sharing them.

Academic interest in news sharing practices on social media has been high during the last decade. In their review of the existing research, Kümpel, Karnowski, and Keyling (2015) considered 109 articles published on the topic between 2004 and 2014 and grouped them according to three different foci: features (and motivation) of users who are more likely to engage in sharing practices, nature of the content shared, and structure of sharing networks. More specifically Hasell and Weeks (2016) investigated sharing of political information online in the context of 2012 US presidential elections, showing that partisan news, by generating stronger emotional reactions, can boost sharing practices among social media users. Similarly studying the 2012 US election, Beam, Hutchens, and Hmielowski (2016) found that sharing of political news online could have some limited positive effects on the political knowledge of those who engage in such practice. Finally, in the same context, Lane, Kim, Lee, Weeks, and Kwak (2017) found that experience of political disagreement online can motivate social media users to share political news, which in turn can result in greater engagement in political participation offline.

Most of the studies (e.g., Barberá, 2015; Colleoni, Rozza, & Arvidsson, 2014; Faris et al., 2017; Himelboim, McCreery, & Smith, 2013) that have more broadly addressed active political behaviours of social media users – e.g., following choices, patterns of interactions, and content sharing – have found that ideological homophily plays an important role in defining communities' borders, especially on Twitter. Similarly, studies dealing with news media consumption on social media have found some ideological self-segregation, at least in relation to users' active choices (An, Cha, Gummadi, & Crowcroft, 2011). Finally, literature has shown (Weeks, Ardèvol-Abreu, & Gil de Zúñiga, 2017) that partisan users of social media are actively engaged in sharing information that supports their opinions. All these elements suggest that different online partisan communities tend to share stories published by different media sources with different intensities. As a result, certain media are referenced by multiple communities while others are exclusively shared by online actors affiliated to a specific party. Colleoni et al. (2014) have already found that the appetite for homophily in term of following relations was not equally strong between US Democrats and Republicans. Following the lexicon introduced by Benkler, Faris, and Roberts (2018), we use the term insularity to describe the degree to which a news media outlet is predominantly shared by a single partisan community.

It should be noted that almost all the above-mentioned studies focus on the US context where several systemic peculiarities might have a relevant impact on patterns of self-segregation of political users on social media. Guided by the intent of investigating political news communities on social media within a context markedly different from the US one, this study focuses on Italy.

Italy is a multi-party parliamentary democracy and has been included by Hallin and Mancini (2004) among 'polarized-pluralist' countries, also as a consequence of its high level of political parallelism both in the press and in the television sectors. Political partisanship historically characterizing the Italian legacy media environment (Mancini, 2013) could affect also the way citizens employ social media to engage with political content produced by professional media actors (see Iannelli & Giglietto, 2015), making the Italian case of specific interest. Moreover, in considering social media political news communities characterizing a multiparty system such as Italy, we should thus take into account that some partisan communities more than others might count on highly insular sources. In order to address this issue, we consider the peculiarities of two actors in the Italian political system, the Five Star Movement and the League, which can be included in a broad family of controversial political actors that have shaken several Western democracies in recent elections. Members of such a highly heterogeneous group of parties and leaders have been frequently defined by using the tag of 'new populism' (Brubaker, 2017; Inglehart & Norris, 2016; Taggart, 1995). These actors are very different in all sorts of ways and populism has been frequently described as a slippery and controversial concept (see for example Moffitt & Tormey, 2014). However, some core elements that, according to existing literature, characterize populism both as ideology (Albertazzi & McDonnell, 2007; Stanley, 2008) and as a communication style (De Vreese, Esser, Aalberg, Reinemann, & Stanyer, 2018; Jagers & Walgrave, 2007) suggest that supporters of these parties, more than those of others, might need hyper-partisan sources to find the symbolic resources for the development of their identity and to participate in political information cycles (Chadwick, 2017). These elements are: a strong polarization of the in-group versus all out-groups; an adversarial attitude towards the élites and a consequent delegitimization of established media institutions; an appeal to the 'pure' people also through the rejection of the politically-correct and the endorsement of positions considered unacceptable by most, if not all, other political actors in the system.

Several authors (e.g., Waisbord, 2018) have indeed observed how the recent rise of populist actors is strictly intertwined with the nature of contemporary media ecologies. In this sense, Hallin has contended that 'contemporary populist movements develop within a fragmented media ecology in which it is possible for populist leaders to bypass legacy media institutions and challenge their legitimacy' (2018, p. 14).

In light of these considerations, it is plausible that supporters of populist parties – more than those of others – systematically distrust mainstream media, favouring sources ideologically proximate to their party and highly critical of their opponents. At a systemic level, it is thus worth investigating whether such an attitude leads to the emergence of sources of political news whose stories are shared on social media almost exclusively by supporters of populist parties. Our first research question is thus:

Are sources dominantly shared by supporters of the Italian populist parties characterized by a higher level of insularity compared to those shared by supporters of other parties? (RQ1)

Considering the concept of social media communities understood as groups of partisan users actively sharing news produced by an information source (Saez-Trumper et al., 2013), however, does not give us a full picture of the extent to which the attention economy on social media (Tufekci, 2013) in a given system is polarized, even if we measure it by exclusively considering active behaviours. Following Tufekci, we define the attention economy as the patterns characterizing production and distribution of attention in a given information ecosystem. In this sense, focusing on users' actions, it should be first noted that the attention economy related to political news on social media is not only generated by the activity of openly partisan users but, more broadly, by all users engaging with political contents. Secondly, it should be pointed out that sharing is only one of the crucial practices connected to attention economies within social media environments (Tufekci, 2013), and commenting has as much relevance (McCosker, 2014).

Through sharing, users aim at amplifying the reach of a news story in order to 'hack' the status of attention economy by trying to augment the visibility of contents aligned with their views (Shin & Thorson, 2017). It could be argued that amplification is only one of the possible motivations behind the action of sharing content on social media, others being, for example, gaining visibility and reputation among peers, expressing a position on a specific topic, obtaining approval from contacts (see Kümpel et al., 2015, p. 6). In any case, in spite of specific motivations, by sharing digital content, users deliberately try to increase the *visibility*, and thus the relevance of content in a given network (Zhang, Wells, Wang, & Rohe, 2018, p. 3162).

Conversely, user's comments are new content that will be consumed by others together with the original information. In this way, they can affect the *type of attention* paid by others to a piece of information by trying to influence their interpretation (see Lee, 2012). This can be done both by supportive comments and, most importantly, for practices of 'hacking' the attention economy, through critical comments de-legitimizing the source, adding counter-information, irony, trolling, incivility or even hate speech. Thelwall, Sud, and Vis (2012; quoted in McCosker, 2014, p. 203) have found that YouTube videos related to politics are among those generating more comments and that the most commented videos are also those featuring the most robust percentages of negative comments. In commenting this finding, McCosker (2014, p. 204) has argued that it highlights the importance of attention economy codes and the role of commenting practices in gathering together critics performing counter actions potentially generating conflicts. These dynamics can be explained by the fact that the encounter with hostile information can motivate social media users to perform 'corrective actions' (Barnidge & Rojas, 2014), intended as expressive behaviours aimed at reaffirming their interpretation of political reality. In line with this vision, Barnidge, Ardèvol-Abreu, and Gil de Zúñiga (2018) have found that content-expressive behaviours, including commenting on political news, are more frequent among those who find themselves in heterogeneous information networks.

In line with these empirical findings and theoretical claims, stories published by news sources whose active audience is heterogeneous from an ideological point of view (and thus less likely to be characterized by a clear-cut ideological leaning), while satisfying some of the users engaging with them, could stimulate others who are not pleased by the framing of a specific story to perform corrective actions through content-expressive behaviours. As a consequence, we should expect a flurry of comments around the stories produced by these cross-partisan sources. Conversely, the homogenous communities characterizing highly insular sources should be especially concerned to amplify the reach of partisan news they agree with and, as a consequence, might be expected to engage particularly in sharing activities. Investigating the comment/share ratio characterizing the stories of different types of news sources circulating on social media can thus add granularity to our understanding of how users are engaged in trying to influence attention economies on these platforms. Consequently, we ask:

Is there a positive correlation between the insularity level of a news source and the number of shares per comment its stories get on social media? (RQ2)

Also, in this sense, however, we should consider that actors within a system do not behave in the same way. Conversely, supporters of some parties might be better organized, or more motivated than others in engaging in practices aimed at strategically influencing the attention economy on social media. Irrespective of the fact that partisan users could rely mainly on insular media, some of them could patrol social media prairies to support their leaders and attack opponents or, when they incidentally come upon counter-attitudinal contents, some users might be more motivated than others to intervene. Also, in this regard, some elements of populist ideology suggest that populist supporters could be more engaged, and capable, than those of other parties to influence social media attention economy. For example, the visceral attachment to the leader frequently characterizing populist constituencies (McDonnell, 2016) and the critical attitude toward established media institutions might all represent an additional incentive for populist supporters to engage with political information on social media. Such elements could stimulate populists not only to gather around highly insular outlets (which is the focus of RQ1) but also to 'correct' unfavourable information about their party or leader (or giving a positive framing of opponents) and, conversely, to recirculate the positive news related on their side and the negative news regarding their adversaries.

Another factor that can make supporters of some parties more proficient than others in developing strategies to influence the attention economy could be the centrality that digital environments themselves have for the party identity, organization, and communication, as well as for its supporters as an arena for political information. In this sense, in the Italian context, the Five Star Movement stands as an outlier both on the supply and on the demand side. The Five Star Movement has been described (e.g., Hartleb, 2013) as a cyber party, i.e., a party actor which gets rid of classic organizational and participatory infrastructures, replacing them with digital alternatives (Margetts, 2003). As a consequence, supporters of these parties have to develop at least basic digital skills in order to get information on the party's activities and get involved in internal decision-making processes. In this sense, it should be noted that the Five Star Movement relies on an ad-hoc digital platform to involve supporters in relevant decisions concerning party life and action (Manucci & Amsler, 2018). Moreover, several studies have shown that supporters of the Five Star Movement are avid consumers of digital news and that the internet and social media represent the most important component of their political information diets (e.g., Demos – Coop, 2018; Mosca & Vaccari, 2013). To sum up, a robust literature has shown that the internet and social media play a crucial role for the Five Star Movement at identity, organizational and communication levels (Bordignon & Ceccarini, 2013; Mosca, Vaccari, & Valeriani, 2015).

These elements, together with the broader discussion on populist actors we presented above, indicate that supporters of Italian populist parties, and especially those of the Five Star Movement, could be more efficient than those of other parties in developing tactics to strategically influence the attention economy on social media. If this is the case, then news items offering a positive presentation of these parties – as well as those giving a negative framing of other parties – will generate more shares per comment on social media, since supporters of populist parties will be keenly engaged in amplifying these stories, while supporters of other parties will not be as active in contesting them. Conversely, stories offering a negative presentation of these parties, as well as those giving a positive framing of other parties, will generate more comments per share, since supporters of populist parties will be extremely active in contesting this news through their comments. To examine this possibility, which is crucial in order to understand the recent success of populist and tech-savvy parties across Western democracies and beyond, we formulate the following research question:

Do articles presenting a positive framing of Italian populist actors generate more shares per comment and stories presenting a negative framing of populist actors generate more comments per share, while the opposite pattern applies to non-populist actors? (RQ3)

Measures and methods

In this paragraph, we describe the data and the analytical approaches we employed. First, we illustrate the measure of online media source insularity we used to characterize the sharing behaviour of political news stories on Twitter, in the whole system and by specific partisan communities (RQ1). Building on this measure, we then analyze the patterns of Facebook interactions around online media sources marked by different degrees of insularity (RQ2). Finally, by focusing on a subset of political news stories, we analyze the relationships between the sentiment expressed in the headline (title) and blurb (description) of the news story toward specific political actors and the patterns of Facebook interactions (RQ3) observed around stories expressing diverging sentiments.

While we are well aware of the wide range of dissimilarities that make Twitter and Facebook different socio-technical infrastructures, this study leverages on a combination of data gathered from both platforms to get a richer picture of online news media sources and their audiences. As detailed in the following section, we employed Twitter data, a social medium mainly used in Italy to circulate news among an elite of users often interested in politics (AGCOM, 2018), to estimate the partisan attention of news media sources and thus sources' insularity. We instead used Facebook data, a widely popular platform with a broad and diverse audience (Vincos Blog, 2018), to analyze the patterns of engagement around those news media sources. Furthermore, due to the different structure of the two platforms in terms of data access and privacy policies it is not possible for an external researcher – at the time of writing – to perform an analysis of the links shared by individual Facebook users with known political leanings. In other terms, the strategy we conceived leverage on the peculiarities of the two platforms both in terms of audience and data access limits.

Measuring the insularity of an online media source

Building upon the Media Partisanship Attention Score (MPAS) developed by Faris and colleagues for their study of the media landscape during the 2016 US Presidential Election (2017), we relied on Twitter data to characterize the partisan attention toward a news source circulating within the Italian ecosystem of digital news. MPAS is based on the frequency of sharing media sources among users who retweeted messages from either of the two main presidential candidates (@realdonadtrump and @hillaryclinton). The general idea is to categorize users first (based on the proportion of their retweets) and then, in turn, categorize the news source they shared. Faris and colleagues subsequently validated their Twitter metric against partisan aligned measures estimated by researchers with special access to Facebook data (Bakshy et al., 2015), reporting a high correlation (rho = 0.94) between the two methods.

In order to apply the MPAS method to the Italian multi-party-political system, we initially built a set of official Twitter accounts belonging to the major Italian political parties[1] and respective political leaders aggregated per party.[2] Using Twitter Enterprise search API via DiscoverText, we then collected the retweets of this set of accounts during January 2018 ($N = 216{,}765$). This dataset was employed to estimate the partisan affiliation of each contributor in the dataset based on the proportion of their retweets for each party. Subsequently, we employed DMI-TCAT[3] to follow the Twitter timelines of the top 5,000 contributors in this retweet dataset and collected all their tweets between 1 February and 4 March,[4] 2018 ($N = 4{,}385{,}877$). We extracted and resolved the nearly 1.3 hundred million URLs shared by these users to measure the attention devoted to different sources by partisan Twitter users. After selecting only, the tweets containing a link, the final Twitter dataset we analyzed included 3,945 users and 3,500,575 tweets, which included 19,274 unique domains. We further cleaned up the list of domains by removing news aggregators and portals and content sharing websites and by retaining only domains mentioned by at least 31 tweets (or above the average value of the tweet distribution per domain). Following this procedure, we obtained a list of 1,372 unique domains (further reduced to 634 news sources following the datasets merge described in the next paragraph).

Using the average partisan affiliation of contributors who referenced a certain domain, we calculated a set of ten scores (one for each party we considered, excluding 'Progressive Camp' and 'Popular Alternative' that did not participate in the elections) and unique domain. Each score ranges from 0 to 1 and sums to one. The set of scores thus indicate a distribution of the partisan attention received by each domain in our dataset. Building upon the set of scores of such Multi-party Media Partisanship Attention Score (MP-MPAS), we designed an insularity score to measure the degree by which a news media source is prominently shared by online actors affiliated to a single party. In other terms, insularity is a measure of the audience ideological homogeneity of an online media outlet. Considering each party (j) and media source (i) whose MP-MPAS scores and the Gini coefficient (G) we calculated, we defined the insularity of a news media source ($I_{(i)}$) the index [0,1] calculated according to the following formulas:

$$I_{(i)} = \frac{(\mathrm{MPMPAS}_{\max(i,j)} + G_{(i,j)})}{\mathrm{MAX}(\mathrm{MPMPAS}_{(i,j)} + G_{(i,j)})}$$

The measure takes into account two properties of the MP-MPAS set of scores obtained by each news outlet. The maximum score [0,1] indicates the amount of attention devoted to the news source by the dominant partisan community. The Gini coefficient [0,1], a widely used measure of the statistical dispersion of the set of scores' distribution, is used instead to fine-tune the measure by assessing cases where the attention toward a news outlet is concentrated (higher Gini index) or spread across different communities (lower Gini index).

Finally, using the properties of the insularity distribution ($M = 0.65$, $SD = 0.16$) and the distance from the mean, we identified four classes of news media sources with different degrees of insularity: 'High insularity' ($N = 116$), 'Moderate insularity' ($N = 181$), 'Low insularity' ($N = 216$), 'No insularity' ($N = 121$). Using these scores, we proceeded to adjudicate the media source with low to high insularity to the partisan community with the highest scores in the set. Media sources attributed to the 'No insularity' class were instead added to a 'Cross Partisan' category (Figure 1). In other words, when a media source is adjudicated to a party, it means that the source received a degree of attention (in terms of sharing activity) that was significantly partisan (concentrated among users who retweeted that party). On the other hand, a media source was attributed to the 'Cross Partisan' category when it was shared by a highly heterogeneous audience.[5]

We employ these measures to answer our RQ1 which investigates levels of social media insularity among Italian political online news sources preferred by the online communities

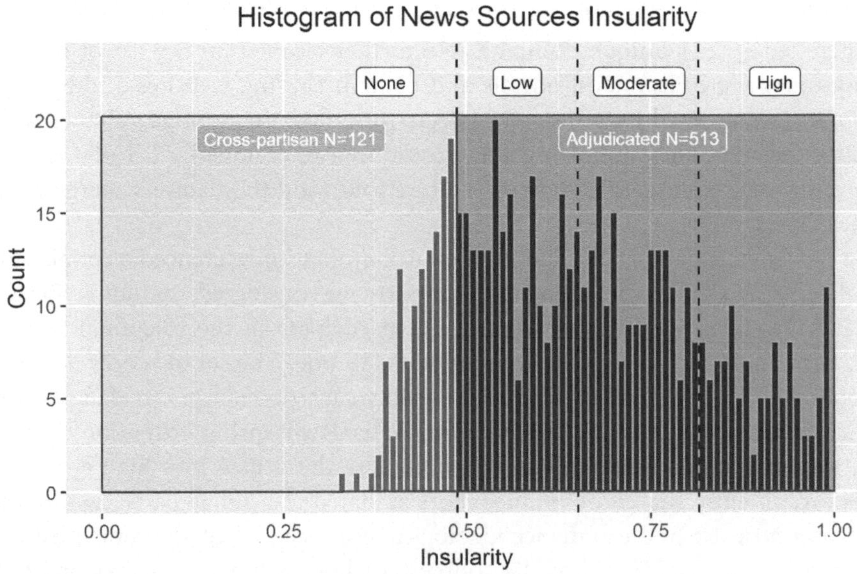

Figure 1. Histogram of insularity scores with classes.

of populist parties compared to those preferred by supporters of other parties. For RQ1 we specifically limited our analysis to the four main online partisan communities (League, M5S, PD and LeU) due to the very small number of news sources adjudicated to minor partisan communities (see Table 2, presented in Findings section).

While based on an existing method developed for a two-party system, our implementation thus (1) works for multi-party systems, (2) includes an original method to measure the insularity in a given online media system, (3) use the distribution of the insularity scores to categorize news sources.

Patterns of Facebook engagement around insular online media sources

During the six months before the Italian 2018 election – between 1 September 2017 and 4 March 2018 – a technological infrastructure based on the open source software Huginn collected in real time a comprehensive dataset of Italian news stories about politics, and their respective level of Facebook engagement (comments, shares and reactions). The news stories were collected from three sources: Google News, the Global Database of Society (GDELT) and Twitter (filtering for tweets including a link and mention of a candidate or a political party). This list was then used to periodically query Facebook Graph API (URL endpoint) in order to gather the global engagement metrics around the collected news stories. The social media lifecycle of a news story was followed every two hours for an entire week, starting from the time the story was published.

The final news stories dataset consisted of 84,815 news stories from 4,113 unique digital media sources, which collected a total of over 65 million comments, shares and reactions on Facebook during the observation period (Table 1).

Our RQ2 asks whether news stories published by highly insular sources tend to receive a higher number of shares per comment compared to news stories published by sources characterized by lower levels of insularity. In order to answer this research question, we joined the list of domains and related MP-MPAS scores obtained from Twitter with the list of unique domains of political news stories collected with respective Facebook aggregated engagement (sum, average, median and standard deviation), removing domains with less than two URL in the news stories dataset, and ending up with a list of 634 news media sources that appeared in both lists. By summing comments (C) and shares (S) received by all the news stories of a news source (i), we calculated the following comments/shares ratio:

$$\frac{C_i - S_i}{C_i + S_i}$$

A value equal to zero means a number of comments equal to the number of shares, a value of '1' means there are only comments, and a value of '−1' there are only shares.

Table 1. Facebook engagement in the whole dataset ($N = 84{,}815$).

	Reactions	Comments	Shares	Total engagement
Absolute values	39,818,195	16,874,919	8,739,960	65,433,074
Percentage	61%	26%	13%	100%

Patterns of Facebook engagement around positive and negative parties coverage

Finally, RQ3 asks whether the positive or negative framing of a news item toward different parties result in different patterns of social media engagement around that specific story. To tackle RQ3, we performed a manual content analysis on a subset of news stories with a high level of Facebook engagement. Following the rationale of our research question, we used the distribution of the sum of comments and shares to identify a subset of highly engaged news stories. After selecting those directly mentioning a political party or politician, we focused on the 3,731 news stories in the top 10th percentile of this distribution. The unit of analysis was the Facebook news stories headline and blurb, i.e., the textual content that social platforms prominently show to their users. From this content, we assessed the sentiment - positive, negative or neutral - towards the four main (as resulted from the popular vote) political actors (party or politician) who ran in the Italian general election: Five Star Movement (M5S), Democratic Party (PD), the League (LN) and Forza Italia (FI).

The analysis was performed by three coders (all authors): first, a code-book detailing the procedure was compiled by the researcher and distributed to the coders; then, the coders had three training sessions. During each session, each coder was assigned a set of 150 randomly selected news stories. After each session, intercoder reliability was checked using Krippendorff's alpha (Hayes & Krippendorff, 2007). Differences between the coders were discussed and consensus coded. Following this training, the coders reached an adequate level of intercoder agreement (Krippendorff's alpha = 0.842 for news stories mentioning the Five Star Movement, 0.724 for the League, 0.820 for the Democratic Party and 0.755 for Forza Italia). The remaining news stories were independently classified by the coders.

Findings

The process of adjudication results in an uneven distribution of news sources per partisan community (see Table 2). Over half of the news sources has been indeed adjudicated to one of the two populist parties. The prominent online activism of the League online community on Twitter also affected the low number of news sources adjudicated to the other members of the centre-right coalition (Forza Italia and Brotherhood of Italy).

Table 2. Results of the adjudication process.

	Media sources	%
League (LN)	215	33.9
Five Star Movement (M5S)	177	27.9
Cross-partisan	121	19.1
Democratic Party (PD)	60	9.5
Free and Equal (LeU)	49	7.7
Forza Italia	4	0.6
Power to the People (PP)	4	0.6
+Europa	3	0.5
Insieme	1	0.2
Civica Popolare	0	0
Brotherhood of Italy (FdI)	0	0
All	634	100

To investigate whether certain political communities predominantly rely on highly insular news sources – i.e., sources prominently shared on Twitter by online actors affiliated to a single party (Faris et al., 2017; Giglietto, Righetti, Marino, & Rossi, 2019) – and considering whether this could be particularly the case of populist parties' online communities (RQ1), we compared the insularity of news sources adjudicated to Italian populist parties (Five Star Movement and the League) with non-populist ones (Democratic Party and Free and Equal).

To this extent, we performed a Kruskal Wallis test and found a highly statistically significant relationship (Kruskal–Wallis $\chi^2(3, N = 501) = 25.68, p < .001$).

Looking at Figure 2, we also observe that:

(1) The news sources shared on Twitter by the Five Star Movement' online community are characterized by a significantly higher degree of insularity in comparison to the other communities;
(2) The news sources shared by the League's online community tend to be characterized by a lower degree of insularity than those shared by Five Star Movement; however, their degree of insularity is also higher than those of the news media shared by the other two 'non-populists' communities and slightly above the mean (see Table 3).

To identify which groups of news media sources are significantly different from the others, we performed a Dunn's post hoc test (Table 4), finding out that the news media sources' group attributed to the Five Star Movement is significantly different from those attributed to PD ($p < .001$), LeU ($p < .01$) and LN ($p < .01$).

Based on this evidence, we concluded that the insularity of news media sources shared by the two Italian populist parties' communities is higher than those of the non-populist

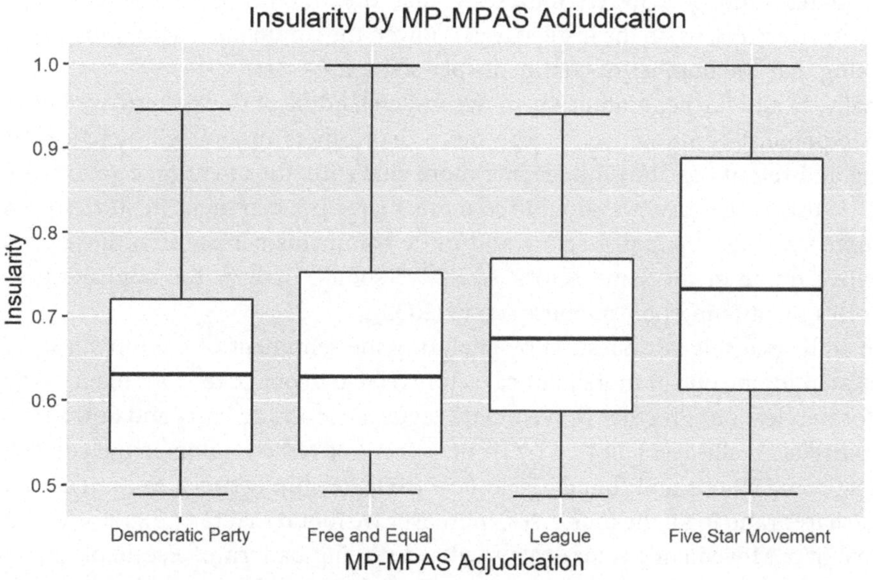

Figure 2. Insularity by MP-MPAS adjudication.

Table 3. Median insularity by MP-MPAS adjudication.

News sources adjudicated to	Median insularity
Five Star Movement (M5S)	0.73
League (LN)	0.67
Free and Equal (LeU)	0.63
Democratic Party (PD)	0.63
Average	0.65

Table 4. Dunn's test with Bonferroni correction for multiple comparisons.

	Free and equal	League	Five Star Movement
League	−0.983939		
Five Star Movement	−3.276976**	−3.677342**	
Democratic Party	0.470071	1.686712	4.146928***

$^{**}p < .01$, $^{***}p < .001$.

ones, and the insularity of news sources shared by Five Star Movement's online community is significantly higher than those shared by all the other ones.

Relying on the scientific literature about the attention economy within social media environments reviewed above, we then investigated whether news sources characterized by different degree of insularity generate different patterns of social media interactions, and more specifically whether news stories published by highly insular sources – compared to the lower insular ones – are characterized by a higher degree of social media amplification (attained through sharing actions), while comments – intended as re-framing attempts – are more frequent in the stories published by cross-partisan sources (RQ2).

We tackled this research question by running a Spearman correlation test to measure the relationship between insularity and comments/shares ratio. The test resulted in highly statistically significant and showed a weak/moderate negative correlation between the two variables ($r_s = -.31$, $n = 634$, $p < .001$). Thus, when the insularity gets higher, the comments-shares ratio gets lower, indicating that the number of shares per comments increases; vice versa, when the insularity gets lower, the comments-shares ratio gets higher, indicating that the number of comments per share increases.

Finally, to add further granularity to our understanding of this pattern, we investigated whether populist communities engage more than others in strategic practices of news sharing and reframing, thus influencing more efficiently the attention economy of social media. If this is the case, we should see more shares per comment in stories presenting a positive framing of populist actors and more comments per share in those presenting a negative frame of the same actors, while we should observe the opposite pattern in the stories mentioning non-populist actors (RQ3).

We addressed this last question by analyzing the sentiment of the top engaging news stories mentioning one or more political actors related to one of the four main parties running for the election (Five Star Movement, League, Democratic Party and Forza Italia). We ran a Kruskal–Wallis test followed by Dunn's post-hoc test with Bonferroni correction for multiple comparisons and found a significant relationship between sentiment and comments/shares ratio in all the four cases, moreover we found that the news stories mentioning Five Star Movement's actors catalyzed a diverging pattern of Facebook interactions when compared to the stories mentioning political actors affiliated with the other parties (Figure 3).

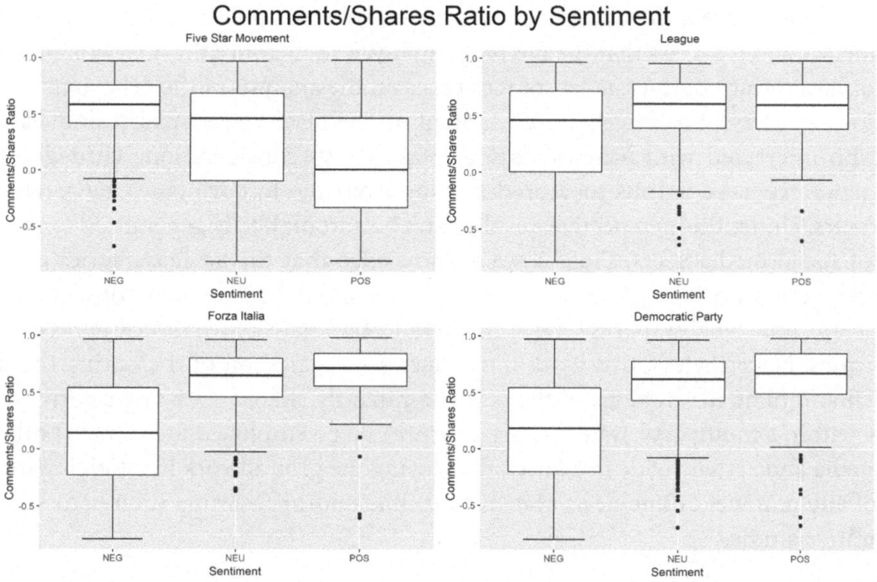

Figure 3. Comments/shares ratio by negative, neutral and positive sentiment of the news stories. Negative values on the *y* axis indicate that news stories have more shares per comment, whereas the positive ones have more comments per share.

Indeed, positive news stories on M5S or on one of its leaders (Kruskal–Wallis $\chi^2(2, N = 1970) = 331.99$, $p < .001$) are characterized by a higher degree of Facebook shares ($p < .001$), while negative ones by a higher degree of comments ($p < .001$). The opposite pattern characterizes the Facebook activity around news stories mentioning the Democratic Party ($\chi^2(2, N = 1581) = 347.92$, $p < .001$), Forza Italia ($\chi^2(2, N = 936) = 253.46$, $p < .001$) and the League ($\chi^2(2, N = 804) = 38.83$, $p < .001$). In all these cases, negative news stories received more shares per comment ($p < .001$) while the positive ones received more comments per share ($p < .001$). Based on this evidence, we concluded that the answer to our RQ3 is affirmative only for Five Star Movement.

Limitations

In the first place, we acknowledge that for a proper investigation of the practices of hacking the attention economy through sharing and commenting, a content analysis of comments, as well as of messages that sometimes accompany the recirculation of third-party messages should be performed. However, given the increasing restrictions that social media companies – and especially Facebook – are introducing for the retrieval of individual data, to carry out such an analysis, special access to social media data would be required. Secondly, considering the activity of social media communities in influencing the circulation of political news, our study does not investigate how spontaneous, coordinated, orchestrated or even unauthentic this activity is. However, while methods to detect botnets' activity on Twitter have been successfully employed in literature (e.g., Bastos & Mercea, 2017), effective strategies to identify similar malicious actions on Facebook are not available. For these reasons, we believe that our research design, blending Twitter and Facebook data, offers an effective way to address the questions we focus on by using public access data. Along the same line, we should stress that the method employed to measure the attention of partisan communities toward online media sources relies on the analysis of the behaviour of a subset of Twitter users who actively create content on the platform. Similarly, only Facebook users who interacted with a news story are taken into consideration. Throughout this study, news exposure is thus measured starting from the footprints left by active social media users. Under this perspective, results can't be automatically generalized to the entire realm of social media users. Finally, we acknowledge that the ad-hoc metrics employed have been tested on a single country in a precise point in time and consequently our findings are unavoidably partial since they could be related to national and contextual peculiarities. Nevertheless, this work introduces a new method of measuring the degree to which an online news media outlet is predominantly shared by a single partisan community within a multiparty system. This measure can be employed to estimate both single news media and system-wide insularity, thus laying the groundwork for studying the evolution of any national online news system over time and/or fostering future cross-country comparative studies.

Discussion and conclusion

Our study sheds new light on the nature of the digital ecosystems of political news. We found that levels of insularity on Twitter tend to be higher for sources which are predominantly shared by supporters of Italian populist parties (the League and the M5S), and especially by those supporting the Five Star Movement. We believe this is an important finding that confirms the idea (Hallin, 2018; Speed & Mannion, 2017; Waisbord, 2018) that the recent success of populist actors in several Western democracies has been favoured by the kaleidoscopic nature of contemporary media systems. The emergence of hyper-partisan niche outlets, presenting themselves as a viable alternative to the crooked mainstream media and self-describing as the voice of the pure people, is crucial to develop the strong in-group vs. out-group's juxtaposition which is central to the populist identity. These media offer an opportunity for the development of highly partisan narratives where opponents are fiercely stigmatized, possibly increasing levels of political polarization of their already homogeneously partisan audiences.

While both M5S and the League relied on insular news sources, this tendency is significantly stronger for the Five Star Movement's online community. This is probably due to the fact that the League took part in the election as a member of the centre-right coalition. While the prominent online activism of the League community resulted in the low number of news sources adjudicated to the other members of the centre-right coalition (Forza Italia and Brotherhood of Italy), the attention overlaps vis-à-vis a similar set of media sources by party members of the same coalition also affected the insularity level observed for sources adjudicated to the League. Our research also revealed a nuanced reality when it comes to a broader understanding of how attention economy develops on social media. Considering patterns of engagement around political news on Facebook, we observed that stories published by sources with a lower degree of insularity generate more comments than those published by more insular outlets. We believe that this finding works against the 'social media as echo-chamber' hypothesis (Sunstein, 2017) since it shows that not only are there sources shared by highly diverse communities but also that these sources, more than others, become arenas for political discussion and confrontation between social media users. While our study does not investigate the nature of these discussions, the fact that sources attracting the attention of cross-partisan audiences are the most commented suggests that these sources give their users the opportunity, if not literally 'to listen', to be exposed to the other side's viewpoints.

Our study revealed that supporters of the Five Star Movement are more proficient and efficient than others in influencing the attention economy within the whole social media environment, which confirms that even a community with its own 'personal' polarized outlets does not fully self-segregate within such a 'reservation'. In this sense, our findings show that, irrespective of the outlet publishing them, stories presenting the Five Star Movement in a favourable light tend to be given wider coverage than those which are well-disposed towards their opponents. Conversely, news giving a negative presentation of the Five Star Movement gets many more comments, suggesting a potential role played by supporters in contesting the bad coverage of their party. Such a pattern, reversed if sentiments towards other parties are considered, reveals how Five Star Movement supporters were more active, numerous or effective even when compared to the other populist actor in the system, the League. We interpret this difference in light of the stronger role played by digital media in the identity, organization and communication of the Movement, which can be considered a perfect example of an 'anti-elitist cyber party' (Hartleb, 2013). This interpretation would seem to imply that a party's capacity to lever its supporters in strategically exploiting the social media arena in order to affect the attention economy might well depend upon a combination of populist ideology and a long-term (symbolic and practical) investment in digital media.

Notes

1. Those polling at 1% or more in the latest December 2017 YouTrend's average of polls (see https://www.youtrend.it/2012/02/10/tabella-riepilogo-sondaggi-politici-elettorali-storico-2008-2009-2010-2011-2012-2013-2014-2015-2016-2017/).
2. We specifically collected tweets that matched a «retweets_of:» rule for the following Twitter accounts: angealfa, alternativa_pop (Popular Alternative, or «Alternativa Popolare»), bealorenzin, civica_popolare (Popular Civic List, or «Civica Popolare»), giulianopisapia, campoprog (Progressive Camp, or «Campo Progressista»), giorgiameloni, fratelliditalia (Brothers of Italy, or «Fratelli d'Italia»), forza_italia, berlusconi (Forza Italia), verditalia, insieme2018, partsocialista (Together, or «Insieme»), pbersani, articolounomdp, si_sinistra, nfratoianni, possibileit, civati, pietrograsso, robersperanza, lauraboldrini, liberi_uguali (Free and Equal, or «Liberi e Uguali»), matteosalvinimi, leganordpadania, noiconsalvini, legasalvini (Northern League, or «Lega Nord»), luigidimaio, beppe_grillo, mov5stelle (Five Star Movement, or «Movimento Cinque Stelle»), matteorenzi, pdnetwork, paologentiloni (Democratic Party, or «Partito Democratico»), emmabonino, radicali, piu_europa (+Europa), maurizioacerbo, direzioneprc, potere_alpopolo (Power to the People, or «Potere al Popolo»).
3. https://github.com/digitalmethodsinitiative/dmi-tcat/wiki.
4. 1 February 2018 was the official starting point of the electoral campaign, subsequently closed by the election day on 4 March 2018.
5. For an assessment of MP-MPAS method against survey data please see Giglietto et al., 2019.

Disclosure statement

No potential conflict of interest was reported by the authors.

Funding

This work was supported by Foundation Open Society Institute in cooperation with the Information Program of the Open Society Foundations: [grant number OR2017-38824].

ORCID

Fabio Giglietto http://orcid.org/0000-0001-8019-1035

References

AGCOM. (2018). Report on the news consumption.

Albertazzi, D., & McDonnell, D. (2007). *Twenty-first century populism: The spectre of Western European democracy*. London: Palgrave Macmillan.

An, J., Cha, M., Gummadi, P. K., & Crowcroft, J. (2011, July). Media Landscape in Twitter: A World of New Conventions and Political Diversity. In *ICWSM*.

Bakshy, E., Messing, S., & Adamic, L. A. (2015). Exposure to ideologically diverse news and opinion on Facebook. *Science*, *348*(6239), 1130–1132.

Barberá, P. (2015). Birds of the same feather tweet together: Bayesian ideal point estimation using Twitter data. *Political Analysis*, *23*(1), 76–91.

Barnidge, M., Ardèvol-Abreu, A., & Gil de Zúñiga, H. (2018). Content-expressive behavior and ideological extremity: An examination of the roles of emotional intelligence and information network heterogeneity. *New Media & Society, 20*(2), 815–834.

Barnidge, M., & Rojas, H. (2014). Hostile media perceptions, presumed media influence, and political talk: Expanding the corrective action hypothesis. *International Journal of Public Opinion Research, 26*(2), 135–156.

Bastos, M. T., & Mercea, D. (2017). The brexit botnet and user-generated hyperpartisan news. *Social Science Computer Review, 37*(1), 38–54.

Beam, M. A., Hutchens, M. J., & Hmielowski, J. D. (2016). Clicking vs. sharing: The relationship between online news behaviors and political knowledge. *Computers in Human Behavior, 59*, 215–220.

Benkler, Y., Faris, R., & Roberts, H. (2018). *Network Propaganda: Manipulation, Disinformation, and Radicalization in American Politics*. Oxford: Oxford University Press.

Bhat, P. (2018). Advertisements in the age of hyper-partisan media Breitbart's #DumpKelloggs campaign. In R. E. Gutsche Jr. (Ed.), *The trump presidency, journalism, and democracy* (pp. 192–200). London: Routledge.

Bordignon, F., & Ceccarini, L. (2013). Five stars and a cricket. Beppe Grillo shakes Italian politics. *South European Society and Politics, 18*(4), 427–449.

Brubaker, R. (2017). Why populism? *Theory and Society, 46*(5), 357–385.

Chadwick, A. (2017). *The hybrid media system: Politics and power*. Oxford: Oxford University Press.

Colleoni, E., Rozza, A., & Arvidsson, A. (2014). Echo chamber or public sphere? Predicting political orientation and measuring political homophily in Twitter using big data. *Journal of Communication, 64*(2), 317–332.

Cosenza, V. (2018). Facebook in italia: 31 milioni di utenti. giovani -40%. Vincos Blog da. Retrieved from http://vincos.it/2018/08/16/facebook-in-italia-31-milioni-di-utenti-giovani-50/

Demos – Coop. (2018). Osservatorio Capitale Sociale - N. 60 - Gli italiani e l'informazione. Retrieved from http://www.demos.it/a01550.php?fbclid=IwAR2wFJaM3qyr5yc5AUDZbBOyQxpLXzkVVcctLbBooaSgZbMH4VilO0cKCEY

De Vreese, C. H., Esser, F., Aalberg, T., Reinemann, C., & Stanyer, J. (2018). Populism as an expression of political communication content and style: A new perspective. *The International Journal of Press/Politics, 23*(4), 423–438.

Dubois, E., & Blank, G. (2018). The echo chamber is overstated: The moderating effect of political interest and diverse media. *Information, Communication & Society, 21*(5), 729–745.

Faris, R., Roberts, H., Etling, B., Bourassa, N., Zuckerman, E., & Benkler, Y. (2017). Partisanship, propaganda, and disinformation: Online media and the 2016 US presidential election.

Flaxman, S., Goel, S., & Rao, J. M. (2016). Filter bubbles, echo chambers, and online news consumption. *Public Opinion Quarterly, 80*(S1), 298–320.

Fletcher, R., & Nielsen, R. K. (2018). Are people incidentally exposed to news on social media? A comparative analysis. *New Media & Society, 20*(7), 2450–2468.

Garrett, R. K. (2009). Politically motivated reinforcement seeking: Reframing the selective exposure debate. *Journal of Communication, 59*(4), 676–699.

Giglietto, F., Righetti, N., Marino, G., & Rossi, L. (2019). Multi-party media partisanship attention score. Estimating partisan attention of news media sources using Twitter data in the lead-up to 2018 Italian election. *Comunicazione Politica, 1/2019*, 89–112.

Hallin, D. C. (2018). Mediatisation, neoliberalism and populisms: The case of Trump. *Contemporary Social Science, 14*(1), 14–25.

Hallin, D. C., & Mancini, P. (2004). *Comparing media systems: Three models of media and politics*. Cambridge: Cambridge university press.

Hartleb, F. (2013). Anti-elitist cyber parties? *Journal of Public Affairs, 13*(4), 355–369.

Hasell, A., & Weeks, B. E. (2016). Partisan provocation: The role of partisan news use and emotional responses in political information sharing in social media. *Human Communication Research, 42*(4), 641–661.

Hayes, A. F., & Krippendorff, K. (2007). Answering the call for a standard reliability measure for coding data. *Communication Methods and Measures, 1*(1), 77–89.

Hilbert, M., Vásquez, J., Halpern, D., Valenzuela, S., & Arriagada, E. (2017). One step, two step, network step? Complementary perspectives on communication flows in Twittered citizen protests. *Social Science Computer Review, 35*(4), 444–461.

Himelboim, I., McCreery, S., & Smith, M. (2013). Birds of a feather tweet together: Integrating network and content analyses to examine cross-ideology exposure on Twitter. *Journal of Computer-Mediated Communication, 18*(2), 154–174.

Hollander, B. A. (2008). Tuning out or tuning elsewhere? Partisanship, polarization, and media migration from 1998 to 2006. *Journalism & Mass Communication Quarterly, 85*(1), 23–40.

Iannelli, L., & Giglietto, F. (2015). Hybrid spaces of politics: The 2013 general elections in Italy, between talk shows and Twitter. *Information, Communication & Society, 18*(9), 1006–1021.

Inglehart, R., & Norris, P. (2016). Trump, Brexit, and the rise of populism: Economic have-nots and cultural backlash.

Iyengar, S., & Hahn, K. S. (2009). Red media, blue media: Evidence of ideological selectivity in media use. *Journal of Communication, 59*(1), 19–39.

Jagers, J., & Walgrave, S. (2007). Populism as political communication style: An empirical study of political parties' discourse in Belgium. *European Journal of Political Research, 46*(3), 319–345.

Kümpel, A. S., Karnowski, V., & Keyling, T. (2015). News sharing in social media: A review of current research on news sharing users, content, and networks. *Social Media+ Society, 1*(2), 1–14.

Lane, D. S., Kim, D. H., Lee, S. S., Weeks, B. E., & Kwak, N. (2017). From online disagreement to offline action: How diverse motivations for using social media can increase political information sharing and catalyze offline political participation. *Social Media+ Society, 3*(3), 1–14.

Lee, E. J. (2012). That's not the way it is: How user-generated comments on the news affect perceived media bias. *Journal of Computer-Mediated Communication, 18*(1), 32–45.

Mancini, P. (2013). The Italian public sphere: A case of dramatized polarization. *Journal of Modern Italian Studies, 18*(3), 335–347.

Manucci, L., & Amsler, M. (2018). Where the wind blows: Five Star Movement's populism, direct democracy and ideological flexibility. *Italian Political Science Review/Rivista Italiana di Scienza Politica, 48*(1), 109–132.

Margetts, H. (2003). Electronic government: A revolution in public administration. In B. G. P. J. Pierre (Ed.), *Handbook of public administration* (pp. 366–376). Thousand Oaks: Sage Publishing.

McCosker, A. (2014). Trolling as provocation: YouTube's agonistic publics. *Convergence, 20*(2), 201–217.

McDonnell, D. (2016). Populist leaders and coterie charisma. *Political Studies, 64*(3), 719–733.

Moffitt, B., & Tormey, S. (2014). Rethinking populism: Politics, mediatisation and political style. *Political Studies, 62*(2), 381–397.

Mosca, L., & Vaccari, C. (2013). Il Movimento e la Rete, by Corbetta P., & Gualmini E. (2013), "Il Partito di Grillo", Bologna, Il Mulino.

Mosca, L., Vaccari, C., & Valeriani, A. (2015). An internet-fuelled party? The Movimento 5 Stelle and the web. In F. Tronconi (Ed.), *Beppe Grillo's five star movement* (pp. 143–168). London: Routledge.

Prior, M. (2007). *Post-broadcast democracy: How media choice increases inequality in political involvement and polarizes elections.* Cambridge: Cambridge University Press.

Saez-Trumper, D., Castillo, C., & Lalmas, M. (2013, October). Social media news communities: gatekeeping, coverage, and statement bias. In *proceedings of the 22nd ACM international conference on conference on information & knowledge management* (pp. 1679–1684). ACM.

Shin, J., & Thorson, K. (2017). Partisan selective sharing: The biased diffusion of fact-checking messages on social media. *Journal of Communication, 67*(2), 233–255.

Speed, E., & Mannion, R. (2017). The rise of post-truth populism in pluralist liberal democracies: Challenges for health policy. *International Journal of Health Policy and Management, 6*(5), 249–251.

Stanley, B. (2008). The thin ideology of populism. *Journal of Political Ideologies, 13*(1), 95–110.

Stroud, N. J. (2010). Polarization and partisan selective exposure. *Journal of Communication, 60*(3), 556–576.

Sunstein, C. (2017). *Hashtag Republic.* Princeton: Princeton University Press.

Taggart, P. (1995). New populist parties in Western Europe. *West European Politics*, *18*(1), 34–51.

Thelwall, M., Sud, P., & Vis, F. (2012). Commenting on YouTube videos: From Guatemalan rock to el big bang. *Journal of the American Society for Information Science and Technology*, *63*(3), 616–629.

Tufekci, Z. (2013). "Not this one" social movements, the attention economy, and microcelebrity networked activism. *American Behavioral Scientist*, *57*(7), 848–870.

Waisbord, S. (2018). Why populism is troubling for democratic communication. *Communication Culture & Critique*, *11*(1), 21–34.

Weeks, B. E., Ardèvol-Abreu, A., & Gil de Zúñiga, H. (2017). Online influence? Social media use, opinion leadership, and political persuasion. *International Journal of Public Opinion Research*, *29* (2), 214–239.

Zhang, Y., Wells, C., Wang, S., & Rohe, K. (2018). Attention and amplification in the hybrid media system: The composition and activity of Donald Trump's Twitter following during the 2016 presidential election. *New Media & Society*, *20*(9), 3161–3182.

Algorithms and agenda-setting in Wikileaks' #Podestaemails release

Nicholas Proferes and Ed Summers

ABSTRACT

In the month before the 2016 U.S. Presidential election, Wikileaks released 37 serialized batches of e-mails authored by former Clinton campaign manager John Podesta. Each release was announced using a unique PodestaEmail related hashtag (#PodestaEmails2, #PodestaEmails3, etc.). In total, Podesta e-mail related hashtags hit town-wide, country-wide, or worldwide Trending topics lists a total of 1,917 times, remaining on Trending Topic lists everyday within the U.S. for 30 days before election day. In this article, we discuss how Wikileaks' release methodology increased the potential reach of Podesta E-mail related content. We describe how Wikileaks' tweets spoke to two audiences: Twitter users and Twitter algorithms. In serializing its content and using new hashtags for each release, Wikileaks increased the potential persistence, visibility, spreadability, and searchability of this content. By creating the possibility for this content to remain persistently visible on the Trending Topics list, Wikileaks was able to potentially realize a greater degree of agenda-setting than would have been possible through singular hashtag use.

Introduction

During the run-up to the November 2016 U.S. Presidential election, Wikileaks—the website devoted to 'analysis and publication of large datasets of censored or otherwise restricted official materials involving war, spying and corruption' (Wikileaks, 2017)—released 'The Podesta Emails' (Wikileaks, 2016b). The Podesta Emails were a cache of over 50,000 e-mails from Presidential candidate Hillary Clinton's campaign manager John Podesta's personal e-mail account. These e-mails contained, 'vivid illustrations of some of Clinton's most serious controversies' (Stein, 2016).

Who originally hacked Podesta's email account has been a subject of some debate. The Associated Press reported that a Russian hacking organization known as 'Fancy Bear' that has purported ties to the Kremlin was behind the original hack (Satter, 2017). Wikileaks founder Julian Assange has refuted the claim that the Russian government directly gave Wikileaks the information (Hains, 2016). An investigative article by the *Washington Post* suggests that the e-mail messages may have passed through several middlemen (Nakashima, Mekhennet, & Jaffe, 2018). Regardless of the origin of the hack, political commentators have argued that this release of information was one of several important moments in the election (Enten, 2016).

Wikileaks regularly releases sensitive government material. What made this particular release noteworthy is that Wikileaks *serialized* the content into almost 40 parts and installments in the series were posted once (and sometimes twice) a day, nearly every day in the month before the November 8th public vote. With each new release, Wikileaks used a new sequential hashtag (#PodestaEmails2, #PodestaEmails3, etc.). This use of sequential, but new hashtags for each batched release made it possible for Podesta-related content hit the Trending Topics lists again and again.

As media organizations covered the content of the e-mails, some additionally made note of the fact that the topic was *trending*. For example, one newspaper, *The News-Gazette* (Champaign-Urbana, IL) regularly published recaps of the day's highlights from Twitter, noting multiple times that '#PodestaEmails' was trending (Jackson, 2016a, 2016b, 2016c). An article in *The Washington Times* stated, 'Twitter's trending news feed was dominated by #PodestaEmails25 after a new batch of stolen documents belonging to John Podesta were posted online' (Ernst, 2016). *The Washington Times* story was subsequently shared by then candidate Donald Trump on his own Twitter page (see Figure 1), extending attention to the fact that this content was trending.

What is important about this event is not just the content that Wikileaks released, but also the methodology. We argue that, in releasing the information serially and using new hashtags for each release, Wikileaks took advantage of Twitter's features in a way that led to greater persistence, visibility, spreadability, and searchability for their content than would have likely been realized through a non-serialized release using a single hashtag. By creating the possibility for this content to remain persistently visible on the Trending

Figure 1. A tweet from former President Donald Trump remarking on Wikileaks e-mail leaks.

Topics list through the use of new hashtags for every release, Wikileaks was ultimately able to achieve a greater degree of agenda-setting through a combination of social and technical mechanisms.

In this article, we detail how Wikileaks' messaging 'spoke' to both Twitter users and Twitter's algorithms, detail the degree to which Podesta related content remained visible on the Trending Topics list, and discuss agenda-setting as a potential outcome of becoming a 'Trending Topic' on Twitter. Ultimately, we argue that, as journalists and news media rely more and more on content from social media as part of their reporting, actors that are able to take thoughtful and informed advantage of the features of social media platforms and are able to draw attention to their content through maximizing use of platform features are more likely to be able to act in an agenda-setting capacity.

Review of relevant literature

Twitter for political purpose

Twitter has become part of the media landscape of political discourse in many countries. As Croeser and Highfield (2014) observe, it has become a 'means of communicating information from official sources, such as government agencies and emergency services, and alternative voices alike' (para. 3). Because of its many-to-many structure, social media allows anyone to share content without the intervention of 'traditional' mass media (Weeks, Lane, Kim, Lee, & Kwak, 2017). At the same time that it has risen in popularity as a venue for political discourse, Twitter has also become an important medium for the distribution and discovery of news. Journalists use Twitter to help identify breaking news (Verdegem & D'heer, 2018) and half of social media users have reported sharing or posting news stories on the platform (Mitchell, Gottfried, Barthel, & Shearer, 2016). The Pew Internet and American Life Project has found, 'Nearly two-thirds of U.S. adults who use Twitter get news on the platform' (Barthel & Shearer, 2015) and that 'nearly as many Americans prefer to get their local news online as prefer the TV set' (Pew Research Center, 2019). In sum, the use of social media for politics and the sharing of news has become a staple of the contemporary media landscape (Penney, 2016).

On Twitter, there are a number of ways that users may try to extend the reach of their content using particular features of Twitter. In this work, we focus on two particular features: hashtags and Trending Topics. Definitionally, *features* are static elements built into the design of a technology. For example, a smartphone might have a built-in camera as a feature (Evans, Pearce, Vitak, & Treem, 2017). Features of technology or platforms offer a 'multifaceted relational structure between an object/technology and the user that enables or constrains potential behavioral outcomes' (Evans, Pearce, Vitak, & Treem, 2017, p. 36). Material *features* of Twitter include the functions of retweeting others' posts through the retweet button, favoriting posts, replying to other users, and hashtags. A user may include hashtags to link content to broader conversations going on through Twitter. As Bruns and Burgess (2011) observe, using hashtags is a 'means of coordinating a distributed discussion between more or less large groups of users, who do not need to be connected through existing "follower" networks.' (p. 1). Twitter's interface turns the use of a hashtag within a tweet to a hyperlink that allows a reader to follow a broader conversation through the search function. Through the coordinate use of particular terms, a user or group of users may try to have a particular hashtag appear in Twitter's 'Trending Topics' list.

Twitter's Trending Topics has become a prominent feature of Twitter. This component of Twitter's interfaces identifies topics that are popular discussion topics on the platform. Trends are not typically curated by hand by Twitter, but rather determined algorithmically. Because Trending Topics show up prominently within the Twitter interface, getting a topic to trend is one particular way of drawing attention to a subject matter (Tufekci, 2017).

One way that a topic can reach the Trending Topics list is through the coordinated use of particular hashtags within tweets. This is sometimes referred to as *hashtag activism*. The Digital Activism Research Project defined hashtag activism as, 'what happens when someone tries to raise public awareness of a political issue using some clever or biting keyword on social media ... If your idea—linked to a good hashtag—gains traction you've started a kind of awareness campaign' (Brewster, 2014).

Twitter has become a popular venue for activists attempting to raise awareness about specific issues, causes, or events through an appearance on the Trending Topics list (Yang, 2016; Gerbaudo, 2012; Tufekci, 2017). To accomplish this, users interested in an issue will generate tweets about a topic or event using a single hashtag in a focused manner, such as #GetOutTheVote or #StopKony. When the Trending Topic algorithm determines a specific topic has enough traffic to be counted as 'trending,' the hashtag or commonly used term becomes visible on the interface timelines of other users in the 'Trending Topics' section of the interface. If the user clicks on the hashtag, by default, they are brought to the 'Top' tweets related to that particular hashtag. Twitter indicates:

> Top Tweets are the most relevant Tweets for your search. We determine relevance based on the popularity of a Tweet (e.g., when a lot of people are interacting with or sharing via Retweets and replies), the keywords it contains, and many other factors. (Twitter.com, 2018)

Even if users don't click into a hashtag that appears in the Trending Topics list to explore the conversation, at the very least, they are still exposed to the message. As a result, for hashtag activists looking to promote a particular issue, choosing enticing or interesting language is important (Yang, 2016). If a user *does* click into the hashtag, greater attention can come to the most popular tweets on a particular subject.

One of the difficulties of making something 'trend,' however, is that Twitter does not disclose exactly how the Trending Topic algorithm works (Gillespie, 2012). This lack of algorithmic transparency has led to some confusion about why some topics trend but others do not. For example, during the Occupy Wall Street protests, despite the fact that thousands of users were tweeting with the hashtag #OccupyWallStreet, the term never hit the New York area list of trending topics (Lotan et al., 2011). Some accused Twitter of censoring the trend (Jeffries, 2011). In response, Twitter representatives pointed to an older company blog post, which states:

> Twitter Trends are automatically generated by an algorithm that attempts to identify topics that are being talked about more right now than they were previously. The Trends list is designed to help people discover the 'most breaking' breaking news from across the world, in real-time. The Trends list captures the hottest emerging topics, not just what's most popular ... Sometimes a topic doesn't break into the Trends list because its popularity isn't as widespread as people believe. And, *sometimes, popular terms don't make the Trends list*

> *because the velocity of conversation isn't increasing quickly enough, relative to the baseline level of conversation happening on an average day* ... [emphasis added] (twitter.com, 2010)

Reflecting on lessons that activists might draw on from the Occupy-related hashtag fiasco, Lotan et al. (2011) argues activists trying to raise the visibility of their cause through an appearance on the Trending Topics list, understanding how the algorithm determines what becomes visible is crucial for choosing appropriate messaging. He concludes:

> if one seeks to keep a topic trending, it is important to change it every few days. ... a gradual rise in velocity only makes it harder and harder for the term to trend. (Lotan et al., 2011)

This suggests continuously revisiting the use of a hashtag to make sure it counts as a 'new' and 'emerging' topics of discussion, rather than a previously popular discussion topic, is important practice for users seeking to increase the visibility of their content.

Agenda-setting and social media

Agenda-setting is a term used to describe a theory of media effects in which the media (traditionally news media) are understood as influencing the amount of importance the public places on an issue (Scheufele & Tewksbury, 2006). Agenda-setting is achieved by repeatedly exposing the audience to certain news stories or spending significant screen time on a particular political candidate's viewpoint. The theory, originated by McCombs and Shaw (1972), suggests that recurring attention to an issue by news media makes the topic more accessible and salient in the minds of the audience (Kim, Scheufele, & Shanahan, 2002). For example, the theory suggests that if major news media outlets spent a proportionally considerable amount of time discussing global warming, that an audience would come to view global warming as an important topic. The concept of agenda-setting is connected to (though different from) the concepts of framing and priming (see: Scheufle & Tewksbury, 2006 for more).

Agenda-setting can occur on social media. While one might imagine that the flow of attention goes from stories appearing in traditional news outlets to things being subsequently discussed in social media, this is not necessarily the case. Russell Neuman, Guggenheim, Mo Jang, and Bae (2014) find a dynamic flow between traditional news outlets and social media. News stories appearing on social media can complement news on traditional media outlets in the minds of an audience, compounding agenda-setting effects. For example, Conway, Kenski, and Wang (2015) found a symbiotic relationship 'between agendas in Twitter posts and traditional news, with varying levels of intensity and differential time lags by issue' (p. 363). As journalists rely on social media to help identify breaking news (Diakopoulos, De Choudhury, & Naaman, 2012), the flow of attention can also go from social media to traditional news outlets. As a result, agenda-setting can work in both directions across social media and traditional news-media.

Politicians use social media to achieve agenda-setting and actively tailor the content of their messages to do so (Skogerbø & Krumsvik, 2015; Yang, Chen, Maity, & Ferrara, 2016). This can be particularly exacerbated within the context of an election cycle. For example, Lee and Xu (2018) observe that during the 2016 U.S. Presidential election, 'Some of the issues Trump stressed in his tweets (i.e., media bias and Clinton's alleged dishonesty) drew significantly more favorites and retweets, suggesting public agenda-setting possibilities through Twitter' (p. 201). Yang et al. (2016) argue that Twitter represents a particularly appealing conversation space, particularly for opposition politicians. However, in the literature on political actors' use of Twitter for achieving agenda-setting, the focus is more on the *content* of the messages that have been tailored for the human reader, rather than ways in which politicians or other individuals take advantage of technical features of a platform in order to achieve agenda-setting.

With this particular literature in mind, in the following pages, we turn to examine Wikileaks' serialized release of the Podesta E-mails. We use this case study to illustrate how Wikileaks' messaging simultaneously 'spoke' to both regular users and simultaneously took advantage of the way Twitter's Trending Topics feature works algorithmically. This resulted in a potentially wider reach for their messaging than would have been likely using other means, ultimately increasing the possibility that they could operate in an agenda-setting capacity.

Methodology

Case study

This attempt to unpack a specific event is best understood as a case study. Case study research starts from 'the desire to derive a(n) (up-)close or otherwise in-depth understanding of a single or small number of "cases," set in their real-world contexts' (Yin, 2012, p. 2). It is, in fact, the real-world context that is critical to understand how the use of particular features of Twitter connects to agenda-setting. As such, the methodology of a case study is particularly well-suited, as the method is most appropriate when the boundaries between phenomenon and context are not clearly evident (Yin, 2013).

This work uses a single case rather than a multi-case approach. It is beyond the scope of this paper to be able to offer a multi-case approach due level of detail involved in this particular case. However, researchers interested in this topic may consider both comparative cases within a single platform (such as Twitter), and can provide further depth and nuance by describing how agenda-setting is achieved differently depending on the particular features of a platform (for example, how agenda-setting may or may not be achieved through other popular platforms such as Reddit).

Data collection

This analysis relies on multiple data sources. First, it relies on data collected from the Wikileaks' Twitter account. Tweets authored by Wikileaks were manually collected through a combination of the Twitter web-based search engine, the archival web recording tool webrecorder.io, and python-based parsing code (a Jupyter Notebook that explains the process in greater detail is available at [Summers, 2017]). A total of 34,775 tweets originally authored by Wikileaks were identified. Wikileaks' profile page indicates that they have a total of 47.9k Tweets. However, the profile page tweet count includes re-tweets, which we did not collect. It is assumed that the 34,775 tweets collected are comprehensive of materials that have not been deleted previously and were not retweets. Second, this analysis relies on data collected from the website Trendogate.com. Trendogate provides historical information on trending topics, in particular, information about locations where a particular hashtag trended and at what time. Third, this analysis relies on news stories and other secondary sources that analyze the impact that Wikileaks had on the 2016 election. Lastly, we rely on data points collected from *Nexus Uni* (which indexes over 5,600 news, business, legal, medical and reference publications, primarily newspapers, magazines and journals newspaper articles) and *Access World News* (NewsBank), which includes the full-text of over 600 U.S. newspapers. In particular, we searched each of these databases for articles that mentioned 'Podesta' and 'Wikileaks' within the same article, and any variation of the exact term '#PodestaEmails' ('#PodestaEmails2', '#PodestaEmails3' etc.) that appeared in the month prior to the election (Oct 8, 2016 to Nov 8, 2016).

The multiple data sources are important because, as noted by Yin (2012), case studies require triangulation in order to find converging lines of evidence. In this case, we examine how these converging lines of evidence speak to how Wikileaks' content release methodology increased the reach of this content, and ultimately helped Wikileaks' more readily achieve agenda-setting.

Case

When a topic 'Trends,' more Twitter users are likely to see the content and to engage with Tweets related to the topic. This is because the topic will show up as part of the 'Trending Topics' list, shown by default next to the users' timeline on the web-based Twitter interface. As for the effects of this, in a 2015 blog post, the social media engagement business *Buffer* wrote that in creating content related to things that were trending on Twitter they created, 'our best-performing tweets of all time, earning somewhere in the ballpark of 11,000+ clicks and more than 3x our normal engagement rate' (Seiter, 2015). This suggests that having something appear on the Trending Topics list not only promotes visibility, but also content engagement.

However, as previously noted, one of the difficulties of making something 'trend' is that Twitter does not disclose exactly how the Trending Topic algorithm works (Gillespie, 2012). While it is impossible to say for certain without discussing the matter with Wikileaks operators, Wikileaks' previous behavior on the platform suggests some familiarity with how the Trending Topics algorithm works.

According to Lynch (2014), Wikileaks' use of hashtags has changed over time. In the early years of their Twitter use:

> Wikileaks initially experimented with placing "#Wikileaks" at the end of their tweets" (p. 2682), however, they ultimately abandoned this practice as "it was difficult to track or index Twitter conversations about Wikileaks' activities among multiple followers; more importantly, the absence of hashtags made it difficult for non-followers to discover Wikileaks through conversations keyed to such tags. (p. 2682)

Instead, Wikileaks began to encourage the use of single hashtags to collate conversations around specific leaks. Lynch (2014) observers that the first time Wikileaks invented a hashtag to gather together those interested in discussing a specific leak was in November of 2009, 'when they urged followers to use #911texts to discuss a leak of New York-area pager messages from September 11, 2001' (p. 2682). They also previously asked interested Twitter users to use specific hashtags during events in order to raise awareness around a particular topic or issue. For example, tweeting, 'For tweets reguarding [*sic*]

Julian #Assange's hearing on the 12th and 13th, please use hashtag #wljul.'" (Wikileaks, 2011).

Wikileaks has also been involved with some degree of controversy around the Trending Topics feature previously. For example, in late 2010, Wikileaks released a cache of U.S. diplomatic cables. This release would become known as '#CableGate.' During this release, Twitter was accused by some users of censoring CableGate and Wikileaks related hashtags from appearing on the Trending Topics list. The accusation prompted Twitter to write a response on its company blog entitled, 'To Trend of Not to Trend'. The blog-post stated:

> This week, people are wondering about WikiLeaks, with some asking if Twitter has blocked #wikileaks, #cablegate or other related topics from appearing in the list of top Trends. The answer: Absolutely not. In fact, some of these terms, including #wikileaks and #cablegate, have previously trended either worldwide or in specific locations. (twitter.com, 2010)

The fact that Twitter publicly responded to the controversy suggests Wikileaks may have taken notice. In July of 2016, Wikileaks itself accused Twitter of 'shadowbanning' a topic from appearing within the Trending Topics list, tweeting, '@Twitter Is Twitter "shadow banning" the #DNCLeak hashtag? https://t.co/dsI0NtoOer'" (Wikileaks, 2016a). This history suggests Wikileaks' operators were at least aware of some of the technical characteristics of the way the Trending Topics algorithm functions and, assuming they had read Twitter's public response to the questions of censorship for their content, some of the potential pitfalls of reusing the same hashtag as it relates to content trending.

Roughly one month before the November 8th, 2016 election day, Wikileaks began to release the Podesta e-mails on its website, and announcing the leaks on its Twitter page. Rather than dumping the Podesta e-mails in bulk and making a single announcement, Wikileaks released the information in batches, spread out just over one month. Each newly released batch was announced on Twitter using its own sequential hashtag (#PodestaEmails1, #PodestaEmails2, etc.). By creating a new hashtag for each release, Wikileaks took advantage of the way Twitter's Trending Topics algorithm operates, achieving a broader impact for this leak than it might have been able to achieve through the use of a single hashtag for each release. This is because had they continued to use the same hashtag over and over (#PodestaEmails for the first release, #PodestaEmails for the second release, etc. etc.), the topic would likely have not trended beyond the first release, since the volume of Tweets likely would not have changed significantly from day to day. But, because there were new hashtags for each release (even though it only varied by a trailing digit), the relative velocity that was being measured against was almost always a prior state of zero, thus yielding a stronger velocity slope.

In sum, Wikileaks created 37 specific hashtags related to the Podesta email leak ranging from #PodestaEmails (created 6:42 PM – Oct 7, 2016) to #PodestaEmails36 (created 12:04 PM – Nov 9, 2016). Across just the Wikileaks tweets that have the first use of a new hashtag (#PodestaEmails, #PodestaEmails2), etc. those 37 tweets have a total of 399,795 retweets and 361,399 likes, with each release tweet averaging 10,805 retweets and 9,768 likes.

As shown in Table 1, Wikileaks introduced at least one new Podesta E-mail hashtag every day for their releases from October 10th, 2016 to November 9th, 2016. In the final week before the election, they were sometimes introducing two new hashtags a day. Given the time-ranges involved in the creation of hashtags, it suggests that the intent

Table 1. Hashtags by date.

Month	Day	Hashtag Introduced
10	7	#PodestaEmails
10	10	#PodestaEmails2
10	11	#PodestaEmails3
10	12	#PodestaEmails4, #PodestaEmails5
10	13	#PodestaEmails6
10	14	#PodestaEmails7
10	15	#PodestaEmails8
10	16	#PodestaEmails9
10	17	#PodestaEmails10
10	18	#PodestaEmails11
10	19	#PodestaEmails12
10	20	#PodestaEmails13
10	21	#PodestaEmails14
10	22	#PodestaEmails15
10	23	#PodestaEmails16
10	24	#PodestaEmails17
10	25	#PodestaEmails18
10	26	#PodestaEmails19
10	27	#PodestaEmails20
10	28	#PodestaEmails21
10	29	#PodestaEmails22
10	30	#PodestaEmails23
10	31	#PodestaEmails24
11	1	#PodestaEmails25
11	2	#PodestaEmails26
11	3	#PodestaEmails27, #PodestaEmails28
11	4	#PodestaEmails29, #PodestaEmails30
11	5	#PodestaEmails31
11	6	#PodestaEmails32
11	7	#PodestaEmails33, #PodestaEmails34
11	8	#PodestaEmails35, #PodestaEmails36
11	9	#PodestaEmails37

was to make this information available specifically before Election Day in the U.S. and to try to draw attention to their content in the critical weeks before the election on Tuesday, November 8, 2016.

As shown in Table 2, in total, Podesta Email related hashtags hit town-wide, country-wide, or worldwide Trending topics lists a total of 1,917 times. Podesta related hashtags hit the Worldwide trending topics list 10 times during that month, hit the United States

Table 2. Count of Trending Topics Locations.

Town-Wide Trending Topics Lists (Aggregated to Countries)		Country-wide Trending Topics Lists		Worldwide Trending Topics Lists	
United States	1345	United States	29	Total	10
Vietnam	145	Vietnam	27		
United Kingdom	117	Canada	10		
Canada	100	Russia	6		
Russia	73	United Arab Emirates	6		
United Arab Emirates	21	United Kingdom	3		
Australia	14	Australia	2		
Belarus	4	Latvia	2		
Algeria	1	Algeria	1		
Latvia	1	Total	86		
Total	1821				

trending topics list 29 times during that month, and hit U.S. city or town trending topics lists 1,345 times.

Podesta related hashtags remained on Trending Topics lists from October 8, 2016 until November 8, 2016. In the U.S., a Podesta related hashtag hit the trending topics list in at least one town every day from October 10th until November 8th, 2016. On average between October 8, 2016 until November 8, 2016, in the U.S., a Podesta related hashtag showed up in 42.9 city-wide or nation-wide trending topics lists a day. This activity peaked on November 5th, with Podesta related hashtags appearing in on 120 city-wide trending topics lists within the U.S. Figure 2.

As a result of their use of new hashtags for each release, Wikileaks was essentially able to keep Podesta Email related hashtags on Trending Topics lists for an entire month. Had they simply used a single hashtag to collate the entire release (such as using #PodestaEmails for every new release) it is highly unlikely that the topic would have been as persistently present in the Trending Topics.

It is difficult to capture and isolate the exact and full effects of Wikileaks successfully landing Podesta related hashtags on the Trending Topics lists for over a month versus the impact of the actual content contained in the released e-mails itself. However, we can see evidence of both facets appearing in media outside of Twitter. A search of *Access World News's* database of newspapers revealed 3,199 articles that mention Podesta and Wikileaks together in the same article. In a search of *Nexus Uni*, we find Podesta-Email hashtags (such as '#PodestaEmails4,' etc.) were mentioned *explicitly* a total of 339 times.

In regards to Podesta-Email hashtags showing up outside of Twitter, in some cases, articles were simply quoting Tweets from Twitter as part of their reporting. For example, one Associated Press article stated:

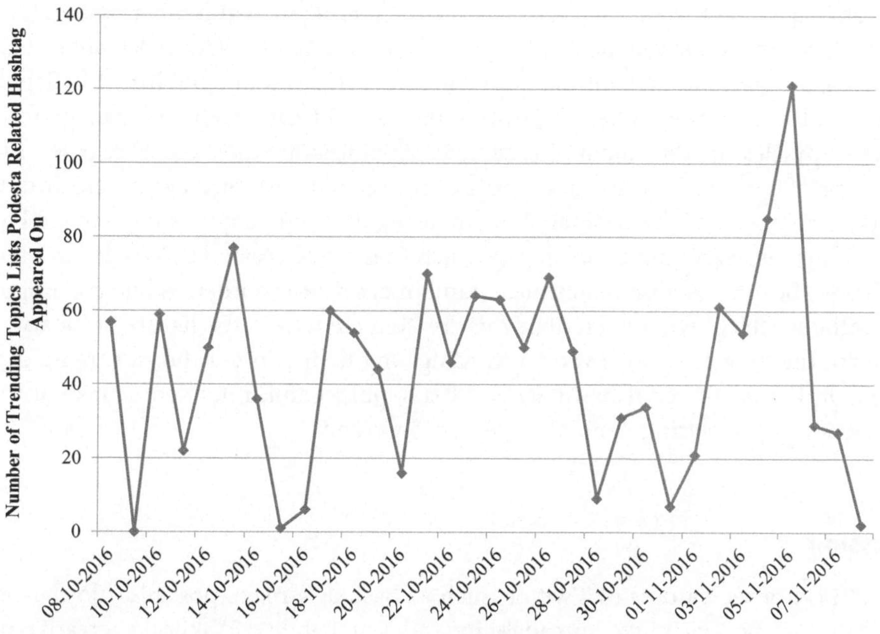

Figure 2. Number of Trending Topics Lists Podesta Related Hashtags Appeared on by Day.

> Questions were raised on social media about the speed with which Russia Today, a news site funded by the Russian government, tweeted about Podesta's e-mails, the latest in a series of hacked emails published by WikiLeaks. The group said the e-mails were visible on its website "well before" it started tweeting them. RT dismissed the questions as conspiracy theories. 'We were fastest on #Podestaemails6, faster than @wikileaks, and the US conspiracy machine can't handle it,' the network said in a tweet. (Daly, 2016)

One newspaper, *The News-Gazette* (Champaign-Urbana, IL) regularly published a recap of on-goings on social media, providing 'a quick glance at the best that Twitter has to offer.' This included noting that '#PodestaEmails' related topics was trending as part of multiple articles (Jackson, 2016a; 2016b; 2016c). These kinds of quotes and references expanded the reach and attention drawn to the content beyond the scope of Twitter users to a wider public.

In some cases, the trending itself also became a part of the story. For example, an article in *The Washington Times* states,

> Twitter's trending news feed was dominated by #PodestaEmails25 after a new batch of stolen documents belonging to John Podesta were posted online. A March 2, 2015, discussion between Mrs. Clinton's top advisers shows Mr. Podesta expressing a desire to 'dump all those emails.' (Ernst, 2016, para. 2).

Then Presidential Candidate Donald Trump himself drew attention to the story in his own tweet, seen in Figure 1. This linking of the story by a presidential candidate likely drew even more attention to the release.

Looking over the entire history of Wikileaks' tweets and hashtag use reveals that, prior to the #PodestaEmail leaks, Wikileaks use of sequential hashtags for multi-part releases was uncommon and far less temporally concentrated. When Wikileaks did create multiple hashtags for content releases, the different hashtags were often spread out across longer spans of time, and involved far fewer parts of the sequence. For example, in late 2011, WikiLeaks began publishing The Spy Files, 'thousands of pages and other materials exposing the global mass surveillance industry' (Wikileaks, 2014). Wikileaks published four 'parts' to this collection, two published in December of 2011, one published in September of 2013, and one in September of 2014. Wikileaks did use multiple hashtags for these releases–#SpyFiles for the initial release, and #SpyFiles4 for the fourth release—but did not create a #SpyFiles2 or #SpyFiles3. Instead the second and third parts were announced using the original #SpyFiles hashtag. In comparing the volume of hashtags created for the #PodestaEmail leak and the frequency at which these were created to Wikileaks' other use of hashtags, the #PodestaEmail hashtags stand out as a clear outlier. While it is impossible to say without interviewing the individuals creating the tweets, the nature of the use, combined with the previous controversy regarding why their content did not trend, suggests that Wikileaks' use of serial hashtags was likely purposeful, intended to take advantage of the possibility of getting content to repeatedly trend.

Discussion

boyd (2014) argues features of Twitter, such as hashtags, make possible affordances that include: persistence, visibility, spreadability and searchability. Wikileaks' creative messaging 'spoke' to Twitter's Trending Topics feature by using new hashtags for each release, thereby furthering the realization of persistence, visibility, spreadability and searchability. By creating new hashtags for every release, Wikileaks made it possible for each new release related to the Podesta leak to appear *persistently* on Trending Topics in at least one U.S. town every day from October 10th until November 8th, 2016. Wikileaks' use of sequential hashtags also increased the potential *visibility* of this release. It provided the opportunity for parallel narratives about Podesta and Clinton to appear within Twitter, and made it possible for these narratives to be more easily *spread* to different individuals and different media spaces.

The careful use of multiple hashtags may have also impacted the *searchability* and *discoverability* of content related to the Podesta e-mails. Twitter's search algorithm shows the most recent top tweets by default. Twitter indicates it determines top tweets by determining 'relevance based on the popularity of a Tweet (e.g., when a lot of people are interacting with or sharing via Retweets and replies), the keywords it contains, and many other factors' (twitter.com, 2018). However, if a topic appears on the Trending Topics list, it becomes more likely that people will interact with tweets related to that topic in some way. As a result, the use of multiple hashtags to improve the chances of landing on Trending Topic lists created a virtuous circle where related content then additionally became more likely to float to the top of search results.

Wikileaks' hashtag use shows how agenda-setting capacity can be furthered through taking advantage of social media features. Wikileaks' ability to function as an agenda-setter was shaped not just by the *content* of the release, but also by the way their messaging spoke to the technical features of Twitter. In many ways, what Wikileaks did was enact Twitter's algorithms through a particular, novel practice (Seaver, 2017). However, we wish to emphasize there is not a *deterministic* relationship between the use of multiple hashtags, appearing on the Trending Topics list, and agenda-setting. It is important to note that, were it not for the hundreds to thousands of Twitter accounts liking Wikileaks' tweets or retweeting them, or creating their own content in response, the use of multiple, sequential hashtags may not have made any difference to how robustly Wikileaks was ultimately able achieve any level of agenda-setting. However, *without* the use of sequential hashtags, the degree to which Wikileaks successfully realized persistence, visibility, spreadability, and searchability of this release through the features of the platform would have been stunted.

Knowledge of technical features of social media platforms, particularly platforms that are often opaque, will continue to provide an edge in realizing specific goals and outcomes, achieving agenda-setting, and ultimately, in expressions of power. Symbolic power is the ability to 'impose the principles of construction of reality – in particular, social reality – [and] is a major dimension of political power' (Bourdieu, 1977, p. 165); or as Watts (2011) describes Bourdieu's concept, the 'power to make people see and believe certain visions of the world rather than others' (p. 4). Increasingly, techniques for successful realization of symbolic power depend on technical knowledge about social media systems and their particular features.

We argue that, based on its history of interactions with Twitter's platform and the Trending Topics algorithm, Wikileaks' use of sequential hashtags at the rate of roughly one a day for the entire month up to election day, rather than using a single hashtag, was likely a strategic choice. Through this choice, Wikileaks' messaging had a higher chance of showing up on the Trending Topics lists for an extended length of time than a one-time, bulk release with a single hashtag. In structuring their messaging campaign in this way, Wikileaks' ability to successfully achieve agenda-setting was deeply shaped by its ability to work the features of Twitter platform to realize persistence, visibility, spreadability, and searchability for its content.

Wikileaks' messaging spoke to both social media audiences and algorithms, furthering a dynamic flow between Twitter and traditional news outlets. News stories about the Podesta E-mails trending complemented news stories about the content of the e-mails. As journalists rely on Trending Topics to identify breaking news, and report trending as newsworthy in itself or as part of a larger story, agenda-setting is now a potential by-product of getting content to trend. We suggest that scholars consider how agenda-setting theory might need to be expanded to account for how sociotechnical systems and their features fit into contemporary agenda-setting practices.

In their original article defining the theory of agenda-setting, McCombs and Shaw (1972) write,

> In choosing and displaying news, editors, newsroom staff, and broadcasters play an important part in shaping political reality. Readers learn not only about a given issue, but also how much importance to attach to that issue from the amount of information in a news story and its position (p. 176).

On social media, news, editors, and newsroom staff are often not the ones making choices about what content appears prominently on a site. Instead, algorithms are often making these decisions, based on data produced by the activities of users. Users who are aware of this, and who have some degree of technical knowledge, may be able to take advantage of the ways these algorithms work. In doing so, these users may find they are more likely (but not guaranteed) to potentially influence what others see by taking strategic advantage of system features. As traditional media cover events happening on social media, the agenda-setting potential is multiplied.

Conclusion

The goal of this article was to discuss how Wikileaks' release methodology took creative advantage of the way that the Trending Topics algorithm works, thereby creating the potential to further the reach of Podesta E-mail related content. Wikileaks did this by crafting tweets that spoke to two audiences: Twitter users and Twitter algorithms. In serializing its content and using new hashtags for each release, Wikileaks was able to create the potential for persistence, visibility, spreadability, and searchability of Podesta e-mail related content, ultimately furthering their ability to function in an agenda-setting capacity.

Knowledge about how social media sites operate will continue to be a key component in achieving agenda-setting. However, as we noted above, Wikileaks use of serial hashtags only created the possibility for this to occur more readily. One does not get to the Trending Topics list merely by using lots of different hashtags. Instead, content must be shared repeatedly for this to occur. Indeed, there is an outstanding question of how collective action during the 2016 election made agenda-setting possible in these digital spaces. It is beyond the scope of our data and this manuscript to comment on this aspect. However, as researchers move towards creating a more robust account of agenda-setting through social media, it will be critical for scholars to additionally contend with that facet, and consider questions about the kinds of power and resources necessary to coordinate such activities.

Disclosure statement

No potential conflict of interest was reported by the authors.

ORCID

Nicholas Proferes http://orcid.org/0000-0002-0295-9616
Ed Summers http://orcid.org/0000-0001-7320-8150

Works Cited

Barthel, M., & Shearer, E. (2015). How do Americans use Twitter for news? *Pew Research*. Retrieved from Pew Research Center website: http://www.pewresearch.org/fact-tank/2015/08/19/how-do-americans-use-twitter-for-news/

Bourdieu, P. (1977). *Outline of a theory of practice*. Cambridge: Cambridge University Press. (R. Nice, Trans.).

boyd, danah. (2014). *It's complicated: The social lives of networked teens*. New Haven, CT: Yale University Press.

Brewster, S. (2014). After Ferguson: Is "Hashtag Activism" Spurring Policy Changes? *NBC News*. Retrieved from http://www.nbcnews.com/politics/first-read/after-ferguson-hashtag-activism-spurring-policy-changes-n267436

Bruns, A., & Burgess, J. E. (2011). The use of Twitter hashtags in the formation of ad hoc publics. *Proceedings of the 6th European Consortium for Political Research (ECPR) General Conference* 2011. Presented at the 6th European Consortium for Political Research General Conference, University of Iceland, Reykjavik. Retrieved from http://www.ecprnet.eu/conferences/general_conference/reykjavik/

Conway, B. A., Kenski, K., & Wang, D. (2015). The rise of Twitter in the political campaign: Searching for intermedia agenda-setting effects in the presidential primary. *Journal of Computer-Mediated Communication*, *20*(4), 363–380.

Croeser, S., & Highfield, T. (2014). Occupy Oakland and# oo: Uses of Twitter within the occupy movement. *First Monday*, *19*(3). https://journals.uic.edu/ojs/index.php/fm/article/view/4827

Daly, M. (2016, October 13). Email: Clinton campaign tried to move back Illinois primary. *Associated Press News*. Retrieved from AP NEWS website: https://apnews.com/7fc6c853cfd848168e8ad4d5168bdb24

Diakopoulos, N., De Choudhury, M., & Naaman, M. (2012). Finding and Assessing social media information sources in the context of journalism. *Proceedings of the SIGCHI Conference on Human Factors in Computing Systems*, 2451–2460. doi:10.1145/2207676.2208409

Enten, H. (2016). How Much Did Wikileaks Hurt Hillary Clinton? *FiveThirtyEight*. Retrieved from FiveThirtyEight website: https://fivethirtyeight.com/features/wikileaks-hillary-clinton/

Ernst, D. (2016). WikiLeaks emails reveal John Podesta urging Hillary Clinton camp to "dump" emails. *The Washington Times*. Retrieved from https://www.washingtontimes.com/news/2016/nov/1/wikileaks-emails-reveal-john-podesta-urging-hillar/

Evans, S. K., Pearce, K. E., Vitak, J., & Treem, J. W. (2017). Explicating affordances: A conceptual framework for understanding affordances in communication research. *Journal of Computer-Mediated Communication*, *22*(1), 35–52. https://doi.org/10.1111/jcc4.12180

Gerbaudo, P. (2012). *Tweets and the streets: Social media and contemporary activism*. London: Pluto Press.

Gillespie, T. (2012). Can an algorithm be wrong? *Limn*, *1*(2), Retrieved from http://eprints.cdlib.org/uc/item/0jk9k4hj

Hains, T. (2016). WikiLeaks' Julian Assange: Russian Government Was Not Source For Podesta, DNC Emails. *Real Clear Politics*. Retrieved from Real Clear Politics website: http://www.realclearpolitics.com/video/2016/12/15/wikileaks_julian_assange_russian_government_was_not_source_for_podesta_dnc_emails.html

Jackson, M. (2016a, October 14). #TheMJs. *News-Gazette, The (Champaign-Urbana, IL)*, pp. B-1. Retrieved from NewsBank: https://infoweb-newsbank-com.ezproxy.uky.edu/apps/news/document-view?*p*=AWNB&docref=news/161271FFBA10F998

Jackson, M. (2016b, October 28). #TheMJs. *News-Gazette, The (Champaign-Urbana, IL)*, pp. B-1. Retrieved from NewsBank: https://infoweb-newsbank-com.ezproxy.uky.edu/apps/news/document-view?*p*=AWNB&docref=news/161B57CFCE3F2FB0

Jackson, M. (2016c, November 4). #TheMJs. N*ews-Gazette, The (Champaign-Urbana, IL)*, pp. B-1. Retrieved from NewsBank: https://infoweb-newsbank-com.ezproxy.uky.edu/apps/news/document-view?*p*=AWNB&docref=news/161FA425666DFF58

Jeffries, A. (2011). Twitter Says It's Not Censoring Occupy Wall Street–People Really Are More Concerned With Doritos Right Now. *The Observer*. Retrieved from Observer website: http://observer.com/2011/09/twitter-says-its-not-censoring-occupy-wall-street-people-really-are-talking-more-doritos/

Kim, S.-H., Scheufele, D. A., & Shanahan, J. (2002). Think about it this way: Attribute agenda-setting function of the press and the public's evaluation of a local issue. *Journalism & Mass Communication Quarterly*, *79*(1), 7–25.

Lee, J., & Xu, W. (2018). The more attacks, the more retweets: Trump's and Clinton's agenda setting on Twitter. *Public Relations Review*, *44*(2), 201–213.

Lotan, G., Graeff, E., Ananny, M., Gaffney, D., Pearce, I., & Boyd, D. (2011). The Revolutions were tweeted: information flows during the 2011 Tunisian and Egyptian Revolutions. *International Journal of Communication*, *5*, 1375–1405.

Lynch, L. (2014). "Oh, WikiLeaks, i would so love to RT you:" WikiLeaks, Twitter, and information activism. *International Journal of Communication*, *8*(10), 2679–2692.

McCombs, M. E., & Shaw, D. L. (1972). The agenda-setting function of mass media. *Public Opinion Quarterly*, *36*(2), 176–187.

Mitchell, A., Gottfried, J., Barthel, M., & Shearer, E. (2016). The modern news consumer: News attitudes and practices in the digital era. *Pew Research Center*. Retrieved from https://www.journalism.org/2016/07/07/the-modern-news-consumer/

Nakashima, E., Mekhennet, S., & Jaffe, G. (2018, January 17). A German hacker offers a rare look inside the secretive world of Julian Assange and WikiLeaks. *Washington Post*. Retrieved from https://www.washingtonpost.com/world/national-security/a-german-hacker-offers-a-rare-look-inside-the-secretive-world-of-julian-assange-and-wikileaks/2018/01/17/e6211180-f311-11e7-b390-a36dc3fa2842_story.html

Penney, J. (2016). Motivations for participating in 'viral politics': A qualitative case study of Twitter users and the 2012 US presidential election. *Convergence*, *22*(1), 71–87. doi:10.1177/1354856514532074

Pew Research Center. (2019). Americans almost equally prefer to get local news online or on TV set. *Pew Research Center*. Retrieved from https://www.journalism.org/2019/03/26/nearly-as-many-americans-prefer-to-get-their-local-news-online-as-prefer-the-tv-set/

Russell Neuman, W., Guggenheim, L., Mo Jang, S., & Bae, S. Y. (2014). The Dynamics of public attention: Agenda-setting theory Meets Big data. *Journal of Communication*, *64*(2), 193–214. doi:10.1111/jcom.12088

Satter, R. (2017). Inside story: How Russians hacked the Democrats' emails. *Associated Press News*. Retrieved January 16, 2018, from AP News website: https://www.apnews.com/dea73efc0159 4839957c3c9a6c962b8a

Scheufele, D. A., & Tewksbury, D. (2006). Framing, agenda setting, and priming: The evolution of three media effects models. *Journal of Communication*, *57*(1), 9–20.

Seaver, N. (2017). Algorithms as culture: Some tactics for the ethnography of algorithmic systems. *Big Data & Society*, *4*(2), 2053951717738104.

Seiter, C. (2015). The Impact of the Trending Topic: The True Story (and Real Stats!) of a Top Tweet. Retrieved from Social website: https://blog.bufferapp.com/trending-topics

Skogerbø, E., & Krumsvik, A. H. (2015). Newspapers, Facebook and Twitter. *Journalism Practice*, *9* (3), 350–366. doi:10.1080/17512786.2014.950471

Stein, J. (2016). What 20,000 pages of hacked WikiLeaks emails teach us about Hillary Clinton. *Vox*. Retrieved from http://www.vox.com/policy-and-politics/2016/10/20/13308108/wikileaks-podesta-hillary-clinton

Summers, E. (2017). warc-twarc. Retrieved from Jupyter Notebook Viewer website: https://nbviewer.jupyter.org/github/edsu/warc-twarc/blob/master/warc-twarc.ipynb

Tufekci, Z. (2017). *Twitter and tear gas: The power and fragility of networked protest*. New Haven, CT: Yale University Press.

twitter.com. (2010). To Trend or Not to Trend ... *Twitter.com*. Retrieved from Twitter Blogs website: https://blog.twitter.com/2010/trend-or-not-trend

twitter.com. (2018). Search result FAQs. Retrieved from https://help.twitter.com/en/using-twitter/top-search-results-faqs

Verdegem, P., & D'heer, E. (2018). Social media logic and its impact on political communication during election times. In *Managing Democracy in the digital Age* (pp. 119–135). New York City, NY: Springer.

Watts, R. J. (2011). *Language Myths and the History of English*. OUP USA.

Weeks, B. E., Lane, D. S., Kim, D. H., Lee, S. S., & Kwak, N. (2017). Incidental exposure, selective exposure, and political information sharing: Integrating online exposure patterns and expression on social media. *Journal of Computer-Mediated Communication*, *22*(6), 363–379.

WikiLeaks. (2011). For tweets reguarding Julian #Assange's hearing on the 12th and 13th, please use hashtag #wljul. [Tweet]. Retrieved from @wikileaks website: https://twitter.com/wikileaks/status/89660895248130049

Wikileaks. (2014). WikiLeaks - The Spy Files. *Wikileaks*. Retrieved from https://wikileaks.org/the-spyfiles.html

Wikileaks. (2016a). @Twitter Is Twitter "shadow banning" the #DNCLeak hashtag? https://www.youtube.com/watch?time_continue=33&v=4at2gH12XBg ... [Tweet]. Retrieved from @wikileaks website: https://twitter.com/wikileaks/status/756956011043385345?lang=en

Wikileaks. (2016b). WikiLeaks - The Podesta Emails. *Wikileaks*. Retrieved from https://www.wikileaks.org/podesta-emails/

Wikileaks. (2017). What is WikiLeaks. *Wikileaks*. Retrieved from https://wikileaks.org/What-is-Wikileaks.html

Yang, G. (2016). Narrative agency in hashtag activism: The case of #BlackLivesMatter. *Media and Communication*, *4*(4), 13. doi:10.17645/mac.v4i4.692

Yang, X., Chen, B.-C., Maity, M., & Ferrara, E. (2016). Social politics: Agenda setting and political communication on social media. *International Conference on Social Informatics*, 10046, 330–344. Springer.

Yin, R. K. (2012). *Applications of case study research*. Thousand Oaks, CA: Sage.

Yin, R. K. (2013). *Case study research: Design and methods*. Thousand Oaks, CA: Sage.

Disinformation, performed: self-presentation of a Russian IRA account on Twitter

Yiping Xia, Josephine Lukito, Yini Zhang, Chris Wells, Sang Jung Kim and Chau Tong

ABSTRACT

How disinformation campaigns operate and how they fit into the broader social communication environment – which has been described as a 'disinformation order' [Bennett & Livingston, (2018). The disinformation order: Disruptive communication and the decline of democratic institutions. *European Journal of Communication*, 33(2), 122–139] – represent critical, ongoing questions for political communication. We offer a thorough analysis of a highly successful disinformation account run by Russia's Internet Research Agency: the so-called 'Jenna Abrams' account. We analyze Abrams' tweets and other content such as blogposts with qualitative discourse analysis, assisted by quantitative content analysis and metadata analysis. This yields an in-depth understanding of how the IRA team behind the Abrams account presented this persona across multiple platforms and over time. Especially, we describe the techniques used to perform personal authenticity and cultural competence. The performance of personal authenticity was central to her persona building as a likeable American woman, whereas the performance of cultural competence enabled her to infiltrate American conservative communities with resonant messages. Implications for understanding disinformation processes, and how some aspects of the hybrid media system are especially vulnerable to hijacking by bad actors are discussed.

Introduction

We now know that several disinformation campaigns operating during the 2016 US Presidential Election were quite successful at attracting widespread attention and inserting their messages into public discourse. Among the most prominent was the program run by Russia's Internet Research Agency (IRA) which, among other things, created thousands of social media accounts impersonating Americans from a variety of backgrounds and political views (US v. Internet Research Agency LLC, 2018).

How such campaigns operate, how they exploit properties of a complex hybrid media system (Chadwick, 2017) and how they fit into the broader social communication environment, described as a 'disinformation order' (Bennett & Livingston, 2018), are increasingly critical questions for political communication scholars.

Our analysis privileges depth and contextualized understanding over breadth. Many extant studies of online media disinformation have employed 'big data' approaches to count interactions and quantify dissemination and exposure (e.g., Boyd et al., 2018). In contrast, we examine the multifaceted ways in which a single, and singularly successful, disinformation account was represented and developed practices of authenticity and resonant messages across multiple platforms and over time. This was the so-called 'Jenna Abrams' account. (Our use of 'Jenna Abrams' and 'she' in this study denotes the IRA team behind the 'Jenna Abrams' account.)

Our study thus complements existing quantitative-computational work and contributes theoretically to two ongoing conversations in the field of communication research. First, this study provides insights into the political implications of the 'fluidity' of self-identity in networked online spaces (Boyd, 2010; Papacharissi, 2010, 2018). The case of Jenna Abrams illustrates how strategic self-presentation could be co-opted by bad actors, becoming a tool to deceive and manipulate. As an account that was wholly not authentic, she represents the hardest possible test of strategic self-presentation processes.

Second, by illustrating how Jenna Abrams cultivated a conservative persona appealing to right-wing publics, we expand our understanding of disinformation as not only a matter of message dissemination, but also a process of cultural resonance. The Abrams account exploited the cultural identities of the American right, formed through years of inculcating by the right-wing media system (Grossmann & Hopkins, 2016) and deepened by the affordances of digital media (Marwick & Lewis, 2017). Therefore, our goal is to illuminate how interactions between Abrams' self-expression and the structural features of the media environment yielded a formidable weapon of information warfare.

In the following section, we introduce our case – the Jenna Abrams account operated by the IRA. It will be followed by a literature review of online disinformation, self-presentation and authenticity on social media, and U.S. conservative political culture. We then explain our data collection and methods before presenting the findings. Implications and suggestions for future research are discussed in the concluding section.

Enter the case of IRA and 'Jenna Abrams'

To properly contextualize the self-presentation of Jenna Abrams, it would be helpful to understand the objectives of her creators. While it is impossible to establish with certainty how the operators of the Abrams account understood their objectives, existing evidence suggests that the larger goals of the IRA campaign were to exacerbate division and sow discord among the American public (United States of America vs. Internet Research Agency et al, 2018) – a strategy that fits within a longer history of Soviet and Russian information warfare (Abrams, 2016).

The Russian campaign was multifaceted and included strategies such as information hacking, strategic leaking, purchased advertisements, and the management of 'organic' social media accounts. The preponderance of the Russian-driven content presented on social media through these techniques involved highlighting racial tensions and deep partisan divides on issues such as immigration, gun rights, and so on (Jamieson, 2018).

Impersonating a young, white, American woman, Jenna Abrams (@Jenn_Abrams) was the second most-followed English-speaking IRA Twitter account, with more than 70,000 followers by the time of her unmasking in November 2017. Her presence was not limited to Twitter: she also operated accounts on Wordpress, Medium, Telegram, and Gab. An analysis by The Daily Beast revealed that Abrams was featured in articles by more than 30 media outlets, among them a number of mainstream news media like The New York Times and CNN (Collins & Cox, 2017) – clear evidence of her success at impersonating American political opinions. An illustrative example is her April 2016 tweet, provocatively noting:

> To those people, who hate the Confederate flag. Did you know that the flag and the war wasn't about slavery, it was all about money.

The tweet stirred up a sizeable controversy and drew in prominent commentators from both sides to criticize, ridicule, and defend her claim; one refutation from a journalist got tens of thousands of retweets and hundreds of thousands of likes (Tornoe, 2017; see Figure 1).

Apart from news media uptake, evidence that we gathered from Polititweet (https://polititweet.org) shows that her tweets were also directly retweeted by several of the most influential far right personalities in the United States, including Paul Joseph Watson (@PrisonPlanet), Richard Spencer, Mike Cernovich, and Mike Flynn Jr. Twitter metrics such as likes and retweets similarly attest to her meteoric rise within that space (Twitter, n.d.). While her tweets barely received likes and retweets at the beginning, they were able to attract on average as many as 700 likes and 500 retweets in her later stages on Twitter.

We take these data points as evidence that Abrams successfully generated substantial influence and response within the American public. How did Abrams construct an identity to do this? What affordances, cultures, and practices of digital media did Abrams draw on to create a persona compelling and persuasive enough to dupe so many audiences? Our multi-method analyses of Jenna Abrams presented below aim to answer these questions.

Literature review

Online disinformation and cultural identity

Research on disinformation is not new to the field of political communication (e.g., early studies by Floridi, 1996; Martin, 1982). Scholars have defined such influence campaigns as aiming for large-scale, pervasive information operations to influence a targeted

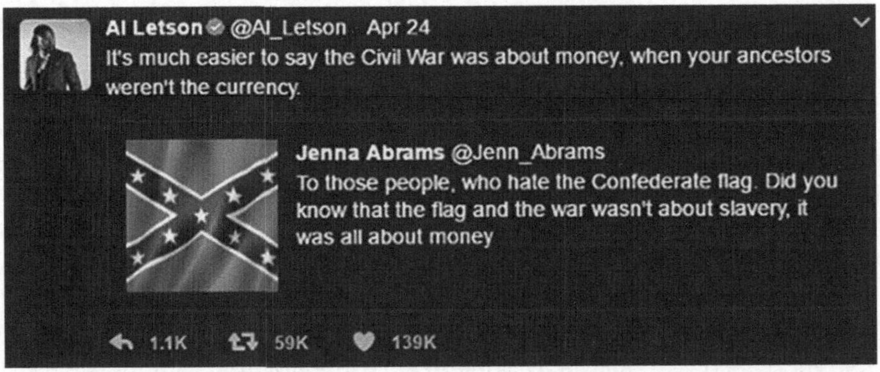

Figure 1. A journalist's refutation of Abrams' tweet (Tornoe, 2017).

population, in order to achieve political goals (Abrams, 2016). While such campaigns and practices have a long history, recent studies show that a lack of gatekeepers makes digital platforms particularly susceptible to disinformation, since users have to rely more heavily on cultural signifiers to evaluate other actors' statements (Kreiss, 2019; Marwick, 2018). For example, according to Daniels (2009), white supremacists used 'cloaked websites' to project a sense of cultural legitimacy in order to promote their political agenda. Along the same line, racial identity was performed and racial antagonism staged by fake Facebook accounts to stir up racial tension (Farkas, Schou, & Neumayer, 2017, 2018). Tripodi (2018) demonstrated how American conservatives' pre-existing belief that mainstream media are 'fake news' has led them to problematic sources like *Breitbart*.

Most of recent scholarly attention to online disinformation has been devoted to Russia's IRA disinformation program (e.g., Boyd et al., 2018; Farkas & Bastos, 2018; Jamieson, 2018). Although scholars have made important contributions in terms of how the current media ecosystem can facilitate the spread of disinformation (e.g., Faris et al., 2017; Golovchenko, Hartmann, & Adler-Nissen, 2018; Lukito et al., 2018b; Starbird, 2017), less is known about how IRA's activities exploited the ability to create and cultivate cultural identities that resonate with the targeted audiences.

In addition, research has shown that IRA-operated accounts are not homogeneous in content (Boatwright, Linvill, & Warren, 2018), and their influence in terms of follower count and media uptake is uneven (Lukito et al., 2018a). This warrants the need for in-depth analysis that focuses on the characteristics of the more successful accounts. In our case, Jenna Abrams' savvy persona-building was found to be a standout feature that arguably helped tap into her audiences' cultural identity.

Hence, this article aims to analyze two dimensions of Jenna Abrams' self-presentation that constitute her cultural appeals to her audience: her construction of an authentic persona, and her exploitation of the conservative partisan identity. The following two sections review pertinent literatures. Specific research questions raised by each body of literature are presented at the end of each section.

Self-presentation and authenticity on social media

Existing literature reveals a great deal about how individuals navigate online experiences in the age of 'context collapse' (Boyd, 2010). Scholars have adopted Goffman's (1959) idea of self-presentation in daily life to conceptualize the 'performance' of ordinary people on these sites (e.g., Ellison, Heino, & Gibbs, 2006; Papacharissi, 2012). Strategic self-presentation before an 'imagined audience' (Marwick & Boyd, 2011a) is one of the central pieces in people's digital life. Baym (2015) argues that Twitter shapes identities via the 'norms of authenticity and of self-branding' (p. 137).

More recently, the idea of strategic self-presentation and persona building has extended to the political realm. Not only is this evident in politicians' embrace of persona building (Usher, 2016), but also in the rise of 'political influencers' who make a career out of 'selling' political ideology online. Lewis (2018) wrote that right-wing influencers on YouTube constructed a sense of 'alternative credibility' that centered on relatability, authenticity, and accountability.

While authenticity has been a central concept in this line of research, communication scholars generally avoid explicitly defining it, citing the malleability and context-specificity of such a concept (see Banet-Weiser, 2012; Marwick, 2013). Although their concern is valid, a clear definition that takes into account the slipperiness of authenticity would help guide empirical analysis. This study adopts a definition developed by cultural sociologist Jeffrey Alexander, who states,

> authenticity is thematized by such questions as whether a person is 'real' – straightforward, truthful, and sincere … If authenticity marks success, then failure suggests that a performance will seem insincere and faked: the actor seems out of role, merely to be reading from an impersonal script, pushed and pulled by the forces of society, acting not from sincere motives but to manipulate the audience. (Alexander, 2004, p. 548)

Most of all, what we draw from this conceptualization is that authenticity is always constructed through performance, and is based on the perception of the audience.

Disinformation practices entail manipulating authorship, obfuscating the true source of the content (Tudjman & Mikelic, 2003). Therefore, the ability to construct authenticity is a necessary prerequisite for the successful dissemination of disinformation.

In Abrams, we see an example of a deft performance leading to a fake persona that nonetheless represented authenticity for her targeted audience. To be specific, her motives were insincere, her goal was to manipulate the audience, and she was likely acting upon some directives by the IRA instead of performing honestly, yet she managed to amass tens of thousands of followers by pretending to be a young, female conservative living in the U.S. Therefore, we argue that Abrams represented the most challenging scenario wherein a user has to construct an authentic persona from scratch, a pure if pervert case of 'achieved micro-celebrity' (Marwick, 2013, p. 117). This paper aims to establish a systematic understanding of how the authenticity work of Abrams was carried out through performance.[1]

> **RQ1**: What strategies did Jenna Abrams employ to construct a persona that conveys authenticity to her target audience?

U.S. conservative political culture and 'deep stories'

Notably, Abrams did not merely establish an authentic individual identity; rather, in line with many other accounts controlled by the IRA, she performed a specific political identity – that of a strong conservative.

Growing evidence suggests that the political culture of U.S. conservatives is ideologically-driven, shaped by the right-wing media ecosystem. As Grossmann and Hopkins (2016) pointed out, Republicans have become much more ideological than Democrats since the 1980s. Over time, the former successfully built an extensive web of conservative ideological networks, including talk radio shows (Jamieson & Cappella, 2008), Fox News cable television channel (Hemmer, 2010), and a number of conservative think tanks. More recently, Faris et al. (2017) showed that conservative hyperpartisan websites also played a big role in perpetrating polarization.

The long-term result of such a network is a collective narrative that scholars called 'deep story', or 'feel-as-if story' (Hochschild, 2016, p. 206; also see Polletta & Callahan, 2019) that bonds conservative communities together through a set of cultural appeals. Citing Peck (2019), Marwick (2018) notes, 'Fox News uses a set of cultural referents like country music stars in their political rhetoric, which interpolates a particular class and race identity: namely, white, blue-collar, and masculine – a strategy that [Peck] calls cultural populism' (Marwick, 2018, p. 494). Kreiss (2018) provided yet another account of the cultivation of partisan identity in the context of *Breitbart* stories.

This deep story of American resentment-conservatism is now widely enough recognized that its expression is available to a wider set of actors. As we shall see, its evocation and performance can be a critical component of affiliation in online spaces – indeed it was for Jenna Abrams. Hence, our second research question:

RQ2: With what techniques did Abrams perform affiliation with the conservative deep story narratives?

Data collection

Abrams' tweets were collected from a Twitter archive that accesses Twitter's Streaming API. This archive collects a random 1% of all global tweets. We searched in the archive for all tweets originating from the Abrams account and retweets of her tweets. We then extracted Abrams' original tweets from the retweets and combined them with the original tweets. This resulted in 3,878 unique tweets between 24 January 2015 and 3 August 2017. Though bias is possible since highly retweeted tweets were more likely to be collected in our sample, we found that the metadata patterns of our dataset were largely consistent with the complete archive of Abrams' tweets in Twitter's release (Twitter, n.d.).

We observed that some tweets in this dataset were out of context. Some had a link that directed to a 'Account Suspended' page, likely denoting media content (e.g., pictures and videos) that were since deleted by Twitter. Some, starting with an @ sign, indicate they were replies. In many cases, these two issues rendered a tweet incomprehensible, or having little discernible meaning. Three coders were trained to code for out-of-context tweets that were subsequently removed (Krippendorff's alpha: 0.75). Our final dataset contains 2,894 tweets.

We used three other data sources to triangulate our findings. First, we studied Jenna Abrams' 45 blog posts (https://jennabrams.com/) from 21 May 2016 to 8 November 2017, when her Twitter account was suspended. In our dataset, there are 15 occasions where she tweeted a link to her blog, indicating that she was using multiple platforms as part of a unified identity presentation. Second, we accessed Jenna Abrams' Twitter profile pages over time via the Internet Archive (https://archive.org). Finally, we used Media Cloud (https://mediacloud.org) to gather media articles that mentioned Jenna Abrams during the period when she was active on Twitter.

Methods

We conducted an in-depth case analysis that takes advantages of archived social media content, and aimed to develop our understanding of Abrams' actions in both qualitative and quantitative terms. The primary method used in this paper is qualitative discourse analysis of Abrams's tweets and other digital content. This inductive approach aims to identify, conceptualize, and contextualize the unique strategies that Abrams used to construct her persona.

That said, our expectation is that a few widely-used self-presentation strategies identified by scholars (e.g., Marwick & Boyd, 2011b; Papacharissi, 2012), as described below, will be at play regardless of the specific aims of the actor. Quantitative coding based on these predefined strategies (as well as an additional category identified in pilot coding) helps us verify and locate their usage in Abrams' content, thus guiding us to properly incorporate them into our explanatory account of Abrams' self-presentation.

Qualitative discourse analysis

Our primary analytical technique is a qualitative discourse analysis performed on the 2,894 tweets in our dataset. In discourse analysis, 'language is taken to be not simply a tool for description and a medium of communication (the conventional view), but as social practice, as a way of doing things' (Wood & Kroger, 2000, p. 4). In this study, we considered the collectivity of texts and visual content in our data (including tweets, blog-posts, and Twitter profile pages) as discourse, in which lies ample indications of the actions by Abrams. The aim of this discourse analysis was to discover 'systematic links between texts, discourse practices, and sociocultural practices' (Fairclough, 1995, p. 17) in the self-presentation strategies employed by this account.

Our analytical protocol consisted of three rounds of coding. It started as we read through all of our data thoroughly and took notes regarding the thematic and rhetorical features of the tweets that pertained to the goal of strategic self-presentation. As we went through the notes again, we conducted an initial round of open coding, using a host of thematic codes that emerged in our notes.[2] At this stage, we observed a conceptual split among the codes: some dealt with strategies for constructing a likeable persona, while others dealt with appealing to the right-wing target audience. The second round of coding, hence, aimed to examine the boundaries of as well as interconnections between those codes in light of our conceptual set-up, similar to axial coding in grounded theory (Glaser & Strauss, 2017). In this process, some codes were merged, some clarified with further notes, resulting in a parsimonious set of categories. This inductive approach resulted in two major points of focus: 'performed authenticity' and 'performed cultural competence,' which structure our presentation of results below. Finally, we went through coded data again in order to verify the explanatory capacity of the categories, make final adjustments, and ensure that we reached saturation.

Quantitative content analysis

We tested inter-coder reliability between three human coders using 27 percent of the sample ($n = 800$), following three training sessions. This is an acceptable sample for testing intercoder reliability rates (Gwet, 2014; Lombard, Snyder-Duch, & Bracken, 2002). For sparse or unevenly distributed variables, kappa agreement statistics produce a paradox (i.e., the statistic is low, but agreement is high) because it treats positive codes as chance agreements (Neuendorf, 2016). For this reason, average pairwise percent agreements are used instead. The rest of the tweets were split evenly and coded by the three coders.

Five variables were labeled dichotomously (1 = yes, 0 = no). A tweet was allowed to be coded as yes in multiple categories. The variables are described below:

(1) *Fan engagement* (Percentage of agreement: 93.67%): Marwick and Boyd (2011b) noted that public interaction with fans is a common strategy used by celebrities on Twitter,

because it lets the fans feel the 'closeness' to their idols. Although this strategy obviously works best with traditional celebrities with large fan bases, it is still reasonable to expect some degree of its use by Abrams.

This was coded as yes (1) if the tweet wanted to interact with the general audience. This included open-ended questions and questions asking followers to like or comment.

(2) *Rapport-building* (Percentage of agreement: 92.67%): 'Small talk' messages are another important strategy identified by Marwick and Boyd (2011b) in fans management: 'The many seemingly insignificant messages serve as phatic communication ... reinforcing connections and maintaining social bonds.' (p. 147)

This was coded as yes (1) if the tweet included information about Jenna Abrams' 'personal life'. Motivational statements, greetings, and hashtag games were also considered rapport-building messages.

(3) *Affective expressions* (Percentage of agreement: 94.33%): Papacharissi (2012, 2015) emphasized the significance of affect in online communication, 'Emotion and feeling define modalities of belonging that are articulated as strangers connect and attach to each other.' (Papacharissi, 2015, p. 117). Affective expressions, thus, have the potential to incite engagement especially when paired with designed partisan messages.

This was coded as yes (1) if the tweet contained strong emotional language. Tweets with exclamation marks, repeated question marks, and capitalized statements (e.g., 'LOCK HER UP') were also coded as yes (1).

(4) *Cultural References* (Percentage of agreement: 94.33%): Marwick and Boyd (2011b) pointed out that 'Links and retweets provide good examples of the affiliative use of cultural markers and symbols. Generally, highly followed users RT or link to items that interest them and presumably their followers.' It is reasonable to expect Abrams tweeted about topics in American culture to appeal to her followers.

This was coded as yes (1) if the tweet contained references to American culture, including well-known holidays, sporting events, celebrities, and pop culture references.

(5) *News* (Percentage of agreement: 93.33%): This category originated from our pilot coding due to the frequency of news sharing. Tweets were coded as yes (1) in this category if the tweet shared information about a recent news story. Tweets that contained a combination of news and opinion were coded as yes (1) as well.

Metadata analysis

Finally, we analyzed the temporal metadata patterns of all the 3,878 tweets by Jenna Abrams, focusing on the types of tweets (original tweets, retweets, or replies) and the use of hashtags. A tweet was treated as a retweet if it started with 'RT @'; a reply tweet was determined if the 'in_reply_to_status_id_str' variable was not empty. The trajectory of Abrams' follower growth was also plotted and analyzed.

Findings

In the following, we present our analysis of the Abrams account holistically, by drawing on qualitative, quantitative, and metadata analyses together. The findings are organized in three sub-sections: the performance of authenticity, the performance of cultural competence, and how the two types of performance work together as a 'dual force'.

The performance of authenticity

A lot of Abrams' tweets are not serious takes on politics, some not about politics at all. Her tweet with a video of a dog 'singing and playing the piano' made it into UK media Independent after getting 'thousands of retweets' (Hooton, 2017). In comparison to her tweets about politics, what one would imagine from those funny, innocuous tweets is a likeable female personality who enjoys her life in the United States, much like a micro-celebrity (Marwick, 2013; Senft, 2008). One person even commented, under one of her Wordpress blogposts:

> You have a very unique way of expressing yourself… you're by far one of the most interesting 'expressionists'. This world lacks personalities. You have one. People are products. You're not.

This section will flesh out the techniques that Abrams employed towards building up a crafted persona that facilitated her engagement with her audiences.

An American girl

Jenna Abrams' Twitter profile indicated that she lived in the 'USA'. Throughout its operation, the account performed as a passionate American girl, displaying the behaviors of someone who cares about her country. First, there were explicit mentions of her 'home country':

> I am afraid that one day incompetent and greedy politicians will ruin the #US, our home! #WhatAreYouAfraidOf

Shortly after her account was suspended by Twitter, she posted on her blog a fairly long attack of The Daily Beast (an online media that exposed the Abrams account as fake) titled, ironically, 'Our democracy has been hacked' (Abrams, 2017), in which she offered point-by-point refutation of some claims made against her.

She also used a few common signifiers of an American citizen, the most blatant one being voting:

> I voted: #myvote2016 #voted #ElectionDay.

Other such tweets include a number of tweets honoring veterans, and some that commemorated the victims of 9/11, with the hashtag #NeverForget.

Pop culture or mass culture references (5.3%, $n = 154$) were another strategy that showed off her 'cultural affiliation' (Marwick & Boyd, 2011b) with fellow Americans:

> Best fancy outfit? Sure! #Grammys2015

> Kim Kardashian is pregnant! Hope she will have twins!

When it was a national holiday, Jenna Abrams would often tweet greetings or relevant quotes. This practice extended to some obscure, superficial celebrations such as 'National Taco Day' and 'National Kissing Day.'

> Patriotism is not always pride in what your country has, but what it doesn't have so that you can strive for it. (tweet on Independence Day, 2016)

While this set of tactics seem obvious and outright, these signals could be powerful cognitive cues that would enhance the trustworthiness of her persona. Sometimes the rhetoric about her American citizenship was in more subtle forms, but could be equally convincing:

> #YoSoyAmerican? Really? Could you please at least write it in English?!

This sort of tweets creates boundaries for who can and cannot be American, indicating that Abrams was well-versed in the cultural signifiers of American citizenship.

A likeable personality

The above example also displays her use of affective expressions, a powerful device to humanize a persona and appeal to the audience. Content analysis suggested that 10% of her tweets ($n = 289$) contained affective expressions, evoked both through words and punctuations. Both question marks and exclamation marks were often used in tandem, as a call to response. Many of these tweets were also political in content:

> President #Obama lied about gay marriage. This is why we're cynical. Sorry WHAT??! Obama lied??? No way!!!

To engage with her fans (7.9%, $n = 229$), Jenna Abrams actively asked questions or tweeted out simple 'polls':

> Are you happy with the choice of #AttorneyGeneral? Comments appreciated

> RT if you voted for Trump, like if you voted for Hillary #ElectionDay #myvote2016 #voted

Extraordinarily, Jenna Abrams even announced at least three Q&A sessions with her Twitter followers (with the hashtag #askjennaabrams), and posted her answers on her blog – this is a testament to her extensive effort to interact with fans.

Jenna Abrams also used everyday greetings, lifestyle content (e.g., puppy videos), and hashtag games to build rapport with her Twitter followers (12.5%, $n = 362$). Numerous occurrences of 'Good morning' and 'Have a great day' were seen in our dataset. Examples for hashtag games, in which Twitter users create tweets for fun or expressing fandom using a common hashtag, include #IfThe80sNeverStopped and #WhenIAmOldAndGrey.

Finally, when engaging with her followers, she often evokes the rhetoric of 'friends' to frame herself as part of the American in-group. She often used this term as part of a salutation (e.g., 'Good morning, my friends'). This was also occasionally supplemented with political statements:

> Have a good Tuesday, my friends and remember that it's 416 days till Obama leaves the Office.

> Ever feel useless? Remember that Germany has a president:) Good morning.

In fact, the pairing of political statements with lifestyle content, hashtags or salutation can be widely found across our dataset. Similarly, the ways she discussed politics was not always serious. Some tweets were merely political jokes or funny anecdotes:

> Get yourself a significant other who looks at you like Justin Trudeau looks at George Soros.

The performance of cultural competence

We use 'cultural competence' to denote Abrams' eloquence in tapping into U.S. conservative political discourse, which was rooted in her capability of digesting the cultural-political mindset of the American right.

An avid consumer of political information

In her tweets, Jenna Abrams performed as if she possessed a good amount of 'knowledge' regarding American politics, especially with divisive issues such as the Black Lives Matter movement, immigration, and feminism. We should note that this 'knowledge' is often shallow, not much more than 'talking points,' such as the aforementioned viral tweet about the Confederate flag. However, this kind of 'talking points-knowledge' is often enough to stir online controversy once tweets containing it was circulated far and wide.

Some tweets explicitly displayed her 'just enough' political knowledge, albeit not intellectually rigorous:

> If all Republicans were like Reagan and all Democrats were like JFK, this country would be going places

> Socialism is the number one killer of humanity in the twentieth century. It starts with 'free stuff' and ends with blood

A number of random quotes from George Orwell hinted at a dystopian view of politics and presumably served to incite cynicism towards the government:

> The most effective way to destroy people is to deny and obliterate their own understanding of their history - G.Orwell

Also, 13% of her tweets ($n = 377$) in our dataset contained news. While some are innocuous local news or anecdotes, a lot of the news shared by Jenna Abrams pertained to the aforementioned divisive issues:

> Christian student suspended after confronting Muslim professor for saying the Crucifixion was a hoax

The act of news sharing demonstrated her (performed) capacity as an avid follower of politics.

Moreover, she was able to send on-pitch right-wing partisan messages based on her understanding of political issues. Those messages were mostly reactionary discourse against liberal figures, activism, and political correctness:

> That's too much! #BlackLivesMatter is a disgusting hate movement

> Hi, I'm Ahmed! I can rape you or your sister and get away with it cause #refugeeswelcome'

Hashtags were uniquely created (e.g., #FeminismIsAwful'; #MuslimIsTheProblem) or 'hijacked' to counteract liberal agenda:

> Bernie Sanders proposes a small tax increase, totaling $19.6 trillion #FeelTheBern

> How did we go from protesting the hijab to celebrating it? #MuslimWomensDay

A deep story

In line with other research reviewed earlier, we found a deep story focusing on liberals' lack of 'common sense' and their 'hypocrisy' running through Jenna Abrams' tweets (Figure 2).

In July 2017, her Twitter bio included the claim 'Calm down. I'm not pro-Trump. I am pro-common sense.' Despite the affirmative use of 'common sense' in the bio, this phrase

Figure 2. Screenshot of Abrams' Twitter homepage on July 18, 2017.

was mostly used to mock liberal people's alleged lack of it. Similarly, 'hypocrisy' was used to expose the alleged inconsistencies between beliefs and actions seen in left-wing political figures. Explicit use of them includes:

> Happy 55th Birthday to our .@POTUS! Thanks for 7 years of ongoing lies and hypocrisy!
>
> #RightNowICouldUse my common sense to say that Islam oppresses women

However, tweets that convey this 'deep story' did not always use the two catchphrases explicitly. Rather, we found a common rhetorical strategy in the tweets: a juxtaposition of (most often distorted) facts or liberal statements, which either (1) attributes an absurd, nonsensical fact to a left-wing political figure's actions or liberal social activism:

> It's almost 8 years of Obama and people don't know which bathroom to use

or (2) displays incongruence between a liberal's ideological beliefs and actions, or between actions over time:

> Hypocrite starter pack: 1. Run against Wall Street corruption 2. Give endorsement to Hillary Clinton

In a word, to seed this deep story in her tweets, she was able to associate and contrast a range of liberal political deeds and reveal the so-called liberal 'hypocrisy' from an American conservative's perspective.

Speaking to the community

To tell the above deep story to the American conservative communities, Jenna Abrams frivolously used terms, catchphrases, and slogans typically circulated within the liberal circles, but also known (and distorted) among conservative people. For example, among the top ten most-used hashtags in our dataset, #FeelTheBern, #BlackLivesMatter, and #ReligionOfPeace are all popular phrases used by left-wing activists and political campaigns. These hashtags were used by Abrams to ridicule corresponding liberal ideas through sarcasm, so the tweet text that surrounds them were usually either critical or disrespectful towards said ideas:

> Muslims can't even coexist with each other #ReligionOfPeace

Words and phrases popular in liberal circles, such as 'patriarchy' and 'white supremacist,' also appear frequently in the non-hashtag form:

> That awkward moment when you can't call a pro-Trump person a misogynistic white supremacist

Therefore, Jenna Abrams showed an ability to hijack elements of left-wing political discourse and re-interpret them using a logic that is familiar to her target audience. This ability likely contributed to her appeal as a knowledgeable political influencer.

We observed that sarcasm was often used by Jenna Abrams to discredit liberal ideas. In August 2016, she even tweeted:

> #ForgiveMeForSayingThisBut I'll label you stupid if you don't understand obvious sarcasm

Aside from sarcasm, she used a 'compare and contrast' approach that implies where the comparison point is rather than reveals it. For example, she once tweeted:

> Japan has accepted 27 refugees last year, has rejected 99%. Haven't heard about any terrorists' attacks there

The significance of the indirect delivery strategy lies in the fact that in order to fully grasp her 'deep story' of common sense and hypocrisy, one has to be a member of the conservative community and familiarize themselves with certain conservative beliefs and counter-beliefs against liberals. By doing so, Jenna Abrams will likely be perceived as an in-group member, thus enhancing her influence on the American conservative community.

A dual force within an attention-driven platform

It is important to note that these performances of personal authenticity and cultural competence cannot work individually; they have to work in concert as a 'dual force' to produce a suitable self-presentation for the purpose of disinformation. Without an authentic, engaging persona to carry the 'deep stories,' the stories would likely be deemed less relatable and trustworthy. Without a consistent narrative that taps into a cultural-political line of thought, the authenticity work would be rendered pointless given that the overall goal of the IRA is to sow discord among the American public.

Meanwhile, it should be noted that both strategies in this 'dual force' are fundamentally cultural. The performance of authenticity drew on cultural resources in American pop culture, collective memory, and symbols of national identity; the performance of cultural competence, evidently, exploited the cultural worldviews of a targeted subgroup.

In this regard, we can find a parallel in the American right-wing media system. As Polletta and Callahan wrote:

> Conservative media commentators often styled a personal relationship with the viewer or listener, in which allusive stories reinforced the bond between speaker and audience.
>
> The people who believed in the deep story and who voted for Donald Trump heard compelling stories on conservative media, but they also heard a style of talk that was engaging. (p. 13)

Jenna Abrams' task was arguably tougher than American conservative commentators in that she began with little recognition among other American Twitter users. Therefore, as we have shown, she devoted considerable effort to build a likeable persona through a host of tactics.

Furthermore, the 'dual force' of performances was assisted by exploiting the attention dynamics on Twitter in the early stage of Abrams' activity. Our metadata analysis showed that 83% of Abrams' replies to others' tweets in our dataset were sent in 2015, many of which were responding to mainstream news media or high-profile politicians. We also observed that in 2015, her most-used hashtags included more generic ones concerning current events and politicians, like #isis and #obama, while some more original hashtags were used much more often in later stages. Both replying to prominent users and using generic hashtags are useful tactics to seek attention from general Twitter users, thus increasing her visibility and potential to gain followers.

The growth of Abrams' following had three hikes in early 2015, but after those early hikes, her follower growth was largely steady except a minor bump in early 2016. As Webster and Ksiazek (2012) pointed out, metrics of attention such as follower count on Twitter could lend further credibility to content providers like Abrams, facilitating her status as opinion leader (Figure 3).

Discussion

This paper has presented an in-depth investigation of the strategic self-presentation and content curation of a high-profile IRA account, Jenna Abrams. We have demonstrated

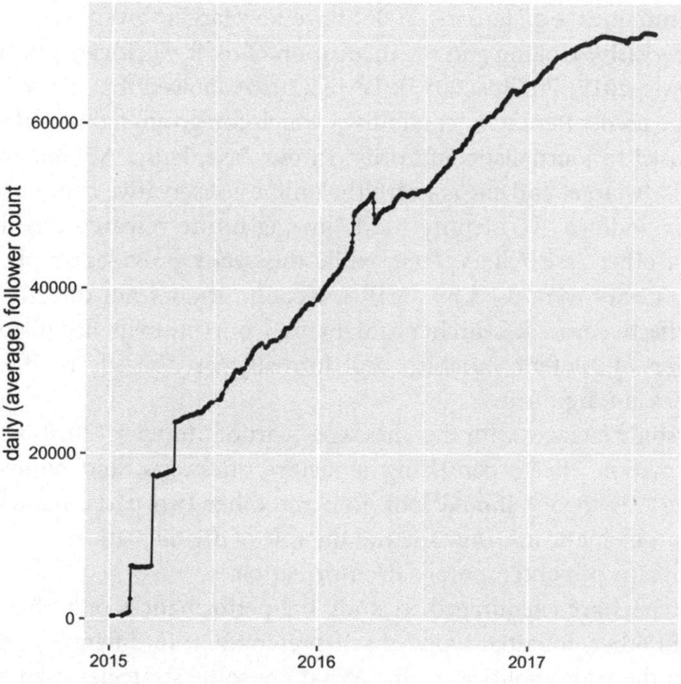

Figure 3. Abrams' Twitter follower growth.

that her performances of personal authenticity and cultural competence were adept, and it likely propelled Abrams' success at recruiting a sizeable following and entering both conservative and mainstream media discourse. Two points of discussion emerge:

First, Abrams' persona-building approach is a reminder that just like other kinds of communication processes, disinformation should not be viewed only as a matter of transmission and diffusion; it is also one of cultivation (Gerbner, Gross, Morgan, & Signorielli, 1986) and ritual (Carey, 2002), where rich cultural dynamics between the sender and the receiver mediate the effects of media messages. Hence, this paper echoes with Marwick (2018)'s call to go beyond the 'magic bullet theory' of disinformation, namely the view that people share problematic information simply because they believe it to be true. To paraphrase Carey (2002), while Jenna Abrams did impart information upon her followers, it was 'the representation of shared beliefs' (p. 39), accomplished through an authentic persona and savvy message design, that marked the essence of this approach.

Technological affordances are the focus of our second discussion point. Specifically, the case of Jenna Abrams shows that a number of features once portrayed mainly as positive aspects of digital media can be co-opted by bad actors. On one hand, freedom of identity expression online has been seen as a source of agency, an opportunity for individuals to 'play with' their own image and control how others perceive them (e.g., Papacharissi, 2012), or even achieve higher social status (Marwick, 2013; Marwick & Boyd, 2011b). In our case, however, Jenna Abrams was able to exploit this feature of self-presentation in social media to deceive for political goals. If the possibilities of identity play are left wide open on digital platforms, coordinated efforts such as those by the IRA are able to pose significant danger to the democratic publics.

On the other hand, the Abrams account is yet another example of the current internet culture of 'engagement' being exploited. Early celebratory accounts of participatory culture and online communities (e.g., Jenkins, 2006) have now largely given way to grave reckonings about the pervasive trolling and the incubation of toxic worldviews in sites like 4chan (Marwick & Lewis, 2017; Phillips, 2015). Lewis (2018) showed that conservative influencers on YouTube used 'alternative credibility,' which foregrounded relatability and authenticity as opposed to journalistic authority. In our case, Jenna Abrams created a niche persona to precisely target and engage with the online conservative community in the U.S.

Based on our findings, we identify the following future research possibilities for the consideration of other researchers. First, while this study provides ample evidence that performative strategies were used by an IRA account, it does not directly engage in the measuring of effectiveness. Researchers might find our findings useful to inform their operationalization of content variables, and formally test the effects of such strategies and the variances among them.

Second, this study engages with the 'messages' part of Marwick (2018)'s three-part theory of disinformation effects consisting of actors, messages, and affordances. Future studies adopting this theory should look into the other two parts, namely people who are affected by problematic information and the role of digital platforms, in order to complete a full landscape of contemporary disinformation.

Third, researchers are encouraged to study the performances of authenticity, cultural competence, and other potential types of self-presentation in different contexts of disinformation, or in the wider political realm. What are some strategies used by disinformation accounts targeting liberal activist communities, racial minorities, nationalist groups, etc.? How about the self-presentation strategies of the new generation of digital-savvy politicians (e.g., see Gerbaudo, 2019)? Comparative studies of identity expression among political actors can also be revealing.

Notes

1. Thus, though Hogan's (2010) contention that 'performance' does not capture online interactions as well as 'exhibition' is well-taken, in our specific case we adopt Papacharissi's (2012) terminology of 'performance' to conceptualize Jenna Abrams' self-presentation. We would like to show that in a space where all identities need to be performed – as Papacharissi and others suggest, fake ones are perfectly welcome to join in.
2. Five categories used for quantitative content analysis were not included in discourse analysis categories, though we still wrote notes when they applied.

Disclosure statement

No potential conflict of interest was reported by the authors.

ORCID

Yiping Xia http://orcid.org/0000-0002-1483-2006

References

Abrams, J. (2017). *Our democracy has been hacked.* Retrieved from https://jennabrams.com/2017/11/08/our-democracy-has-been-hacked/

Abrams, S. (2016). Beyond propaganda: Soviet active measures in Putin's Russia. *Connections : The Quarterly Journal; Garmisch-Partenkirchen, 15*(1), 5–31. doi:10.11610/Connections.15.1-01.

Alexander, J. C. (2004). Cultural pragmatics: Social performance between ritual and strategy. *Sociological Theory, 22*(4), 527–573.

Banet-Weiser, S. (2012). *AuthenticTM: The politics of ambivalence in a brand culture.* New York: NYU press.

Baym, N. K. (2015). *Personal connections in the digital age.* New York: John Wiley & Sons.

Bennett, W. L., & Livingston, S. (2018). The disinformation order: Disruptive communication and the decline of democratic institutions. *European Journal of Communication, 33*(2), 122–139.

Boatwright, B. C., Linvill, D. L., & Warren, P. L. (2018). *Troll factories: The internet research agency and state-sponsored agenda building.* Leipzig: Resource Centre on Media Freedom in Europe.

Boyd, D. (2010). Social network sites as networked publics: Affordances, dynamics, and implications. In Z. Papacharissi (Ed.), *A networked self* (pp. 47–66). New York: Routledge.

Boyd, R. L., Spangher, A., Fourney, A., Nushi, B., Ranade, G., Pennebaker, J., & Horvitz, E. (2018). Characterizing the Internet Research Agency's social media operations during the 2016 US presidential election using linguistic analyses. *PsyArXiv.* October, 1.

Carey, J. (2002). A cultural approach to communication. In D. McQuail (Ed.), *Mcquail's reader in mass communication theory* (pp. 36–45). New York: Sage Publishing.

Chadwick, A. (2017). *The hybrid media system: Politics and power.* London: Oxford University Press.

Collins, B., & Cox, J. (2017, November 3). Jenna Abrams, Russia's Clown Troll Princess, Duped the Mainstream Media and the World. *The Daily Beast.* Retrieved from https://www.thedailybeast.com/jenna-abrams-russias-clown-troll-princess-duped-the-mainstream-media-and-the-world

Daniels, J. (2009). Cloaked websites: Propaganda, cyber-racism and epistemology in the digital era. *New Media & Society, 11*(5), 659–683.

Ellison, N., Heino, R., & Gibbs, J. (2006). Managing impressions online: Self-presentation processes in the online dating environment. *Journal of Computer-Mediated Communication, 11*(2), 415–441.

Fairclough, N. (1995). *Media discourse.* New York: Bloomsbury.

Faris, R., Roberts, H., Etling, B., Bourassa, N., Zuckerman, E., & Benkler, Y. (2017). *Partisanship, propaganda, and disinformation: Online media and the 2016 US presidential election.* Retrieved from https://dash.harvard.edu/handle/1/33759251

Farkas, J., & Bastos, M. (2018). *IRA propaganda on twitter: Stoking antagonism and tweeting local news.* In *Proceedings of the 9th International Conference on social media and society* (pp. 281–285). ACM.

Farkas, J., Schou, J., & Neumayer, C. (2017). Cloaked Facebook pages: Exploring fake Islamist propaganda in social media. *New Media & Society,* 146144481770775. doi:10.1177/1461444817707759

Farkas, J., Schou, J., & Neumayer, C. (2018). Platformed antagonism: Racist discourses on fake Muslim Facebook pages. *Critical Discourse Studies, 15*(5), 463–480.

Floridi, L. (1996). Brave. Net. World: The Internet as a disinformation superhighway? *The Electronic Library, 14*(6), 509–514.

Gerbaudo, P. (2019). The age of the hyperleader: when political leadership meets social media celebrity. *New Statesman.* Retrieved from https://www.newstatesman.com/politics/media/2019/03/age-hyperleader-when-political-leadership-meets-social-media-celebrity

Gerbner, G., Gross, L., Morgan, M., & Signorielli, N. (1986). Living with television: The dynamics of the cultivation process. *Perspectives on Media Effects, 1986,* 17–40.

Glaser, B. G., & Strauss, A. L. (2017). *Discovery of grounded theory: Strategies for qualitative research.* New York: Routledge.

Goffman, E. (1959). *The presentation of self in everyday life.* New York: Anchor.

Golovchenko, Y., Hartmann, M., & Adler-Nissen, R. (2018). State, media and civil society in the information warfare over Ukraine: Citizen curators of digital disinformation. *International Affairs, 94*(5), 975–994.

Grossmann, M., & Hopkins, D. A. (2016). *Asymmetric politics: Ideological Republicans and group interest democrats.* London: Oxford University Press.

Gwet, K. L. (2014). *Handbook of inter-rater reliability: The definitive guide to measuring the extent of agreement among raters*. New York: Advanced Analytics, LLC.

Hemmer, N. (2010). *Messengers of the right: Media and the modern conservative movement*. New York: Columbia University Press.

Hochschild, A. (2016). *Strangers in their own land*. NY: The New Press.

Hogan, B. (2010). The presentation of self in the age of social media: Distinguishing performances and exhibitions online. *Bulletin of Science, Technology & Society*, *30*(6), 377–386. doi:10.1177/0270467610385893

Hooton, C. (2017). Singer-songwriter beagle plays avant garde ballad. *Independent*. Retrieved from https://www.independent.co.uk/arts-entertainment/music/news/piano-playing-beagle-definite-good-boy-a7720221.html

Jamieson, K. H. (2018). *Cyberwar: How Russian hackers and trolls helped elect a president*. London: Oxford University Press.

Jamieson, K. H., & Cappella, J. N. (2008). *Echo chamber: Rush Limbaugh and the conservative media establishment*. London: Oxford University Press.

Jenkins, H. (2006). *Fans, bloggers, and gamers: Exploring participatory culture*. New York: NYU Press.

Kreiss, D. (2018). The networked self in the age of identity fundamentalism. In Z. Papacharissi (Ed.), *A networked self and platforms, stories, connections* (pp. 28–44). New York: Routledge.

Kreiss, D. (2019). The fragmenting of the civil sphere: How partisan identity shapes the moral evaluation of candidates and epistemology. In *Politics of meaning/meaning of politics* (pp. 223–241). New York: Palgrave Macmillan.

Lewis, R. (2018). *Alternative influence: Broadcasting the reactionary right on YouTube*. New York: Data & Society Research Institute.

Lombard, M., Snyder-Duch, J., & Bracken, C. C. (2002). Content analysis in mass communication: Assessment and reporting of intercoder reliability. *Human Communication Research*, *28*(4), 587–604.

Lukito, J., Suk, J., Zhang, Y., Doroshenko, L., Su, M., Kim, S. J., … Wells, C. (2018b). *Zero Day Twitter: How Russian Propaganda Infiltrated the U.S. Hybrid Media System*. Paper presented at the Association for Education in Journalism and Mass Communication, Washington, DC.

Lukito, J., Wells, C., Zhang, Y., Doroshenko, L., Kim, S., Su, M., … Freelon, D. (2018a). *The Twitter exploit: How Russian propaganda infiltrated U.S. News*. University of Wisconsin-Madison Research Paper. Retrieved from https://uwmadison.app.box.com/v/TwitterExploit

Martin, L. J. (1982). Disinformation: An instrumentality in the propaganda arsenal. *Political Communication*, *2*(1), 47–64. doi:10.1080/10584609.1982.9962747.

Marwick, A. E. (2013). *Status update: Celebrity, publicity, and branding in the social media age*. New Haven: Yale University Press.

Marwick, A. E. (2018). Why do people share fake news? A sociotechnical model of media effects. *Georgetown Law Technology Review*, *2*, 474–512.

Marwick, A., & Boyd, D. (2011b). To See and Be seen: Celebrity practice on Twitter. *Convergence: The International Journal of Research Into New Media Technologies*, *17*(2), 139–158. doi:10.1177/1354856510394539

Marwick, A. E., & Boyd, D. (2011a). I tweet honestly, I tweet passionately: Twitter users, context collapse, and the imagined audience. *New Media & Society*, *13*(1), 114–133. doi:10.1177/1461444810365313

Marwick, A., & Lewis, R. (2017). *Media manipulation and disinformation online*. New York: Data & Society Research Institute.

Neuendorf, K. A. (2016). *The content analysis guidebook*. New York: Sage Publishing.

Papacharissi, Z. (Ed.). (2010). *A networked self: Identity, community, and culture on social network sites*. New York: Routledge.

Papacharissi, Z. (2012). Without You, I'm Nothing: Performances of the self on Twitter. *International Journal of Communication*, *6*, 1989–2006.

Papacharissi, Z. (2015). *Affective publics: Sentiment, technology, and politics*. London: Oxford University Press.

Papacharissi, Z. (Ed.). (2018). *A networked self and platforms, stories, connections*. New York: Routledge.

Peck, R. (2019). *Fox populism: Branding populism as working class*. Cambridge: Cambridge University Press.

Phillips, W. (2015). *This is why we can't have nice things: Mapping the relationship between online trolling and mainstream culture*. Boston: MIT Press.

Polletta, F., & Callahan, J. (2019). Deep stories, nostalgia narratives, and fake news: Storytelling in the Trump era. In *Politics of meaning/meaning of politics* (pp. 55–73). New York: Palgrave Macmillan.

Senft, T. M. (2008). *Camgirls: Celebrity and community in the age of social networks*. New York: Peter Lang.

Starbird, K. (2017). *Information wars: A window into the alternative media ecosystem*. Retrieved from https://medium.com/hci-design-at-uw/information-wars-a-window-into-the-alternative-media-ecosystem-a1347f32fd8f

Tornoe, R. (2017). Two popular conservative Twitter personalities were just outed as Russian trolls. *Philly.com*. Retrieved from: https://www.philly.com/philly/news/politics/presidential/russia-fake-twitter-facebook-posts-accounts-trump-election-jenna-abrams-20171103.html.

Tripodi, F. (2018). *Searching for alternative facts: Analyzing Scriptural Inference in conservative news practices*. New York: Data & Society Research Institute.

Tudjman, M., & Mikelic, N. (2003). Information science: Science about information, misinformation and disinformation. *Proceedings of Informing Science+Information Technology Education*, *3*, 1513–1527.

Twitter. (n.d.). *Elections Integrity*. Retrieved from https://about.twitter.com/en_us/values/elections-integrity.html#data

United States of America v. Internet Research Agency et al. (2018). United States district court for the district of Columbia. Retrieved from: https://www.justice.gov/file/1035477/download.

Usher, B. (2016). ME, YOU, And US: Constructing political persona on social networks during the 2015 UK general election. *Persona Studies*, *2*(2), 19–41.

Webster, J. G., & Ksiazek, T. B. (2012). The dynamics of audience fragmentation: Public attention in an age of digital media. *Journal of Communication*, *62*(1), 39–56.

Wood, L. A., & Kroger, R. O. (2000). *Doing discourse analysis: Methods for studying action in talk and text*. New York: Sage Publishing.

Index

Note: Page numbers in **bold** refer to tables and those in *italics* refer to figures.